CREDITS

CONCEPT AND CONTENT
Natalia Bielczyk, PhD

Twitter: @nbielczyk_neuro, @nBielczykCrypto
LinkedIn: www.linkedin.com/in/nataliabielczyk
Personal website: www.nataliabielczyk.com

COVER DESIGN
Roger Tung

Email: roger20402@gmail.com

ISBN: 9789083057910
Published in the Netherlands by Welcome Solutions, Nijmegen.
Bielczyk, N. *What Is out There for Me? The Landscape of Post-PhD Career Tracks*. 2nd Ed (2020).

DEDICATION

To my Mother.
She is an amazing person.

INSPIRATION

"If one doesn't know to which port one is sailing, no wind is the right wind."

Lucius Annaeus Seneca

ACKNOWLEDGMENTS

Firstly, I would like to thank **Guillen Fernandez** who, in the summer of 2016, was the first to inform me about the whole problem associated with the lack of career guidance for PhDs moving towards industry. It took me a long time to realize that what Guillen said was actually right, and I fully agree that more needs to be done in this area.

Contributors

I would like to thank contributors who shared testimonies about their personal experience related to switching career tracks to industry: **Klaudia Ambroziak, Adriana Bankston, Ruud Berkers, Mirjam Bloemendaal, Miriam de Boer, Gary McDowell, Eliane Farnhauser, Jeffrey Glennon, Chris Hartgerink, Stephan Heunis, Marlieke van Kesteren, Mark Melnykowycz, Piotr Migdał, Gina Oana Popa, Raimon Pruim, Adeel Razi, Marzia Scelsi,** as well as a number of other contributors who preferred to stay anonymous. I would also like to cordially thank **Mozhan Soltani** for her help and advice with the book, **Elisenda Bonet-Carne** for her help in developing the landscape of post-PhD career tracks, and **Leonardo Morelli** for his help with the section dedicated to consultancy jobs. I would also like to thank **Vera Chan** and **Claire Braboszcz** for sharing their experience and for the insightful comments on the effective strategies for approaching job interviews.

Furthermore, I'd like to thank all the researchers and career experts who visited the Welcome Solutions' *Career Talks*[1] as guests and shared their personal experience and knowledge about post-PhD careers with us. This information greatly helped me in preparing the second edition of the book. Thank you, **Claudio Corrao, Annika Rausch, Maciej Jedynak, Leonardo Morelli, Ian Cameron, Peter Lewiński, Natalia Vtyurina, Andre Marques-Smith, Mattias Hansson, Maria Otworowska, Patrick Britz, Alessandro Montalto, Mariam Kostandyan, Victoria Sherwood, Adriana Bankston, Jeffrey Glennon, Danni Reches, Alican Noyan, Ricarda**

---

[1] www.welcome-solutions.com/index.php/career-talks

Braukmann, Lindy Ledohowski, Parag Mahanti, David Mendes, Eric James Stephens, Nick Edwards, Davide Rigoni, Carmen Rietdijk, Jen Polk, Matthias Hombauer, Irina Sheftel, Fabio Gori, Nadia Holden, Niels Zondervan, and **Jonathan Weitzman.**

I was also lucky to meet a number of extremely helpful people who edited and proofread this book: **David Guthwin** (*Introduction*), **Missy Green** (chapters 1, 5), **Jennifer Smith** (chapters 2, 7, *Last Words*), **Jeffrey Glennon** (chapters 3, 4), **Daniel Sharoh** (chapter 6), and **Stephan Heunis** (chapters 8, 9).

Mentoring circles

My adventure related to mentoring and working on career development for PhDs started in the *Organization for Human Brain Mapping Student and Postdoc Special Interest Group* (OHBM SP-SIG, also known as OHBM Trainees[2]). I was a member of this wonderful committee, serving as Career Development and Mentorship Manager in 2017-2019. During work toward my PhD, I had multiple ups and downs, and sometimes I felt that it was very hard to find like-minded people in my immediate environment. In the OHBM SP-SIG however, I found wonderful people with whom I shared common goals. We were all eager to improve the quality of life for early career researchers as far as we could with the resources we had. I believe that we got much further than we had expected! I hope that we will stay in touch for many years and that I will encounter people of this kind around academia more often. Lastly, I would like to add that I couldn't imagine a better platform to work on mentoring, but also to learn about leadership and teamwork. Therefore, I would like to give special thanks to **Michele Veldsman** and **AmanPreet Badhwar**, two wonderful and natural leaders who created the *OHBM International Online Mentoring Program*[3]. I would also like to thank all the other members of the committee: **Ayaka Ando, Alex Barnett, Chiara Caldinelli, Heidi Foo, Mengxia Gao, Shabnam Hakimi, Amelie Haugg, Leanna Hernandez, Lia Maria Hocke, Kaori Ito, Christian La, Meena Makary, Navot Naor, Aki Nikolaidis, Marzia Scelsi** and **Shruti Vij**. Working with this council was so enjoyable also because of the energetic and cooperative OHBM Executive Staff: **Stephanie McGuire, Kayla Stidger** and **JoAnn Taie**, as well as our OHBM council liaison, **Shella Keilholtz.**

I would like to further thank people who helped me with the foundation I am leading, *Stichting Solaris Onderzoek en Ontwikkeling*[4]: **Stephan Heunis, Lara Todorova, Alicja Łuszczak, Daniel Borek, Patrick Britz, Ali Khatibi, Adeel Razi, Mozhan Soltani, Chris Hartgerink, Sonal Sengupta, Daniele Marinazzo, Charl Linssen, Piray Atsak** and many other contributors and advisors. I greatly appreciate your support and hard work!

---

[2] www.ohbmtrainees.com

[3] www.ohbmtrainees.com/mentoring-programme

[4] www.stichting-solaris.github.io

My thanks go to the *eLife Ambassadors* community, especially to **Kora Korzec** who gave me an opportunity to serve as an eLife Associate in the *eLife Community Ambassadors* program 2019-2020, working with 243 fresh *eLife Ambassadors* on a broad range of topics concerning daily academic life, from responsible mentoring to mental health in academia. Thanks also to other members of the board of the program: **Lotte de Winde, Tracey Weissgerber** and **Mark Patterson**. Thanks as well to other associates I am working with: **Adriana Bankston, Samantha Hindle, Daniela Saderi, Huajin Wang** and **Steven Burgess**.

I would like to cordially thank **Veronika Cheplygina, Aidan Budd, Stephan Heunis**, and **Malvika Sharan**, with whom we co-organized a 5 day-long retreat (or rather, an un-conference) entitled *Avengers for Better Science*[5]. This event aimed at promoting Open Science, mentoring and inclusivity in the research community. It was great working on this with you!

Lastly, I would like to thank **Natalia Vtyurina**, a Chairperson of the *CRS Benelux & France Local Chapter*, a professional association oriented at helping PhDs in developing careers in industry. Natalia introduced me to a lot of wonderful people interested in post-PhD career tracks. *CRS Benelux & France Local Chapter*[6] is a great initiative!

Open Science movement

I would also like to express my appreciation to **Stephan Heunis** for inviting me to speak at the Open MR Benelux event, Leiden 2019, and to other speakers: **Daniele Marinazzo, Veronika Cheplygina, Gilles de Hollander, Tim van Mourik** and **Matthan Caan**. I was strongly encouraged to further pursue my mentoring activities at this event, and I got a lot of inspiration. I would also like to thank the *Open MR*[7] community launched and managed by Stephan for keeping this awesome initiative going. I am sure that *Open MR Benelux* will flourish! Furthermore, I would like to thank **Alessandro Crimi** and **Martyna Płomecka** for inviting me to speak at *Brainhack Zurich 2019*[8]. It was a great opportunity to actually share some of the content introduced in this book with a live audience and get valuable feedback before publication.

I would also like to thank the *AoN Brainhack Warsaw*[9] team. With this team, we organized the Brainhack event as a satellite of *Aspects of Neuroscience* conference in Warsaw, November 2017. So, thanks to **Daniel Borek, Krzysztof Bielski** and **Martyna Łempicka**, as well as the next committee AD 2019, which we had an opportunity to supervise: **Aleksander Molak, Karolina Baranowska, Ada Kochlewska** and **Martyna Płomecka**. *AoN Brainhack Warsaw* was the first major

---

[5] www.avengers-for-better-science.github.io

[6] www.bnlf-crs.org/home

[7] www.openmrbenelux.github.io

[8] www.brainhackzurich.ch

[9] www.brainhackwarsaw2017.github.io

international event I co-organized, but my peers made it very easy for me. It was a pleasure to work in this team from the first day until the last; we had a really good vibe, high synergy, and everything went really smoothly in the end. This event opened many doors for me and allowed me to make many new contacts.

I would like to thank two teams with whom I had the pleasure to work with at Brainhacks. Firstly, I would like to thank the team with whom I pursued the project *Functional connectivity: can we find the common ground?* at the *AoN Brainhack Warsaw* 2017: **Małgosia Wierzba, Grzegorz Link, Paulina Dąbrowska, Agnieszka Dębska, Aleksander Molak, Anna Alińska, Marcin Koculak, Cagdas Topcu, Agnieszka Tymorek, Juan Camilo, Emilia Kolada, Anastasia Neklyudova** and **Monika Derda**. Secondly, I would like to thank the team with whom I pursued the project *Trends in the resting brain* at *Brainhack Networks* 2018[10]: **Onerva Kohonen, Greg Koehler, Fabrizio Damicelli, Sarah Morgan** and **Pouya Ghaemmaghami**. It was great working with you all!

Friends

I would like to cordially thank all the other people who helped me after my academic PhD contract expired.

I would also like to thank **Lara Todorova**, with whom we carried out a few events, and spent countless Saturdays working hand in hand. I would like to thank **Joanna Widomska**. I really enjoyed goofing around together at Ibiza and in Orlando, and all the other little moments spent together—and especially the gratitude walks around Goffert park; and **Alina Lartseva**, with whom we kept on dancing, and dancing and dancing, and who taught me a lot about Dutch ways of thinking and customs. I would like to thank to **Max Hinne** for helping me with translating the deed of formation for Stichting Solaris, and for all the career advice. Thanks to **Piray Atsak** for our regular late-night sessions by a glass of wine and long talks about life and whereabouts. Also, cordial thanks to **Veronika Cheplygina** and **Mattias Hanson** for their advice and help. Thank you for working on my self-confidence, and for your warm words in hard times! Thanks also to **Ewa Roszak**, my long-lasting friend and a professional coach who was always on the line for me, as well as to **Caroline Pakel** who mentored me through Skype and shared advice on how I should work on my sense of self-value as a professional, and how to negotiate for myself.

I would also like to thank people I have met in the blockchain circles. Firstly, I would like to thank **Jana Petkanic** and **Luuk Weber** from the Blockchain Talks team. It is very nice to work with you; thank you for sharing what you know about how this industry works! I would also like to give my words of acknowledgment to **Richard Kohl** for encouraging me to write about blockchains and crypto. I wouldn't even think of it if Richard did not advise me to try! Furthermore, I would like to thank **Eleonore Blanc, Justin Bons, Olivier de Jong, Dirk Kadijk, Alvin Leito, Bart van Maarseveen, Natalia Nowakowska, Dax Nagtegaal, Ekin Tuna, David, Adriana Truong**, and **Hans Vanmechelen**. Lastly, I would like to highlight the good influence of **Sanne Groeneveld** and **Hugo Schoenbeck** on my activities in the blockchain

---

[10] www.brainhack-networks.org

community, and on my well-being in general. They are both very empathetic and understanding and helped me a lot in hard times when I was at the end of my PhD. I would also like to thank the *Qnext* team led by **Javad van Landewijk** and **Justin Floeter**: **Christian Martin, Bram de Lange, Lucca Spaapen, Yann van Ewijk, Yacine Bourouba,** and **Hoang Nguyen** (in collaboration with **Jelte Veldmeijer** and **Hein-Pieter van Braam**). Specials thanks to Javad for teaching me how to play black jack! I would also like to thank the *Impakt Tribe* team, **Marijn Kegel, Jeroen van der Heide** (with the help from **Dirk Kadijk**), for teaching me about entrepreneurship and salesmanship.

My other tribes

This year, I also started working on my own innovative project—which I hope grow in the future! I would like to thank **Alina Bielczyk, Rwik Mukhopadhyay, Moazzem Hossen** and **Marcin Grzybowski** for their engagement in the project, and their efforts in making it work. I would also like to thank **Ewa Bielczyk, Radosław Chrapkiewicz, Cees van Diemen, Sanne Groeneveld, Jeroen van der Heide, Jacob Issa, Olivier de Jong, Dirk Kadijk, Niels Keurentjes, Michał Krych, Mattie Lafleur, Alvin Leito, Grzegorz Link, Alicja Łuszczak, Kornel Maczyński, Piotr Migdał, Iwona Mochol** and **Hugo Schoenbeck** for constructive comments on the concept and business plan.

I would also like to thank my colleagues from the *OHBM Fundraising Committee*: **Kayla Stidger, Michael Mullaly, Jessica Turner, Abhinav Yadav, Alan Evans, Arthur Toga, Lilianne Mujica-Parodi, Alain Dagher**, and **M. S. Zobae**. I learned a lot about fundraising from you!

I would also like to thank wonderful people whom I met at *Hackerspace Nijmegen*: **Jimmy Comack, Ed van Dalen, Sjors Gielen, Michiel Klaarwater, Stefan Marsiske, Sjoerd Timmer, Pol, Joep, Dan, Bart, Bas, Bas, Ant** and others. Hackerspace is an initiative in which anyone is welcome to participate in technical and art-related group projects. I would also like to thank **Rob Hermens, Wim Hamersma,** and other members of *Stip Nijmegen Oost* who taught me a lot about gardening.

Lastly, I would like to thank the members of *Pecunia Causa*, a student investment club at Radboud University. It was lovely to join the meetings and I learned a great deal! So, thanks to **Koen Smeets, Rinze Hartman, Martijn van Os**, and all the monthly attendees!

The unnamed

I would also like to thank all the unnamed individuals with whom I talked about their career paths over the years. From chats with other academics over beer, through encounters with the locals on long distance travels in different parts of the world, to casual chats with strangers at bus stops and train stations.

Family

Thanks to my sis, **Ewa Bielczyk-Maczyńska**, my little sister who is always going forward with her life. You go girl!

Enduring thanks to my mother, **Alina Bielczyk**, who has freely shared with me her 30-year experience in corporate life, always advising me down the line. I have no idea how much time we spent on Skype discussing my PhD work—it must have been hundreds of hours. I must say that I was surprised to find how much of my Mum's wisdom applies to academia. She is also very patient and persistent, a hard-worker and an optimist at the same time. I am grateful that she was always standing by my side, even in the darkest times when I was down and deep in trouble, ambivalent about how to proceed with my life and whether to even pursue science at all. She is just always there, no matter what. Also, I would like to have as much energy as she does—she is the most work-focused person I have ever met.

Lastly,,,

...I feel grateful for the opportunity to live in the Netherlands. This country really gave me everything. The Netherlands is one of these places where you feel safe in daily life, people are helpful and not judgmental and let you live your life the way you want. I am not sure if I would be the person I am now if I lived anywhere else. Although Dutch people sometimes do comically inexcusable things—for instance repainting Big Bird from Sesame Street from yellow to blue and calling it Pino—I still love this place!

INTRODUCTION

A walk through a dark wood

Coming of age can be a long journey. Who could expect that after years and years of under- and postgraduate studies, when you hit your late 20s or early 30s, you would still be highly uncertain of whom you'll become when you grow up? You were always the best student in your classroom. You were always a high-flyer. And now, you feel that perhaps you need to start over from scratch. And, you ask yourself, "What now? What is out there for me? Which path to take?" It's a scary place to be!

My story after PhD

It was a typical, dim fall in the Netherlands when I started sending off my job applications. I had come to the Netherlands a few years before, after I had graduated from a triple MS in Physics, Mathematics, and Psychology at the University of Warsaw, Poland. My primary reason for moving here was to enroll in a prestigious PhD program in neuroscience at the Donders Centre for Brain, Cognition and Behavior at Radboud University Medical Centre in Nijmegen. After my PhD contract expired, I rested for a long time. I needed that, as the program was, generally, hard and frustrating. But now, I have concluded that this was the time to find an occupation in which I could further develop, excel, and spread my wings. And it soon turned out that doing so is not as easy as I had thought it would be.

First, I looked into possibilities for financial assistance during the job search. Unfortunately, I found that in the Netherlands people who happen to be house owners are not offered unemployment benefits unless they sell their property. Having a house under a mortgage that I did not want to sell, I knew that I had to find a source of income as soon as possible and that it couldn't be a random job like a shopping assistant or a waitress because I was insufficiently fluent in Dutch.

I started my job search from browsing through job-listing websites and social networks for professionals such as *LinkedIn*[11]. I soon realized that the job offers were

---

[11] www.linkedin.com

written in a very non-transparent way. It was hard to even decode what a given job was about. In every job offer, I was finding the same pseudo-language. Everyone was searching for "an enthusiastic, highly motivated team worker," and everyone was offering "opportunities for growth"—whatever that meant. I applied for a few jobs that sounded interesting, but I flopped at the first round and I wasn't even invited to the interviews. Just as expected—given that I didn't really know what type of job I was even applying for.

So, I soon changed the strategy and turned to private companies specialized in finding jobs for PhD graduates. As a person who was just finishing a good program, and who personally knocked at their door, I should have been most welcome, right? I had quite an extensive academic background, and a long list of papers as a PhD-to-be. I also had quite a lot of management and mentoring experience through involvement in numerous events and participation in more than a few student boards during my graduate studies. I felt that my resume was really strong and that I was easy money for any prospective employer. What could possibly go wrong?

So, I paid a visit to such an agency, and soon felt rattled by the way I was received. Recruiters were confused and didn't really know how to classify me—a specialist? Or maybe a junior manager? I felt that my value as a professional was really high, and in general, recruiters agreed with me. However, my value did not make me employable in their eyes. The other day, a professional recruiter even told me openly that given my skills and experience, I should be placed in a high executive position at a large corporation. But, since my set of skills was so unique, it would have taken his people *too much time and effort* to find that suitable position for me. Thus, it wouldn't have been profitable for them to try; they were only interested in the "easy cases" which require a minimum of calling and emailing to place PhDs at specialist industry positions in the area of the market corresponding with their previous research field. The result of my inquiries was that all the private recruiters I contacted refused to help me.

Then it occurred to me that I might try to monetize my mentoring activities and turn them into a day job. For the whole previous year, I was doing a lot of nonprofit voluntary work, by helping as a Career Development and Mentoring Manager in the student board of the Organization for Human Brain Mapping. I loved doing this, and the council seemed happy with my work as well—but this function wasn't paid. Therefore, I looked into possibilities to work in one of the institutions that take care of the professional development of researchers: startup accelerators, career centers at universities, governmental agencies responsible for developing new educational policies. I cold-emailed many offices, but I was not lucky with that either. They were politely answering that they did not have any vacancies at the moment, or that they only worked in Dutch (which I don't really know well enough at the moment). Or, they did not answer at all. These positions were very hard to get without any connections. And even in instances where I was relatively well-connected, it seemed that I did not have the right connections. It was sad and depressing to me that people working in these centers might answer my email after a month or two (or not at all); I work really hard and always answer emails fast while those to whom I sent email queries typically did not bother too much about their professional correspondence, and yet were chosen for their jobs.

I turned, next, to the blockchain circles which I had been in touch with since the summer of 2017. At some point in 2017, I started attending monthly conferences in the blockchain industry in Amsterdam, and I never stopped, although my interest in the subject cooled. I met a lot of people there, and knowing that I have strong technical writing skills, I started thinking that I might join some projects and write white papers for them. A white paper is a bit like a business plan, except that it is focused on the technicalities more than on the business model. Unfortunately, it soon turned out that a lot of people are interested in my writing services but only willing to pay in shares, and not in cash. It's exciting to have an equity stake in startups but I would die from starvation before any of these companies ever gains in value to the point when I can capitalize on my shares.

I also applied for some traineeship positions in corporations. The value of these positions was that they were associated with many opportunities for personal growth within the company. But on the other hand, the contracts offered were not attractive. As a person about to graduate with a PhD, I was getting the same job offers as fresh BSc graduates: low pay, uncertain future role within the company, plus a clause that would penalize me for leaving the company any earlier than after two years.

Then, I started knocking at the doors of the institutions that are supposed to help the unemployed. In the Netherlands, there are thousands of career consultants employed by universities, health centers, unemployment agencies, etc. Unfortunately, many of these people are unhelpful: they listen to you for an hour, smile and nod in the process, and in the end, they politely say, "Sorry, I cannot help you. You might be willing to contact the following person..." And that's the end of the conversation! After two or three trials, I was so frustrated that I decided not to try again. What are these people even paid for?

In the end, I discovered that, given all I had done in my life so far, the only way to get a "normal job" and to live on a decent level was to accept one of the jobs in data science that I was offered in the process. In the Netherlands, there is a huge market for jobs in data science, machine learning, and AI at the moment; there is a deep deficiency of high-class specialists in this area. As a result, if you have *any* programming experience, you'll get almost any position you apply for—even if you don't know the exact programming language they need at the moment. Most companies need data science consultants so badly that they'll also try to bind you to the company for as long as possible. Therefore, job contracts often include a clause that enforces you to stay in the company for another 12 or 24 months—with a monetary penalty in case of early departure.

In the Netherlands, data science jobs for PhDs are generally well-paid and usually accompanied by attractive working benefits. This is something that my family and friends were trying to persuade me to do for a long time. In situations like this, people around you usually think that they know better, and give you a lot of advice even if you don't ask for it. Everyone tells you something different, yet you have a feeling that they don't really know what you are like on the inside, and what you really need. To my parents, "data science" sounded like the most logical and natural thing to do, especially after getting a background in Mathematics and Physics, and then in Computational Neuroscience. To my friends, among whom many went into data science and were really happy there, this was a no-brainer too. This occupation meant living on a good standard, 40-50 days of paid vacation per year, a lot of career options, income safety, a continuation of the same lifestyle that I had had before, and overall peace of mind.

The whole problem was that I *did not* want to become a Data Scientist. During my PhD program I had to try a lot of different activities—from conceptual work and planning new projects, through statistics, programming, writing, presenting, and publishing in peer-reviewed literature, to teaching students, organizing events, and other logistic activities. Among all these, I enjoyed the programming part *the least*. I always felt pumped and enthusiastic when I was getting a new research idea, and when I was converting the idea on my mind into a plan on paper. I felt I was accumulating a lot of energy during that initial phase of the project. Then, I felt like slowly dying in pain when I had to put this idea into code. The energy accumulated before was slowly leaking until nothing was left, and I felt like a zombie. Of course, I had a lot of bad feelings associated with this state of mind, from anxiety to mood swings. Whenever I was done with all the analysis, had to write down the results, draft the paper, send it to a journal, and then go out to other people to present the output, I was feeling like both the mental power and the feeling of overall satisfaction from the project were slowly returning to me, and my face was reacquiring life-like color. The scenario was the same every time.

At that point, I felt trapped and frustrated. Companies didn't trust my managing and mentoring skills enough to offer me executive positions. At the same time, I was most welcome to join them as a Data Scientist—which would be a nightmare job for me. The problem was also that, whatever I was thinking of doing with my life next, the range of income in all these occupations was not looking good. In data science and other technical jobs, the distribution of income is uniform, and all jobs are well-paid. If you are a freshman in data science, you can already get, say, double or even triple the mean salary in your country of affiliation, and from that point, your salary will be gradually going up together with your working experience. After a few years of professional development in this area, you can enjoy double or triple that initial salary, and you can live on a very high standard. To sum up, the distribution of salaries in the data science field is relatively uniform and usually spreads between twofold and fivefold of the average salary. This implies that as a Data Scientist you can be *certain* to live well, but at the same time you have rather slim chances of becoming a multimillionaire in the process. On the other hand, all the jobs I was leaning towards, from writing to working on the careers of other people, have a completely different distribution of income. In these disciplines, income is very dependent on the personal brand, and the distribution of income is scale-free rather than flat: a small group of people can live on a very high standard while the vast majority starves. I wasn't greedy but I didn't want to starve either, so it was a very hard choice to make.

I was thinking to myself multiple times, "Natalia, you bloody Millennial! Maybe you expect too much? Just take any job, and be happy that you even have one." This is a state of mind in which you are restless and stressed. Weirdly, at the same time, you feel very much alive—maybe even more alive than ever. But on the other hand, this is a state of mind which you want to escape as soon as you possibly can. One hopes for a lucky escape, of course.

I observed people for a long time while attending meetups and conferences, and while working in student associations. I tried to find out where I best fit as a person. I was attending gatherings of the nearby student business club, I was attending some Hackerspace, I joined many online discussion groups, and I participated in dozens of thematic Slack groups in many areas of science and industry. I knew that one day, I would meet my tribe, a group of my soulmates whom I simply resonate with.

The story ended up well for me. I learned how to get offers for jobs in corporations and smaller companies—not only the data science jobs, but also positions in logistics, project management, and education. However, in the process, I learned a few things about myself, which eventually stopped me from accepting any of these positions.

As mentioned before, I used to attend a lot of blockchain conferences. So, one day it struck me how much I shared with these people, especially in terms of the sense of humor and outlook on life. This couldn't be accidental. The more time I was spending with them, the more astonished I was about how much we were alike. It felt a bit like discovering brothers and sisters I had never met before. I looked back at my life, and everything all of a sudden started to make sense. For instance, for some reason, as much as I liked the academic community, my befriended researchers rarely laughed at my jokes—they used to find them either too dry or too edgy. I always had different hobbies than most people around me when I was in graduate school—while others were enjoying their beers at the local bar, or traveling around Europe with friends on the weekends, I used to sit down glued to my computer, and google to find out what's the hottest stock on S&P 500, or what's the next big technological innovation.

On the contrary, people whom I met in blockchain circles were just like me. Whenever I spent time with them, I felt understood, pumped, and inspired. They laughed at my jokes and in their eyes, I had a bright rather than quirky personality. I looked back at my childhood and youth, and it seemed to me that the signs that I might have a soul of an entrepreneur were always there. While other kids were playing in the yard, I used to collect and sell herbs while on vacation. I also traded little collectibles such as the souvenirs with pictures from the movie *The Lion King* at primary school, and I was restless until I had the biggest collection in the whole school. When it came to choosing studies, I chose to study... *freedom.* Namely, I went to study at the College of Inter-Faculty Individual Studies in Mathematics and Natural Sciences (MISMaP) at the University of Warsaw. At that time in Poland, this was the only college that offered full freedom to choose any subjects within the scope of seventeen natural sciences. And, I was very happy with my choice. To sum up, ever since I remember, I had a lot of entrepreneurial behaviors—I just didn't pay attention to them.

I also remember one situation that finally convinced me to act on these inclinations. In the summer of 2019, I visited the major conference in my research field. It was in Rome, and while being there, I was still hesitating what to do next—I could still consider some Postdoc position if the people and the project would suit me.

One afternoon I bumped into one of the major Principal Investigators (or, PIs) in the field, and we went for a walk to the nearby park to chat about science and life in general. So, we were sitting on some tree trunk laughing and exchanging ideas. At some point, I felt that I was done with the foreplay and that this was the right moment to finally ask about positions in his lab. However, before I managed to open my mouth, he said, "Natalia, you know what… Just let me know if you start a company, I might apply to work there!" I didn't know if to laugh or cry, but eventually, I concluded that it was quite a hilarious situation. Now I realized that the only difference between entrepreneurs and me was that I never decided to become one. And, so I did.

Of course, the beginnings were not easy—but I revived right after I stopped perceiving myself as *an unemployed person* and started looking at myself as an *entrepreneur with zero revenue*. This transition in thinking has instantly put my brain into a hacking and selling mode, and I have been happily building up my businesses ever since.

The problems related to post-PhD career tracks

Anyway, even though I came to a happy ending, in the process of searching for my way I realized that I was not the only person who needs to take a lot of time at the end of the academic contract to find a new career path. Since the number of faculty positions is growing much slower than the number of PhD graduates (Schillebeeckx et al., 2013), there is a whole crowd of highly educated people who need to sail away from academic community towards a new land—either because they change their plans, or because there are not enough good positions for them in academia. I experienced this statistic personally as I know dozens, or even hundreds, of confused PhDs at the end of their contracts. The new, post-PhD reality is usually associated with lots of stress and anxiety, as well as the lack of understanding from family and friends who are not academics. People used to tell you, "You have a good education so you'll be fine, right?" But, finding an enjoyable new job is not as easy as it seems at first—even with good credentials. There is such a huge difference between finding a job, and finding the right job! Also, making a step from academia towards industry is more than just changing *a job*: it also automatically implies changing a *profession*, and that's a whole new level of difficulty.

I was sad to realize that the same people who used to be the smartest and the most hard-working kids in the classroom, now need to line up asking for jobs from those who used to be C-students for all their lives. I was also sad to realize that people who sacrificed their whole youth to studying, and to producing new knowledge in good faith, are often treated like fresh meat by recruiters, and placed at the lowest specialist positions somewhere in a cubicle in the corner. For some jobs, they are overqualified while for some other jobs they don't have enough practical experience to be a serious contender for the position. Many PhDs keep fully focused on their academic projects, and when their contracts expire, they all of a sudden find themselves in some sort of limbo, in which there is no clear path for further self-development.

Also, academia doesn't prepare early career researchers for industry jobs properly. It's a typical case of the *tragedy of the commons* (Hardin, 1968). It would be better for the whole society if early career researchers were helped with getting more information about the open job market, sending them to internships in private companies during their PhD program, or guiding them to professional courses dedicated to building transferable skills. But, for every PI, the priority is to make sure that the students are glued to their PhD projects and produce manuscripts rather than happily explore the job market—otherwise, the grant money will dry up one day, and the PI and their other employees will be in trouble. So, even the good and empathic PIs need to first take care of the financial condition of the lab before they spend any time and money giving their PhD candidates all these opportunities—and that's how PhD students are exploited. Making progress in this area will most probably be impossible without institutional regulations (Sinche et al., 2017)—just as in any other case of the tragedy of the commons.

So, what's the outcome of this phenomenon? A crowd of very well-educated yet confused young people who are full of hesitation as to what to do after their PhD work comes to the end. We like to think that our life is a sort of movie script in which everything happens for a reason and that there will be a happy ending one day. Acquiring the PhD credentials is a hard challenge, time and energy-consuming as well as emotionally draining… and then, one day, it comes to the end. This is when you start thinking, "What was it for? What's the conclusion? What's the pay-off? What's the climax of my story?" It turns out that the story might be just starting now for you, and that you'll need to make your best efforts to find your true calling, and that there is no guardian angel and no one can help you but yourself.

Moreover, what we experience in the open job market these days, is the *curse of abundance*: there are so many options that, paradoxically, the mean satisfaction from work dropped compared to the situation a few decades ago. Actually, in the US, the percentage of employees declaring themselves as satisfied with their jobs, dropped from 61.1% in 1987 to 47.7% in 2014 (Cheng et al., 2014). As highly educated individuals with lots of career options, PhDs are even more vulnerable to this effect than the rest of society.

How this book was conceived

Needless to say, conceiving things is pleasant! When I was looking for my way in the world, I googled a lot, and found that the problems and solutions related to switching careers from academia to industry is a black hole in the scientific literature. Although a lot of attention in the academic press is dedicated to mental health problems, little attention is paid to looking for *practical solutions*, for instance for good directions to ship young, ambitious, creative people from academia to industry. Not many statistics can be found on post-academic career paths, except for a few single studies, e.g., a psychometric study on post-PhD careers of early career researchers in science, technology, engineering, and mathematics (a.k.a. STEM sciences) in the United Kingdom and Canada (Woolston, 2018) which reports that this particular group of PhDs enjoys higher salaries than their non-PhD counterparts in the same age group. There is not much self-help literature for PhDs thinking of a career switch though. This lack of resources struck me given that the group of academics who experience this issue worldwide is in the range of millions.

At some point, it came to my mind, "Why don't you write a book? After this long process of self-discovery and job search, you learned so much, especially about what NOT to do, that this is already a book material." I had a strong desire to share this knowledge, but I felt scared at first. Looking for jobs is not rocket science after all; it's burdened with the strong human factor. You just can't give a mathematical formula for how to find a perfect job. Moreover, the academic community is a very complex organism, and there are multiple groups of PhDs with differing sets of hard and soft skills. In every country, in every institute, and even in every single lab, the working conditions are a bit different—and so are the graduating PhDs. Eventually, I came to the conclusion that this book is really necessary and I decided to take the challenge.

I also decided to write *the truth* instead of coloring the reality—this is why to some, the content of this book might be bittersweet. When we start PhD programs, we are usually told by everyone around us, from promoters to parents, that a PhD program is the acme of education and that it's always a good thing to enter no matter what happens next. No, it is not always the case. With a lack of good winds, graduate school can turn you into 30-year-old wreckage unable to mentally handle any job. Under certain circumstances, the PhD title can also decrease your chances to get a job in industry—and I personally know some people who openly declare that PhD has actually *blocked* them from getting their dream job. Just as everything else that happens to you, the PhD program can turn into something that brings you closer to, or blocks you from becoming happy. It just depends on what you do with the knowledge gained during your PhD time.

Let's improve together!

I'm a researcher myself and I dedicated this book to other researchers. Yet, while talking about jobs, careers, and self-development, I cannot back up many of the statements made in this book with scientific research. The reason is that the mechanisms underlying human motivation, the roots of happiness, and the determinants of professional success are still rather unexplored topics. In this book, I backed my statements with research literature whenever I could, yet still, a large portion of the text comes from street wisdom, from common sense, from motivational and self-help literature, from my conclusions, as well as from observing and interviewing the people I met on my way. On many occasions, I cited press articles and blog posts rather than scientific studies, due to the lack of research in this area. I also had to generalize on many occasions. Some statements are also my personal opinions—and I was doing my best to clearly indicate whenever this was the case.

Writing books, quite the same as writing research papers, is all about being humble and taking others' opinions on board. Therefore, I would be grateful for any feedback on this volume you might have—you are always welcome to write to me, and the *Feedback Information* is given at the end of the book. I'm also curious about your personal career story. If any of the tips found in this book help you, and if you would like to share your story, please write to me as well! I would be most happy to share your success story online.

Take-home message

If I had to choose just one take-home message from this book, I would use a puzzle metaphor. When we are looking for jobs, we often dive into the sea of opportunities. We google, we browse through *LinkedIn* and job boards, we ask around. We want to know about these jobs as much as we possibly can, including all the details of the workspace, the office, the team, the working benefits, etc. And, we tend to fish for the *best job*.

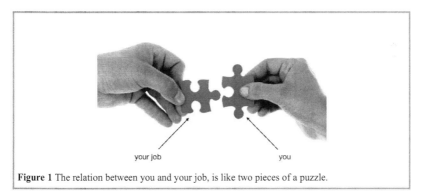

Figure 1 The relation between you and your job, is like two pieces of a puzzle.

But at the same time, we often forget about finding out as much as possible about *ourselves*. You and your job are two parts of the same puzzle (Fig. 1) which should fit together. And, if you are looking for a job, you should choose jobs which are *best suited* to you, and not just those which look best on paper. Most of the job satisfaction comes from non-material values, and if your job doesn't meet your values, you won't be happy there. Moreover, if you don't know your limits and boundaries, finding the right job will take you forever—as you'll keep on walking in the dark, and sampling jobs by trial and error.

This is why self-discovery is so important in the process. Society is a very complex environment. To be able to navigate in this environment, you need to be perfectly conscious of your own strengths and weaknesses, of your hard and soft skills. But you also need to be certain about your personal working style and your preferences towards the working environment. Don't worry though! Self-discovery can be a pleasant and exciting activity, and this is what this book is all about. It's worth dedicating time to this topic, as every minute spent on thinking about whom you are, and about your strengths and weaknesses, will pay back hundredfold in the long run.

This take-home message could be rephrased as "there is no such thing as the best job." While we would all agree on certain aspects of a "good job" (e.g., given a choice, we would all probably choose a higher-paid over a lower-paid position), most of the other features need to meet your personal preferences. Some people enjoy working alone and not being bothered by anyone while others prefer working in teams, and running from one meeting to another. Some people like quiet offices while others prefer an open space. Some people prefer taking a role of a specialist, or a problem-solver, on the team while others prefer managing others.

To sum up, this book aims to give you an overview of post-PhD career opportunities and share some tips on how to find your strengths and limits. None of the possibilities is better than the others; it's a matter of your own, individual working style, your set of skills, and flexibility.

How this book is structured

This book is dedicated primarily to PhDs in science, technology, engineering, and mathematics (a.k.a., STEM sciences), and in life/medical sciences. It is because, in other fields such as humanities and social sciences, certain elements of academic lifestyle can be different from STEM and life sciences. For instance, in humanities and social sciences, it is more common to have individualistic projects and publish research papers as a sole author in the context of PhD candidacy, while in exact sciences this is an extremely rare situation and most publications list multiple authors. Therefore, the scope of skills acquired during a PhD program in humanities might differ from the scope of skills acquired during a PhD program in STEM and life sciences.

However, I believe that there is still a lot of valuable information that researchers in social sciences and humanities could get out of this book! Most of the advice given here is universal across disciplines and I hope that every reader will get some useful insights from this material. I can also recommend supplementing this material with additional solutions such as free online mentoring programs dedicated to humanities. An example of such a program can be the Open Post Academics Mentorship Program[12]. This program aims to empower PhDs in the social sciences and humanities to expand their network to people outside of academia, to understand their skill set, and learn how to apply their training and abilities to projects beyond academia.

Also, as mentioned before, career development is not rocket science, and it's not possible to give one formula to find a perfect job. For me personally, this was the hard aspect to learn as I have an analytic mind and I always try to rationalize problems, simplify them, and come up with algorithmic solutions. In this case, however, it is simply not possible.

Since there are no algorithms for how to find a dream job, this book is based on self-reflection to a large extent. I introduce the scope of possibilities for post-PhD career trajectories, and I also include a lot of self-reflection questions to give you some food for thought. Answering these questions will help you in your self-discovery and

[12] www.openpostac.org

in finding your way if you decide to start a new career in industry. I also placed a brief take-home message at the end of each chapter, to sum up its content.

Good luck!

Natalia

CONTENTS

PART I

How to make the decision, and find your strengths

CHAPTER 1

SHOULD I STAY, OR SHOULD I GO?

Leave academia?

First, let's make one thing clear. The expression "to leave academia" sounds pejorative—as if you were jumping ship, giving up, or something along those lines. If you are in the process of transitioning to industry, you *do* leave the system which you grew up in behind—but it might also be the start of something beautiful, and a chance to bring a lot of value to society (and much more wealth for yourself). And, as I will attempt to convince you in this book, it's even more likely that in industry your overall impact will *grow* rather than drop. However, for now, let's avoid using the expression "leaving academia," and refer to "transitioning to industry" instead.

The right and wrong reasons to make the transition

Can you be happy in academia? Of course! I know many people who are very happy as professional academic researchers. Academic success comes from a combination of a few factors: finding a topic you are passionate about, a healthy environment, people whom you enjoy working with, and the place that offers you good lifestyle and working conditions. If all these stars align, you can become a happy academic and stay around for a lifetime. However, most researchers lose balance in their academic life at some point. And then, they start asking themselves, "Should I stay, or should I go?"

This book is addressed both to those who have already decided to transition to industry and those who are still hesitating. So, if you happen to be a member of the latter group, this chapter might be of particular interest to you. My personal experience is that many researchers consider the transition for all the wrong reasons. This results in a high risk of disappointment in the future. In this chapter, I'd like to discuss the five most common wrong and right reasons why you might consider a career switch to industry.

To my mind, the main wrong reason to move to industry is an attempt to avoid *games* or *politics*. We all know this slow process of turning from an idealistic, fresh PhD candidate obsessed with science to a calculated player who always thinks about possible returns before taking on any new research project. In the first year of a PhD program, most of the lunch discussions with your peers concern your new projects, courses, summer schools, conferences, other new scientific events, and new opportunities. In the last year of your PhD however, you spend your lunch breaks gossiping about your boss, talking about whose contract is ending next, and discussing how to secure enough money to stay around for one more year. One day you realize that the senior researchers spend their whole life like this: hustling, making deals, establishing formal and informal coalitions, managing money. Some early career researchers are disgusted by academia at this point—and to many, this is the ultimate deal-breaker that persuades them to move towards industry.

Is this a valid reason to say "No" to academia? Let's see. If you decide to enter a corporation, you'll soon learn that there are internal fractions—cliques whose members help each other career-wise and back each other up in trouble. In the stereotypical view, corporate cliques are groups of few individuals who habitually smoke together on the balcony and secretly gossiping behind the glass door. In reality, those mutual admiration societies are much harder to notice. If you go to an environment like this, you'll be astonished that those who get promoted are not necessarily the best employees but rather, the most skilled and ruthless corporate rats (Schrijvers, 2002). And, fighting for positions in corporations can be even more cut-throat than it is in academia. It is because the disproportion between salaries at the top and the bottom of the pay scale is way higher in corporations. Fighting for money can trigger the worst in people.

If you decide to go to a startup for a change, you'll soon notice that the startup structure is not as flat. Namely, those who happened to find themselves in the right place at the right time—who joined the company in the early stages—now have a lot of shares and power in the company. These individuals will get more responsible tasks than you, and their opinion will be more trusted—even though you might be much more skilled and hard-working than them.

If you start working as a freelancer, you'll soon find out that it's better to select projects that give maximum returns at the minimum effort and pass more energy-consuming or tedious projects to others—befriended freelancers or subcontractors. You'll also find out that you get at least 80% of your contracts through skillful networking and salesmanship and not because the quality of your services speaks for itself. As it turns out, the best-paid people are those who are in the spotlight and not those who are the most competent. Thus, you will need to invest an incredible amount of time and effort in constant self-promotion and making thousands of new connections.

Lastly, if you choose to become an entrepreneur, you'll be surrounded by con artists all the time. You'll need to quickly learn how to find the right people, stick to them, and negotiate good deals for yourself, or otherwise, you'll starve.

Wherever you go, there will always be fewer seats at the top than the number of contenders interested in these seats. Only people with strong interpersonal and adaptive skills will be able to get there.

Also, isn't this true that in some way, every job sooner or later becomes a game? In every working environment, there are some written and unwritten rules that decide about the ultimate professional success. Once you learn these rules, you have a choice: you can follow the rules, or you can go your own way and risk that you won't be as appreciated as deserved given all your competencies. Perhaps, it's better to accept the reality—namely, to accept the fact that politics is prevalent in the job market—and start building a strong personal network rather than deny it and try to run from it. Therefore, if politics in academia is the main reason why you are thinking of quitting, please think twice.

The second wrong reason to make a career switch towards industry is the *uncertainty* associated with a research career. Most academics are uncomfortable with constantly being compared with others, and with the necessity to think many steps ahead and secure the next contract before the current contract comes to the end. This is a tricky one. Especially for researchers who already have families, *safety* is the factor that has a major influence on the general well-being. However, we live in very uncertain times in which the job market morphs very quickly. You'll need to follow this development and keep on learning, or otherwise, you'll stay behind. These days, large corporations actively stimulate their employees to grow by shifting them from one department to another every 2-3 years. This effectively means that even with a permanent contract within a large company, you are expected to effectively change your occupation every 2-3 years. Furthermore, many new professions appear on the market while other professions become obsolete and disappear. For instance, nowadays, crowds of PhDs go towards data science and machine learning since this field is developing and the offered working conditions are very good. Is this still going to be the case in 10 or 20 years? What if the most machine learning jobs will be taken over by machines—as the name suggests?

Furthermore, wherever you go, you'll need to make someone happy: either your boss or your clients. For this reason, you will always be evaluated in one way or another. In fact, in industry, you are much more often compared to others than in academia—and in much more quantifiable ways. For instance, if you are a consultant, a salesman, or a manager in sales, the sales made by you and/or your people will always be compared to the results of other employees or to your results from the past. Marketing is all about the numbers: bad results for a prolonged period won't go unnoticed, this is for sure. In academia, on the other hand, everyone has their own, individual project with its own limitations. For this reason, differing amounts of output between researchers within the same research group usually meet with understanding. In academia, it is also much more accepted to go on sick leave if you are in a bad mental condition. In industry, your boss might take such an occurrence as a financial loss to the company, and this might jeopardize your future career plans in that place.

To sum up, there will always be a degree of uncertainty and pressure wherever you go. So, if your main reason for switching jobs to industry is to minimize your discomfort, you might be massively disappointed with what you find in the open job market.

The third reason I would like to discuss here is *finances*. In academia, there is a common belief that somewhere out there, *they are paid much better than us*. It might be true that in certain fields of the market, industry jobs will guarantee you a starting salary higher than your current earnings. But this is only true in some areas of the market, and it very much depends on the current market demand in your area. Moreover, bad salaries in science is a myth. In most countries in the world, even if Postdoc salaries are not as high as counterpart salaries in the industry, they are still much higher than the *average* salary. If you don't have any savings as a Postdoc, this might indicate that you suffer from so-called lifestyle inflation (more about this topic in chapter 7: *Work on Your Personal Freedom*). This means that you are so good at spending your money that even if your salary is doubled, you'll still spend it all. In such a case, what difference does your salary make anyway? In such a situation, you should concentrate on cutting your monthly expenses rather than searching for a better-paid job.

Besides, money should never be the main driver to choose the job. If you are looking for personal satisfaction from work, high income won't guarantee you that feeling. It usually works the other way around: good income will naturally become a side effect of doing something you enjoy, something you are good at, and something that creates high value to other people. So again, if you want to jump to industry with the sole purpose of finding a better-paid job, you may become disappointed discovering that your perceived quality-of-life didn't increase as expected.

The fourth reason I would like to mention here is a *personal conflict*. Some researchers are so tired of their current superiors that they step outside academia to "take a break for a while." It often happens that they never come back. People often have incompatible working styles, and perhaps you currently experience such a mismatch. If you happen to have a personality clash with your advisor or some other senior researcher in your team, extrapolating this situation to possible future collaborations and resigning from the academic career might not be the right choice— especially if you are still in love with your research topic. Personal issues can take a lot of life energy, but at the end of the day, it's all about whether *you* believe that your research is valuable. The opinion of other people (especially if this is a single opinion) should not matter to you as much as your own gut feeling.

Also, the judgment of people is a very subjective topic. If one person finds you difficult to work with, it doesn't mean that the person next door won't find you to be a nice and collaborative person. If you feel unappreciated in your current working environment, but you still feel excited about your research, you might consider giving yourself another chance, and going for another research project somewhere else before you make the ultimate decision to switch careers. There are thousands of successful PIs who had personal conflicts with their superiors in the past but never lost drive and passion for science—and eventually, they made it to the top. Almost every PI had some form of a bottleneck in the past, and these bottlenecks made them stronger in the process. If you don't believe this is the case, you might casually ask some fellow PIs about their career path over drinks. If after a few beers you ask them, "What went wrong in your own career?" I am sure they'll have plenty of stories to tell.

Lastly, one clearly wrong reason for switching to industry is the *bandwagon effect*. This psychological phenomenon happens when people blindly follow the decisions of people around them without any valid reasons to do so (e.g., when everyone around you buys the newest and the most expensive model of an *iPhone* and you feel a strong urge to do the same, or otherwise, you wouldn't be cool anymore).

In some areas of the market, it's so easy to find good industry jobs with a PhD that this the transition becomes the default choice. For instance, PhD students in computer science studying at top universities usually get approached by IT companies a long time before they finish their PhD contracts—and typically, they are offered very good working conditions. I've got some questions from befriended researchers who highly enjoy their academic jobs yet experience the fear of missing out (a.k.a., the FOMO). "All my colleagues transfer to industry, and they all seem happy. Should I join them? Am I insane to stay where I am?" Well, not necessarily. There is no point in following the majority if you are not deeply convinced that this is the right way for you. Besides, people often get overexcited about a new job in the initial phase after signing the contract. And, they might also seem happier on their *LinkedIn* profiles than they are in reality. *LinkedIn* is a self-promotion platform and not a diary.

So, what are the *right* reasons to move out of academia? The first situation is when your love for your research topic is gone for good. You no longer feel the excitement that you felt at the very beginning of your academic adventure while getting new ideas or discovering new findings in your research projects. You no longer feel a rush of adrenaline while presenting your research to other people. You become quite indifferent to reading about new findings. All becomes *just a job*. This can happen for many reasons, and sometimes it is hard to tell *why* it happens in a particular situation. It's a bit like waking up next to someone you have been with for many, many years, and discovering that you feel nothing now. Can you expect a happy end once this happens? This is rarely the case. To my mind, if you find yourself in such a situation and you are fairly sure that the love is gone with no chance of coming back, this is a valid reason to think about making a career switch and giving yourself a chance to fall in love again.

The second valid reason to look for a job outside of academia is a desire to work in a real team. Of course, academic projects most often are team projects (at least officially), and most researchers are team players by nature. However, there is a huge *systemic* problem in academia: at the end of the day, everyone who aims to build their academic career needs to take care of their own CV and their own publication record. This causes that people highly prioritize projects in which they are leading researchers, and delay or even ignore the projects in which they are minor contributors; they may even block each other at work. Again, this is not a problem with people per se; this is a problem with the *system of evaluating* them. Anyway, this results in low synergy between researchers—in fact, they slow each other down instead of helping each other to successfully complete the project in time.

One of the most common comments made by those who transfer to industry is that they are positively surprised with the quality of teamwork in their new workplace and with how well-supported they feel at work. Indeed, teamwork in industry is at a whole new level. Typically, the whole team has exactly the same goal: to beat the competition and to win the market—together. Since there are no names of single contributors on the final product, there are no elbows in use and no internal conflicts. It sounds like a paradox: since no one is acknowledged, everyone is happy. Therefore, if the main source of your frustration is the lack of synergy in academia and if you have a strong desire to experience more teamwork in daily life, this is a good reason to try something new somewhere else.

To my mind, the third good scenario is when you are *curious* about what is out there. You feel very young at heart, and you don't feel the need to settle on one career path just yet. You have acquired a rare skillset during your academic career and you have a strong desire to challenge yourself and to explore the job market. You are asking yourself, "How far can I get with the skills I already have? What can I change in this world?" In this case, you'll probably regret it if you don't try. You can commit to spending one year outside of academia and examine whether you enjoy this new life —if you are a proactive, driven person, academia will most probably still welcome you back after this period.

The next good scenario is when you got a very good research idea, you met the right people at the right time, and it might be the opportunity of a lifetime for you. For instance, imagine that during your PhD, you made a discovery that might lead to the development of a new drug, a new online platform that solves a big societal problem, or any other product that might potentially hit it big in the market. You are not sure about the potential of the project, so you knock on the door of the local incubator and ask professionals for their opinion. They are excited about your achievement and pass you through to their network of investors. And then, you find yourself at the crucial decision point: shall I pursue this commercial project—which probably means that I will no longer have time for my research for at least a few years, and commit a sort of research career suicide—or should I forget about this? Many early career researchers encounter this situation but don't have the grit to go for the opportunity—yet most of those who took the challenge, are happy with their decision and never regret it.

Importantly, such opportunities often happen not only while you are in graduate school but also when you are experienced as a researcher—as this is when you are proficient enough to create or recognize a real innovation. For many researchers in the age range of 35-60, it becomes hard to make the ultimate decision to leave their current lifestyle on behalf of a risky adventure. They often have preschool-aged children at this point—and for that reason, they are afraid to dump a stable income for entrepreneurship. For people who are older than 60 and very close to retirement, this decision becomes easier again; they usually feel accomplished enough in their careers: they are wealthy, they are done with paying back their mortgage, and their kids are already independent. The message is: if you get a million-dollar idea during your PhD and some investors are willing to supply this idea with cash, you should consider going for it—with age, this decision will only become harder. With age, people usually make better decisions as they have more knowledge. But at the same time, they are less willing to take risks and have less energy. Thus, if you are not willing to wait until you are 60, the time is now.

One last good reason for why you might be willing to transfer to industry is probably the most important factor among all: *intuition*. If you cannot help the recurring thoughts, "What if…" If you cannot help listening to the stories of friends who switched careers, and you keep on wondering how you would do in this new, unknown land, it might be an indication that you should try. Intuition is a very powerful tool. Especially if you work at a prestigious institution, you produce good results, your boss is satisfied with your progress, your family is proud of you, you like your coworkers, yet still, you cannot help the itch that something is missing in your life and that there might be some other, dream job out there waiting for you behind the horizon—you probably should try. If you don't try in such a situation, there is a high chance that one day, you might regret it. I would even say that you are most likely to regret it.

I summarized the aforementioned reasons in Table 1. Again, these reasons are my own, personal insights—however, after conducting hundreds of conversations with researchers before and after a career switch, I'm quite confident about this list.

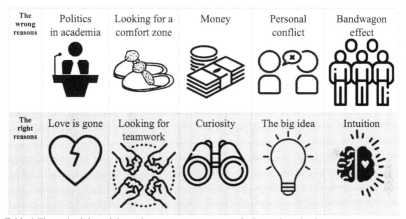

Table 1 The main right and the main wrong reasons to transfer beyond academia.

As a summary, there are two main types of motivation to leave the academic system. Firstly, your motivation can be *reactive*: you can think about leaving academia primarily because you want to *run from* certain aspects of the academic system that you don't enjoy—either your toxic boss, politics in academia, the feeling of being constantly overworked, the feeling of being undervalued in financial terms, or the feeling of abandonment after all your colleagues left for industry. Secondly, your motivation can be *proactive*: you have a gut feeling that somewhere out there, your dream job waits for you, you have a desire to challenge yourself, you have an urge to find your tribe in the job market, or you want to develop your business idea. As a rule of thumb, *proactive* motivation will yield much better results in the long run than *reactive* motivation. Therefore, rather than asking yourself, "Should I leave academia?" it is better to ask, "Is it the right time for me to conquer industry?"

We can also look at the difference between the right and the wrong reasons from a different angle: the right reasons are those associated with *internal* factors, i.e., values, priorities, and creativity, while the wrong reasons are related to *external* factors, e.g., dysfunctional academic system, other people's (seemingly) shiny careers, or a superior hard to manage. Internal motivation works better in any circumstances, navigating in the job market included.

You might have noticed that one aspect is missing in the above list, namely the *personal reasons related to the family situation.* Many PhDs resign from the research career based on the fact that long working hours in academia will not allow them to achieve the work-life balance they desire. Or because their growing family requires financial support that the academic salary cannot provide. These are, of course, valid reasons to leave! I didn't mention them above primarily because everyone has their way of valuing different aspects of their life. For some people, family always comes first, and they can sacrifice their careers for their family without a blink. Others cannot ever be happy without pursuing their dream at work—even if they have a family next to it. After resigning from a career, their mental health will be affected to such an extent that it will negatively influence the family as well. Thus, everyone needs to weight the importance of the academic career versus other areas of life by themselves and make the decision upon it.

Now, the question arises, "Should I stay, or should I go?" Obviously, this is a question that only you can answer for yourself. However, one thing I can tell you here is that, if you are highly unsatisfied with your current job, it's *good* news because it gives you the motivation to change something in your life. The worst possible scenario is when you are in limbo: not too excited about your job but at the same time, everything seems merely good enough: you have a meh-project, meh-boss, meh-colleagues, meh-salary. When you know deep inside that this is probably not the place where you'll grow and optimally develop yourself—but at the same time, you don't have clear reasons to complain. So, you decide to ignore these thoughts and stick to your current lifestyle.

The stages of grief

Let's assume that you eventually decide to go for the big jump and start a new career. What is the scope of your feelings in such a situation? Unfortunately, most people don't feel like butterflies just leaving their cocoons. Instead, they feel confused, anxious, and go through an almost existential crisis, questioning their role in the world and the meaning of life. Sometimes, they even feel like they have just disappointed the very society that invested in them!

First, after the switch, life as we know it will inevitably change. In academia, and especially in graduate school, private/social life is often mixed with professional life to such an extent that you have no friends outside academia. It's also often the case that you have little to no experience with working in industry. This is very scary; it feels like leaving everything you know on behalf of one big question mark, "How will this feel—to become the new kid on the block again? Will I meet nice people out there?"

Most of us started thinking about an academic career many, many years ago—during undergrad studies, or even much earlier: in high school, in times when we were these annoying brainiacs in the classroom. For the vast majority of students starting their PhDs, research is much more than just a job; it is also a way of living. I would even say that academia is a form of a religious movement in which you can—or even should—sacrifice a big piece of yourself. Fresh PhD candidates keep their eyes set on the tenure track. Typically, they don't plan to leave this career path in the future. We were all like this at some point. But then, you realize that for some reason (I mentioned some common examples in the previous section), you might need to change your original, sacred plan. Your research portfolio is something you build for many years. You put a lot of heart into this. Thus, terminating your research career and changing to another profession is associated with a deep feeling of loss; most likely, the nuances of your academic achievements won't be recognized or appreciated in your new working environment.

If you move from academia to industry, you need to *bury* your previous life. Namely, you need to accept that your current way of living is coming to the end, and this change is for good. The more achievement you have acquired in academia, the more painful this realization will be. Burying your life is a bit like burying a person: you'll need to go through a multistage process of grief. I find Kubler-Ross's model of grief (Kubler-Ross, 1969) very helpful to understand what happens to you at the end of your academic career.

The first stage is *denial*. In this stage, the bare thought that you might work outside academia is so surreal that it feels like a movie rather than real life. Then comes *anger*: at some point, it finally reaches your head that you'll need to forget about what you have been building for so many years—and you are not happy about it, not at all! You feel betrayed by the academic system, by your schoolteachers who were telling you to study, by everyone. "What was all this pain for?"—you ask yourself in rage and curse the unfair world. Then, you calm down and start *bargaining*: you rethink the situation and try to still find the reason why it might be worth staying where you are. You look at *Twitter*; all the people seem happy and successful in there. And you ask yourself, "Am I just being a drama queen? Maybe I should be tougher. Maybe I should be more receptive to my everyday little problems, and accept the downsides of my job, just like everyone else seems to accept it." Then, you come back to your own situation, and you realize once again that changing careers is the best option in your case. And then, there comes the *depression*: a deep sadness in reaction to the fact that your professional life, as you know it, is inevitably coming to an end. The last phase is *acceptance:* cheering yourself up, and mentally preparing for the next steps necessary for your transition.

How do you get over grief fast? No one has found an algorithmic approach to this problem yet. First, it is good to realize that you are grieving. Secondly, I suggest you settle on your final decision on whether you are willing to try something new as soon as you can, and start making steps towards that goal. Rather than sitting behind the closed door, thinking about the past and worrying about the future, better to reach out to people who already represent the place where you would like to go, make some new friends, and start making plans for the transition.

The biggest challenge

Lastly, what is the hardest part of the transition to industry? Is this finding a new job? I would dare to say: the hardest part is actually to *repurpose yourself*. Most of us academics dreamt about becoming an independent researcher for long years before ever coming to graduate school. We see a purpose in advancing the current state of knowledge in a certain field, and we often make it our mission. When this stage of our life comes to the end, we need to find a new source of motivation that is bigger than just a job. This process of looking for a new purpose typically takes much longer than the process of getting employed in some new environment. This is because you will need to get through a few stages before defining your new purpose. First, you'll need to secure a position that will give you income and allow you to work on some interesting subject matter. Then, you'll need to learn everything about the branch of industry and the environment you belong to, to spot some new problems that might be worth solving. You'll need to focus for attention on those problems and eventually, your new purpose will emerge. Of course, some people need to see a higher purpose in their job more than others—for some researchers, the need to find a new inspiration will not be a problem. For most of us, it will be though. If this is the case for you, you need to be patient and trust that the inspiration *will* come at some point.

The take-home message

1. There are right and wrong reasons to switch careers from academia to industry. The wrong reasons are primarily *reactive*:
   a) Running from politics,
   b) Running from the feeling of uncertainty,
   c) Running from the feeling of being undervalued in financial terms,
   d) Running from toxic people and personal conflicts,
   e) Fear of missing out.

   The right reasons are primarily *proactive*:
   a) Searching for a new passion,
   b) Searching for real team spirit,
   c) Curiosity about what is out there for you,
   d) Great business idea that someone is willing to fund,
   e) Intuition prompts you to do so.

2. Closing your academic career track can be associated with grief. Healing from grief is a complex, multistage process.

3. The hardest aspect of the transition is not the necessity to find another job, but rather, the need to *repurpose* yourself. This process can last for years.

CHAPTER 2

A BUTTERFLY

Am I, really?

In this chapter, I would like to focus on some qualities that you have developed as a researcher, and that are not necessarily represented by the majority of the workforce in the open job market. It's necessary to first learn that you already have all these good qualities in your hand, *before* you even start thinking about your next career step. Just to feel good about yourself!—as you should be feeling right now. Furthermore, it's important to realize all these qualities before going for job interviews; this will help you in developing the self-confidence necessary to sell yourself to potential employers, and to successfully pass the interviews.

Of course, PhD programs typically allow you to develop more skills than the list provided below. In this list, I narrowed down the options to the qualities represented by the *vast majority* of PhDs.

➤ Ability to self-manage, and multitask.

For us researchers it's obvious that whenever we are left alone in peace, in an empty office, a lot of good things will happen—namely, a lot of research will get produced. Having the ability to work without interruption, is a blessing to us since it allows us to finally get down to our favorite research projects. Interesting projects are why we applied for our jobs in the first place!

However, in most companies the situation is very different: if employees are left unattended, absolutely *nothing* would happen. Most large companies have open space in their offices on purpose; if they put all the employees in closed cozy offices, so that they couldn't see each other's computer screens, everyone would be glued to *Facebook*, or to their phone, for the whole day. Any employee who is self-motivated to work, is gold!

Also, if we are not given clear instructions for how to conduct some tasks, in particular, we will simply google, ask around, or sleep with the problem and come up with some proxy solution on the next day. Obvious, right? For many people outside academia, this is not so obvious though: many employees prefer to be closely guided and instructed. If there is any task without instructions attached to it, they easily panic, or politely refuse the task and pass it on to someone else. Have you ever called the national tax office or any other large public institution in your country? They use to politely say, "I don't know this one, let me pass you through to my colleague in another department." "I don't know"—it's their favorite answer! A typical researcher would rather answer, "I don't know, but I will check and get back to you." An employee with the self-motivation to troubleshoot problems is priceless!

➤ Ability to break up complex problems into smaller, more manageable pieces.

No research study can be planned, conducted, and published in a single day. It's a long process, which can only end with success if the research problem is well analyzed, and if the proposed solution is converted into a systematic plan. And, if that plan is well executed piece by piece, and day by day. Most PhD students are in charge of sorting this plan out all by themselves.

On the contrary, in most companies, problem-solving is as procedural as possible. It's often the case that employees have a hard time approaching any problem which is not captured by the company procedures. Such problems can go through the hands of a few teams, and a few levels of management, before reaching a consensus on how to best approach the issue. An ability to write down your procedure for a given problem using prior knowledge and common sense is a very valuable skill.

➤ Approaching solutions to problems in an iterative way.

Most complex problems need multiple attempts before they eventually work. For every professional researcher, this is quite obvious. While getting closer to the final solution with every iteration, we have a deep feeling of excitement. This is, however, is not as obvious to many people outside academia; they often take the subsequent attempts as failures, and every unsuccessful attempt is irritating, or even depressive to them. Patience is gold, while for most people, waiting for months, or even years, for the results of their work, is an abstraction. Therefore, the ability to delay gratification and approach problems iteratively, is a rare competence which should be cherished.

➤ Experience working with people coming from other cultural backgrounds.

For researchers, it's an obvious one: diverse teams are proven to be more productive than non-diverse teams (Hunt, Layton & Prince, 2015), and inclusivity works on behalf of both productivity and the well-being of the community members. As researchers, we are trained as professionals among people representing minorities, and diversity is in our DNA: since science was always big on labor mobility—maybe even to a higher extent than we would often wish, as we feel this constant pressure to change our research positions and geographical locations—we naturally have an open and welcoming attitude to researchers representing minorities and other cultures. Of course, the situation is still far from perfect and nowadays, a lot of attention is dedicated to improving upon inclusivity and diversity in academia (Bumpus, 2015, Puritty et al., 2017). However, industry is *far behind academia* in terms of developing good practices for inclusivity. This is mostly because staff mobility is industry is lower than in academia, and moving abroad for work is practiced to a lesser extent.

For this reason, the fact that you previously worked in a multicultural environment, and that you successfully conducted projects in multiple diverse teams, in which you were playing different roles (as a student, as a collaborator, as a supervisor of a Master's thesis, etc.), can give you a huge advantage in the open job market. You can become that employee who is sent to the most interesting business conferences and gets delegated to speak to other teams abroad because your employer can trust in your interpersonal and communication skills. You can be that employee who is trusted by your employer to train junior employees, without the worry that you'll be biased and favor some training participants over others. You can be that employee who is trusted to shake hands with new business partners because you'll treat everyone with kindness and without any prejudice.

➤ The hipster, the hacker & the hustler in one.

In the startup culture, there is a saying that every good team contains the hipster, the hacker, and the hustler. The *hipster* is the person who is the most imaginative in the team. Hipster thinks outside the box, comes up with new solutions, and creates the *vision* for the project. The *hacker* is the person who has the technical skills to bring this vision to life: to conceptualize the steps necessary to get there, and then execute these steps one by one. The *hustler* is the salesperson: someone who can excite people outside the team about the vision, and who can persuade a lot of people to invest in the project and buy the final product. Note that usually, three different individuals take on these three roles (although in some startups, the same person plays the roles of the hipster and the hustler).

In academia, we play all these roles at once: we need to conceptualize the problem, to come up with a solution, to execute that solution, and to sell it to a wide audience—all by ourselves. We cannot delegate a colleague to go present our poster at a conference just because we feel like "this is not our thing." Nobody cares if you are an introvert, and if you would rather prefer to stay at home; you are supposed to present, so you do it to the best of your ability. We cannot delegate executing the project to someone else and focus on traveling and talking about it instead either. Well, to some extent this is what senior researchers do—yet still, it's not possible to get there without getting your hands dirty at the early stages of the scientific career.

In the open job market, the ability to take up all these roles at the same time is a huge asset. This is also why so many researchers become successful entrepreneurs. We don't wait for others to take over the parts of the work which we don't enjoy, or which we don't feel comfortable with—we multitask and play various roles in the project according to what the situation requires.

➤ Constant learning.

For us, lifelong learning is a rather obvious assumption: to solve a new problem which has never been solved before, you naturally need to learn something that no one learned before you did. The process of reading, learning, attending lectures, and improving on our—already quite advanced—knowledge, will never stop. And this is something we all accepted and feel comfortable about.

On the contrary, in the open job market, the way of thinking about the learning process is often different. There are lots of ambitious people out there who are hungry for knowledge. But there are also lots of people who have associated learning with painful memories from school. These people would prefer to profit from the knowledge obtained during their undergraduate studies for the rest of their lives rather than keep on learning new competencies. Whenever their employers invest in them and send them to courses and workshops, they treat this as an unnecessary hassle rather than an opportunity. And, they enjoy these excursions as an occasion to travel, drink with colleagues, and type yet another bullet point on their resume rather than an opportunity to learn something new. Many people prefer to end their education with a Master's diploma, and then focus on settling down, finding a safe job, and getting the highest salary using the least amount of energy cost possible—and then aging in peace.

Therefore, if you are a person eager to read, learn new things about the subject of your job, and track the news in your field without being whipped by your boss— you have a great competence which will pay off in your next career. Even if you start as a newbie in an area out of your comfort zone, the ability and willingness to learn daily will let you gradually surpass the competencies of the more senior people around you. I mean all those people who completed Master's studies within that area many years ago but don't bother to update their knowledge any further. So, by acquiring expertise quickly, within a few months to a few years, you can get promoted to the Leader Specialist or Focal Specialist positions and lead big projects within the company.

➤ Ability to take constructive criticism.

In academia, we need to face criticism daily. From a supervisor unhappy with the weekly progress to journal editors kindly rejecting our papers—it's never pleasant, but we need to learn how to live with this. Furthermore, we develop the ability to tell the difference between the *constructive* and the *not-so-constructive* criticism, to filter negative feedback, and to address the constructive criticism appropriately. When we get criticism of our work, we don't start asking, "Who is guilty of this?" but rather, "How can I solve this problem today?"

For a large portion of the workforce, criticism is just hell—even if it's constructive. It can easily lead to burnout, depression, or the decision to quit from one's job. Not many people can stand as much rejection and criticism in daily life as researchers, and still pursue their projects with a smile on their face. They react to criticism with anger or defensive demeanor instead, regardless of whether the criticism is justified. Corporations know about this. Thus, in most corporations, open criticism of others' work is not tolerated—if you dare to say anything negative about another employee's professional ethic or the quality of their results, you'll get scolded even if you were right.

Even though officially, peer criticism is not welcome in most branches of industry, this thick skin will still help you in the open job market. In every company, you will become indispensable as a person who reacts to rejection peacefully: who doesn't take the rejection personally, who never loses their nerves, can rationalize conflicting arguments, analyze them, and respond appropriately. Also, the *accompany* of rational and easy-going people who can constrain their negative emotions is always appreciated. If you don't start a battle every time your initiatives are hammered—but rather, you smile, and propose to talk about the details, and come up with another proposal—you'll earn trust and respect in your new environment very quickly.

➢ Ability to present in public.

According to numerous public surveys, people fear from presenting in public more often than they fear death (Bruskin, 1973, Dwyer & Davidson, 2012). This is partly due to atavistic fears from the old times when standing on stage was usually associated with being publicly punished. Today, this is no longer the case, and standing on stage usually means something positive for a change: getting awarded, performing as an artist, or broadcasting your vision to a lot of viewers. Even though the external conditions have changed, the human brain didn't rewire all that quickly and ancient fears remained in the back of our minds.

As researchers, we don't have a choice here. We need to overcome our fears and learn to present in public—this is a part of the academic game. We also need to be prepared that the public reception of your work won't always be positive—the audience can ask you some critical questions at almost any moment. Pretty much everyone had that experience at least once in their lifetime: some uncomfortable questions from the audience that you just cannot answer from the top of your head. What do you do then? Smile and openly admit that you don't have the capacity to answer the question for now? Throw some joke on the table and skip the question? Disregard the question as irrelevant (the strategy often chosen by senior researchers)? Or perhaps, answer the question by asking yet another question? Whichever tactics you prefer, I am sure that you will do much better than just standing on stage, stuttering in helplessness, and looking around for help. Well, that already makes you stand out in the job market—as most people can't handle the stress associated with such situations; they would simply freeze, instead of playing the question around. So, maybe you should think higher of your presentation skills; an ability to defend your points in front of a live audience is a valuable and scarce competence.

We all have transferable skills and competencies

The above competencies are just examples of *transferable skills*. Transferable skills are the skills you developed during your research career that are also of value in the job market outside academia. As a matter of fact, all PhDs have multiple transferable skills—it's often a matter of nomenclature. When you are preparing for applying to industry positions, you'll need to translate some of your skills from the language of science to the language of business and management.

You will also need to learn how to introduce your competencies to the recruiter in a convincing way. Anyone can say, e.g., "I have strong leadership skills." Even if you do have this skill, the recruiter has no evidence for it yet. One popular approach to tackle this kind of conversation is the STAR technique (Higgins, 2014). STAR stands for *Situation, Task, Approach,* and *Results.* Using this technique, you can give viable examples from your professional history to demonstrate your competencies. *The Situation* means setting the stage. Namely, you need to describe the circumstances in which you used your competency to solve some problem. Example:

> "Five years ago, I was organizing a student conference at my institute.
> I was leading the managing committee of nine PhD candidates preparing the conference and we expected around 250 participants."

Task means the problem you had to solve in this situation. Example:

> "Six weeks before the conference, one of our private sponsors suddenly stepped back for personal reasons, and we calculated that we wouldn't have enough funds to pull off the conference. We had to find new funds as quickly as possible."

Approach stands for the solution you proposed to resolve the situation. Example:

> "I summoned the team and explained that we need to rearrange our responsibilities and diversify our efforts looking for funds. I formed three working groups of three team members each. I gave the first group the task to look for open small grant calls to organize workshops and conferences. I sent the second group to cold email local companies. Finally, I instructed the third group to email the participants at the conference and ask them for small donations on behalf of the conference."

Results mean the outcome of your solution. Example:

> "Eventually, even though we didn't manage to land any grant within this time frame, we received €1,000 from a local startup and another €800 in donations from the conference participants. Thus, we reached the budget three weeks before the conference."

How to learn this technique? You can find many exercises that can help you with preparing for talking about competencies online (Mather-L'Huillier, 2015). Most of these exercises will list many exemplary PhD activities that help you develop transferable skills (e.g., "I wrote a PhD thesis!"), and you will be asked to *translate* these academic activities into the language of management (e.g., "I complete my projects, and I am a proficient writer!"). Here, I would like to propose *inverting* this task and asking you to do exactly the opposite. Please take a look at the list of competencies that recruiters are most often looking for in job candidates (Table 2). Please come up with some evidence from your professional career that can demonstrate these competencies, using the STAR technique. This exercise will further help you in responding to job offers, writing motivational letters, and giving the right answers during the job interviews. Plus, it's a pleasant exercise!

Skill/competence	Your own experience
Problem-solving skills	
Negotiation skills	
Ability to organize information	
Leadership skills	
Self-management skills	
Teaching/mentoring skills	
Self-motivation	
Enthusiasm/passion	
Team spirit	
Adaptation skills	
Ability to focus	
Ability to think out of the box	

Table 2 Think about your prior professional experience as a researcher (and other experiences!). Which projects and events give evidence/arguments that you have the competencies listed above?

Also, keep in mind that you don't need to represent *all* these qualities. For instance, if you are thinking of a data science job, then most likely, negotiation skills will not be essential for this job. But if you are thinking about a Project Manager position, negotiation skills will be quite useful and can be expected of you! Therefore, it is better to have clear evidence to justify 6-10 competencies that are essential for your career than try to hit all the marks at a time.

Transferable skills versus core competencies

The aforementioned text relates to transferable skills that can be of value to numerous employers or clients. If you apply for a job that will require you to join a certain working environment, your employer needs to make sure that you have all the skills necessary for this position, but also, all the skills that are necessary to fit the team. Thus, you will get tested for multiple compulsory requirements for the job. You will need to score all the marks on the list to be even considered for the position. In other words, demonstrating the required transferable skills is the *minimum requirement* to land the job—it's necessary but not sufficient.

However, there is yet another set of skills: core competencies. Core competencies are the skills that make you *stand out* from the crowd. To advance in any career, you will need to recognize and utilize your core competencies. Transferable skills might be enough to get you the job, but in the long run, they might not be enough for you to get promoted and build your career further. Core competence can either be your strongest side, or those of your skills that are very rare and in high demand in the job market. For instance, let us assume that you can write research articles, code, conduct data analysis in genomics, manage students, and present your research in public—but in fact, *writing* is your favorite aspect of the current job. You find writing your strongest skill: you could write almost any type of text. The process of writing energizes you, and at the same time, your writing skills are valued in your environment. You feel that you can successfully pursue all the other tasks on the list, from programming to supervising students, yet your results will be average. With your set of competencies, it might happen that employers will prefer to place you at the data science position—just because analytic and programming skills are in high demand right now and there is a scarcity of strong programmers and Data Scientists. But, will you flourish as a Data Scientist knowing that your programming and analytic skills are just average, and you don't enjoy the process of programming at all? It's a highly unlikely scenario.

Therefore, you need to use some introspection and feedback from your current working environment to determine your core competencies. Then, you will need to verbalize these competencies in your motivational letters and job interviews—otherwise, you can experience a lot of frustration in your next job. Even if you land the position, you might feel that your professional development has stopped due to the wrong tasks assigned to you. Of course, private companies are more capitalistic and practical than academia; in case you are mismanaged and unproductive, you will likely get shifted to another position within the company where you can produce more value for your employer. This process takes time so it's better to avoid/prevent such situations. We will talk more about core competencies in chapter 3: *What Are My options? What Types of Jobs Suit Me?*

You also need to remember that whether or not a certain quality is a core competency depends on the circumstances, For instance, let's assume that you have strong technical writing skills. If you decide to apply for a job in a company that offers grant writing services, your competency will be treated as a core competency as it directly generate profits for the employer. However, if you apply to a tech startup where employees are expected to spend their days writing code, it will only be a nice bonus on your resume and won't be valued by the employer to as high extent as you would wish—unless you find a way of making your skill a core competency. For instance, let's assume that you can convince the employer that you can write a high-class documentation for the whole company and that it's worth to employ one person who will be responsible for this part of the product because this speeds up the process of releasing the product to the market. Then, all of a sudden, your technical writing skills will be treated as a core competency—as they can directly lead to cutting costs by the company.

Furthermore, what is a core competency in one working environment, doesn't necessarily need to be respected elsewhere. For instance, can you keep secrets to yourself? If so, have you ever thought about this skill as a core competency as a researcher? Probably not. In academia, we popularize Open Science, we present our pipelines at international conferences, and we proudly share our projects in every detail. There are virtually no secrets to keep—or at least, to keep after the premiere of our new paper or tool. In business, life is very different. The intellectual property (or, IP) of your company is a closely guarded secret—both before launching the product and afterward. Therefore, the ability to keep confidential about what you do is crucial and can be your core competency.

Caveats associated with looking for jobs in the open job market as a researcher

As mentioned above, as researchers, we all have plenty of transferable skills. However, there are also some mental traps you can get yourself into as a researcher in the open job market. And, paradoxically, accomplished researchers with packed research CVs get trapped much more often than those who feel like underdogs in academia. It happens for a few reasons.

Firstly, if, for whatever reason, you feel like an underdog, you naturally spend more time thinking about yourself, and especially about your weaknesses and how to work around them. Knowing your weaknesses is as important for your career as knowing your strengths! High-flyers who discovered their natural talents early on, focused on those strengths, and *happened* to mentally fit the academic system, often assume that they will fit similarly well everywhere they go. And it often turns out that this assumption isn't true. Also, feeling too good about yourself and taking an assumption that—since you are an intelligent and well-educated person—you will always find a good job whenever you need it, is a mistake and can easily backfire on you. In fact, the job market is complicated, the recruitment process is generally slow, and the recruiters often perceive candidates differently than candidates see themselves (more on this topic in chapter 5: *How to Land My Dream Job?*).

Secondly, high-flyers who stand out in academia are often in a comfort zone of sorts and don't feel motivated enough to look for external jobs. It's difficult to put a stop-loss on your career and decide to change your path if you are recognized and respected by other people as a professional—even if deep down, you feel that this is not an optimal career track for you.

Thirdly, academic high-flyers often have unfocused resumes that indicate both sharp analytic mind and management/logistic skills. This profile is appreciated in academia, but it can confuse the recruiters. Namely, it makes it hard for recruiters to classify you in terms of what type of professional you are—a manager or a specialist. In branches of the job market such as IT or biotech, managers with a technical background are in demand—but only when they have prior management experience in the industry. Management experience from academia rarely counts. For this reason, researchers who never exhibited any leadership skills and never indulged in any extracurricular initiatives on behalf of better science during their academic career often get jobs much faster than those who did.

Lastly, accomplished researchers typically have a strong association with their jobs: they live and breathe what they do. High-flyers tend to perceive their projects as their artwork, have recurrent thoughts about their research in free time, and feel a sense of duty to make their project work whatever it takes. In many working environments in industry, this is not the case—people mentally distance themselves from work, treat working time as a trade-off for salary rather than one of the reasons to live, and switch off the working mode at 5 pm sharp. It is hard to adapt to such an environment, and many researchers don't prepare for this cultural shock.

Multipotentiates in the job market

Lastly, I would like to briefly discuss one topic related to the fact that research is a diverse, multifaceted type of job. Many people going into science, are people of the renaissance. In high school, they not only excelled in mathematics and natural sciences, but also literature, arts, or even sports. Because of so many talents that revealed so early, many researchers had a huge dilemma while choosing the major to study. In the end, they chose a career in which they could play multiple roles at a time: be an actual scientist, while also playing parts as an academic teacher, a salesperson, a journalist, an event organizer, an author, etc. One can say a lot of things about academic life, but surely not that the work is algorithmic. In every profession, it is good to be able to improvise and handle multiple tasks. However, in academia, this is even more of the case than in most other environments. While some researchers would rather focus on research and treat all the other responsibilities as a distraction, most researchers enjoy this vibrant, diverse lifestyle. Such people with a preference for multitasking and combining multiple professions into one are often referred to as *multipotentiates* (Wapnick, 2017).

This trait can become a sort of issue when you think about a career switch to industry: it's often hard to find a non-academic job in which the scope of duties has spectrum as broad as academic jobs. In a private company, you might get a very well-defined set of tasks, and you will need to complement the competencies of your teammates rather than be on top of the whole project.

Hence, the question, "What to do about my multipotentiality?" is a valid concern. Below, I provide a few pieces of advice on how this problem could be alleviated.

➢ Look for open working environments.

The good news is that most industry jobs do require multitasking, after all. In a corporate environment, there is a mass of people dynamically segregated into teams. These teams need to communicate and report to each other. Therefore, even as a specialist, you'll need to attend and prepare for a lot of meetings and presentations. If you decide to go for freelancing or entrepreneurship, you'll need to play the role of a one-man band—you'll need to interact with all the stakeholders of your business. So, every environment where a mass of people gets involved—either as coworkers or as stakeholders—will require multitasking mastery from you.

➢ Compensate with your hobbies, or hustle on the side.

Given that in industry the working hours are generally shorter than in academia, you have a chance to compensate for some deficits of your job with your hobbies. For instance, if you enjoyed organizing hackathons in academia, and your next position is an office job which has nothing to do with logistics and organizing events, you can team up with your friends from academia, and organize some events in your free time. Or, you can join such an event over the weekend as a participant.

You can also think of starting a sole proprietorship and hustling on the side—most employers allow for this, especially if your little business is not competitive towards what your employer does. I have a friend who works full time in fundraising in their daily life. But he has also developed a little side-business as a... producer of home-made, flavored, designer soap. His boss has no issues with the fact that he often spends Saturdays producing soap at home. The story was quite puzzling for me, so I asked him about the origins of his unusual hobby. He just smiled and said, "Just a hustle on the side!"

➢ Be patient and work towards senior positions in industry.

Once you climb the ladder and get promoted to more senior positions in industry, your job will resemble academic life more and more. You won't only work on projects within your department, but you will also travel, and manage junior employees, and set collaborations with other teams. Especially if you reach the senior level in the company, either as a manager or as a specialist, you will be at the frontiers of the company's expansion in the market, and you will have the opportunity to propose and pursue new initiatives.

So, there is hope for multipotentiates in industry!

The take-home message

1. The vast majority of PhDs represent at least eight qualities which are in high demand in the job market:
    a) Ability to self-manage and to multitask,
    b) Ability to break up big problems into smaller, more manageable pieces,
    c) Approaching solutions to problems iteratively,
    d) Experience working with people coming from other cultural backgrounds,
    e) The hipster, the hacker & the hustler all in one,
    f) Constant learning,
    g) Ability to take constructive criticism,
    h) Ability to present in public.

2. Before you start writing your job applications, you need to learn two things:
    a) How to translate all the transferable skills you have acquired into the language of business and management. It's not hard!
    b) What your core competencies are. This is much more difficult but necessary to develop a successful career.

3. Those who finish grad school as high-flyers, often have more issues with finding a job in industry than underdogs—mostly because they don't put enough attention to deliberating their weaknesses and because they have a very strong association with their jobs.

4. As a multipotentiate, you have a natural need for self-development in multiple directions at a time. Therefore, it can take you some time to develop a satisfactory lifestyle in your new career in industry.

CHAPTER 3

WHAT ARE MY OPTIONS?
WHAT TYPES OF JOBS SUIT ME?

What is a good job?

There is no official definition of a good job. There is a popular belief that job satisfaction must be associated with a lavish paycheck but this is not true. In fact, job satisfaction weakly correlates with income (Clark, 2015). If not income, then what determines your satisfaction from work? The public image of social media influencers as successful people can lead to the impression that achieving *an impact* in your community, and a *base of followers* is synonymous with professional success. Of course, such a view of the world is also misleading, and can only lead to frustration.

I personally believe that everyone should work on their own, private definition of a *good job*. Personally, I feel that I have a *good job* when I work at a desk situated beside a window, yet fail to notice the weather outside the window. Of course, I'm happy to know that some things I am doing, help other people—but honestly speaking, that indulgent feeling of living in the moment, is what makes me call the job a good one. This is different for everyone, and a good first step is finding out what is important to you.

Six approaches to the job search

Before you even decide on the type of job to look for, you should decide on your strategy. In other words, what are your selection criteria? Choosing the optimal job searching strategy is like choosing a diet—there is no "one fits all." For this reason, I introduce some of the most popular approaches to job searches below. I also list the pros and cons of each of them.

➤ What is my passion? What gives me the most energy?

As Confucius famously said, "Choose a job you love, and you won't ever have to work a day in your life." In other words, pursue your passion! "Follow your passion" is the slogan we hear from the media a lot these days. However, is this the best possible approach?

Firstly, it is hard to disagree with Confucius' statement. If you have a job that you sincerely enjoy and are passionate about, then every time you perform the job, it leaves you with more energy and enthusiasm than you had before. Having an enjoyable job leads to long-term positive consequences in other areas of your life as well: it impacts your health (Henseke, 2018) and your interpersonal relationships. If you have a job that gives you a sense of power, you will also have enough extra energy to keep the proper work-life balance and pay attention to your family and friends. Furthermore, most people naturally prefer to flock around happy and inspiring individuals who are satisfied with their professional life rather than those who are always depressed and can infect others with this negative attitude. So, if you have a job that puts a smile on your face every day, you will probably also get yourself a lot of new friends, and new opportunities will come along.

We would all choose for jobs which give us energy over those that do not—this sounds quite an obvious choice to make. What could go wrong here? Well, it turns out that choosing your passion as your way of living is not always a good idea. There are four main factors which you have to consider before you decide to do this:

a) *What is the impact on other people?* You can encounter a mental trap here. Namely, it can happen that something that makes you happy, has negative consequences on other people—individuals whom you might not personally know. For instance, most *Instagram* fashion influencers started their activity online because they genuinely enjoyed buying new clothes, composing outfits, doing makeup, playing a homegrown stylist, and sharing their art and vision with other people. They had a desire to live off from their passion. Many of them succeeded. Unfortunately, what happened next went out of control. After a few years of booming, the *Instagram* culture created a false image of the world in which the lives of the influencers truly look like pictured on their *Instagram* accounts. Thousands of young women got depressed from comparing themselves to the idealized *Instagram* models. Research studies revealed the systematic negative influence of *Instagram* culture on the well-being and self-esteem of *Instagram* users by research (Sherlock & Wagstaff, 2018). So, in this case, a group of women who went for their dreams and turned their passion for clothes and makeup into their job caused that the whole generation of young women (a.k.a., the Z-generation) became insecure and unhappy about their bodies.

b) *Competitive market.* People usually have converging tastes for the activities they enjoy. We all enjoy sleeping. Most of us enjoy morning coffee. We would all choose to look good rather than look bad. Similarly, enjoyable jobs are usually associated with more candidates per seat than available seats. Also, in such jobs the distribution of income is often very unequal: a few people who managed to develop their brand, live on a very good standard while the majority struggles to meet ends. YouTube could be an example here; many young people dream about becoming a YouTuber these days (Dirnhuber, 2017), yet there are only some people at the top of the food chain who get all the attention while most YouTubers cannot afford to live off from their online activities. So, before you decide to make

26

your passion your job, it's good to also ask yourself this question: what are the statistics in this field? Is it as easy as it seems at first?

c) *Your passions change over time.* What were you passionate about in high school? Or, ten years ago? Were these the same things you are passionate about right now? I would bet the answer is "No." So, if you go for what you are passionate about, at some point you might discover that you have become indifferent to it in the process. And then, you might need to develop a new passion. In fact, it's quite improbable that you will keep the same passion for the rest of your life!

d) *The Ouroboros effect.* I coined this term to name the phenomenon when you start treating your passion as a profession—and then, the initial enjoyment fades away. Let's assume that you, for instance, enjoy *painting* in free time as it helps you to recharge after your stressful working day. So, whenever you are stressed, bored, or you just want to disconnect from the world, you close yourself alone in a room, put on some music, and start painting. It is a form of meditation to you, and it always makes you happy and relaxed. All your friends and family have been telling you that they enjoy watching your paintings and that you should become a professional artist. And then, one day, you take a brave decision to try. So, you put photos of your work on your website. You get in touch with art galleries, you start attending meetups in the space, and talk to other artists in the field. All of a sudden, you discover that there are plenty of other people like you—passionate and talented painters who are trying to get their work to the same galleries as you. You ask yourself, "Why is this person in, while I am not? How is their art better than mine?" You also bump into professional art critics who review your work—and they are not as positive about your talent as your friends. After all, this is their role to play: a critical review of your artwork. Since you decided to do this for a living, you calculate how much you need to price your work, and how many you should sell per month to make ends meet. And then, when you create your next piece, you start asking yourself, "I aim to sell this piece for $650, is it worth this much already? Maybe I should spend a few more hours on this one and polish it further?" You also start comparing yourself to other artists in the field and ask yourself, "What is my unique selling point? What makes me stand out? Isn't my art too similar to the art of other people? Maybe I should change my style a little?" And then, one day, you discover that you are now experiencing stress similar to the days when you had a stressful day job, in times when painting in your basement was only a hobby to you. And, you can even miss the old times when you could close yourself in a room and paint. The conclusion is: under certain circumstances, *every* activity can become stressful when it becomes your job and has a direct influence on your financials and your living standard, no matter how enjoyable it was before. Of course, there is a small percentage of people who are immune to stress and will never react this way—but let us assume that your susceptibility to stress is within the norm rather than exceptionally high.

➤ *What type of activity is the most comfortable and causes the least stress?*

This strategy for job search usually works only in the short term. Yet, it can work well, especially if you are in the process of healing from some traumatic experience. For instance, if you feel that you are physically and mentally tired after your PhD, you might consider a job that gives you a sense of internal peace and a possibility to rest, regain energy, and find more time to think about the future. For instance, you might choose to take a job as a research assistant in the research area in which you did a PhD. You are an expert in this discipline already so there is a chance that you will perfectly know what to do in your new job since day one. Furthermore, a job of a Research Assistant is not associated with the academic career path. Thus, most likely, you will not be pressured to compete with anyone and to work beyond the official working hours. This type of job can allow you to rest, clear your mind, and at the same time, to have financial security at the minimal level of responsibility and stress. Other examples could be positions where you can use your academic skills but in a different context, e.g., teaching, project management, etc. However, mind that these positions might be associated with other sources of stress than academic jobs.

A peaceful, 9-to-5 job can help you in finding a new career path and is a much better option than staying unemployed and spending whole days googling for jobs from home. The peace of mind which stable employment and the regular weekly schedule give will make you more energetic and mindful to spot good new opportunities. In addition, a new working environment may bring new opportunities. One thing you should remember is that this solution is meant for a period of time (i.e., between half a year and two years) to enable you to recover from your previous contract and find a new career direction—unless you discover that you enjoy your current job so much that you prefer to stay for much longer than planned.

➢ *What am I best at?*

We live in a culture in which we constantly hear, "You can be whoever you want to be." Unfortunately, this sentence is often misunderstood: the word "can" means "are allowed to" rather than "are able to." In fact, life is way too short and the competition is way too severe to aim for professions for which you have no natural talents.

If you are close to completing your PhD, you are probably close to 30 (±3 years). At that age, most people can already tell what they are *good at*. In your teenage years, teachers were pushing you to learn all the material contained in the school curriculum even if you clearly didn't have a talent in certain disciplines. Then, you went to study at the university. Then, in your twenties, you probably traveled to quite a number of places, met many people, and tried out various activities and new challenges—not only during your undergraduate studies but also during your PhD and at internships. Up to now, you have probably developed some sense of where your strengths and talents are, and which professional activities are easier and more natural for you than for most people.

The things you are good at, are *often* the same things you are the most passionate about (see above), but this is not *always* the case. Sometimes, it happens that while you are on the way to reach your personal goals, as a by-side effect, you also develop some skill(s) that have high market value and can get you a good job. For instance, when you were learning all the skills necessary to conduct the experiments for your PhD project, you might have learned competencies such as programming.

28

And, you might have discovered in the process that you actually have a talent for programming. If you now enter the open job market, you might learn that this skill is highly valued today and that it allows you to work on preferential conditions (e.g., remote work at very high hourly rates). You might then find out that you *enjoy the lifestyle* which utilizing your skills gives you—and that, you can call it a good job!

Sometimes, you might also *fail to notice* that you are good at something: this particular activity is so natural for you that you never thought about it in categories of talent. For instance, you probably don't realize that you are a fantastic chef until someone else tells you that. You can overlook many talents in this way!

One anecdote that always makes me smile, is how George R. R. Martin, the author of the famous *The Songs of Ice and Fire* (also known from its TV adaptation entitled *The Game of Thrones*), discovered that he had a talent for writing. As he revealed in a recent interview[13] with a peer author Stephen King, as a high school kid he was quite nerdy and not too popular among other kids. The other day, his teacher in literature class asked all the kids to write an alternative ending to *The Pit and the Pendulum*, a short story by Edgar Allan Poe. In this story, a man tortured by the Spanish Inquisition is helped by rats to get out of a torture machine and is eventually saved. The teenage George wrote an alternative ending in which the main character is eaten alive by the rats instead of being saved, and dies horribly. Against all odds, his teacher found this ending great. For more, he let George read his ending aloud in front of the whole class. The kids who didn't think too highly of George got hooked and started to look at him differently on that day. So, he thought to himself, "I need to do more of this writing stuff, it pays off!" The rest is history.

We like to think that we should make for a living based on what we *enjoy* doing (this is what *YouTube* and *Instagram* careers are based on after all). However, it's often the opposite: we *start enjoying* jobs in which our expertise is respected, and which secure us a good lifestyle. In other words, we enjoy what we are good at. It has also been found in research studies, that passion and the feeling of fulfillment often come after reaching some level of proficiency in a certain area and not the other way around (Wrześniewski et al., 1997). Also, extensive longitudinal studies by *Gallup* suggested that people who are given the opportunity to focus on their strengths at work every day are six times more likely to be engaged in their jobs and three times more likely to report an excellent quality of life than others (Rath, 2007).

So, if you are a highly qualified professional, and if your skill set is highly rewarded and appreciated in your environment, at some point you may realize that you got to enjoy doing your job. This is often experienced for instance by medical doctors. When you think about it, can you imagine that being a dentist can be a satisfying job? Even thinking about tinkering by someone else's teeth, feels hideous. Yet still, many dentists develop a deep sense of satisfaction from their jobs: they know that they do something hard yet useful to other people and that their knowledge is respected. They can also enjoy high earnings, and they can provide for their families. When you ask an average dentist if they enjoy their profession, they'll say, "Of course!"

---

[13] www.youtube.com/watch?v=v_PBqSPNTfg

➤ *Where do I produce the most value for other people?*

Lastly, one strategy to look for the right job is to look at the area in which you can create *the highest value* for other people. As mentioned in Benjamin Todd's TEDx talk[14], at the deathbed, people are the most satisfied with their professional lives when they feel that they did something *meaningful to other people*. As Benjamin explains, developing some skills and utilizing that skill by doing something that has a positive influence on this world will always give you a sense of satisfaction, and will eventually lead to a fulfilling career. Not mentioning that altruists have a high level of social approval, and are helped rather than stopped by bystanders—so you can feel the wind at your back every day. Indeed, most people declare in their old days that they are happy with what they did for others throughout their lives rather than what they achieved in their professional careers.

➤ *Where do I get the best benefits?*

If you were offered two similar positions in the same area of the market and neighboring locations, except that one of them is paid twice as much as the other one, you would probably prefer to take a better-paid position. As a matter of fact, the salary (plus the additional working benefits) is the only quality of the job which is *fully predictable* (as the contract specifies it precisely) and can be quantified objectively. Everything else that the recruiter offers you at the job interviews is subject to interpretation. You might read in the job description that you are going for a start job in a vibrant Research and Development (R&D) team, and then realize that in fact, the R&D department consists of two people including you, one of them being more of an accountant than an R&D expert. You might be told that the atmosphere in the team is nice and relaxed, and then find out that according to your standards, it's not as nice at all. You might be told that there is a lot of room for personal growth within the company while in fact, the first two years of the contract is a traineeship, and you are expected to follow instructions. There could be multiple misunderstandings between you and your employer—only the objective employment conditions are given for certain.

Sometimes, especially if you have specialist knowledge which is in high demand in the job market and you are stepping into a new field with this knowledge (so that you are not sure what to expect in your new job), it's good to take the working benefits into account while making the decision—regardless of how materialistic it sounds. Good salary not only gives you a feeling of being appreciated for your work but also allows for accumulating savings and increasing your amount of freedom over time (see also chapter 7: *Work on Your Personal Freedom*).

➤ *What would you do with yourself if you had just one year left to live?*

Career advisors often encourage you to do this particular exercise: imagine that you find out that you have just *one last year to live*. What would you do with your remaining time on this planet? Would you reconnect with your family? Would you finish all your unfinished projects? Would you go for your dream job? Or perhaps, would you embark on some distant, exotic journey?

---

[14] www.youtube.com/watch?v=MKlx1DLa9EA

This "no regrets" policy can sound like an extremely edgy way of looking for jobs. However, people who get very far with their professional careers often declare that they live *in the shadow of death*: they are conscious of the fact that life is short and nothing lasts forever. Thus, they remind themselves about this sad truth every single day—they are painfully aware of the ticking clock at all times. One famous example, Steve Jobs, once said, "Remembering that you are going to die is the best way I know to avoid the trap of thinking you have something to lose." So, what is on your bucket list?

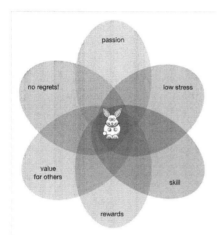

Figure 2 Chasing after the bunny. Ideally, a job should have a few different qualities at a time.

But hey, which job search strategy is the right one then? Choosing between doing something that you particularly enjoy, something that you are good at, something that pays well, and something that you would regret not doing feels like choosing between a partner who is intelligent, a partner who is physically appealing, and a partner who has a sense of humor. So, do you need to lower your standards and resign from any of the important qualities you are looking for in another person to find a partner? Or rather, should you keep on looking for as long as it takes?

I like to believe that the job market is so huge, and there are so many professions and working environments out there, that if you put enough effort, you should be able to find a job which hits at least a few marks on the list. Something that you can excel at, something that gives you energy, and somewhere where you feel safe and sound. Something that serves other people, and something that you would choose to do if you had just one last year to live. Not easy to find such a job—but it's worth chasing after the bunny (Fig. 2)!

The professions in which PhDs usually excel

As explained above, there is more than just one way of choosing a career. Let's now consider the following question related to your core competencies:

Which of the following aspects of your academic job do/did you *enjoy the most*? What do you feel you *are the strongest at*?
a) Actual research: defining new research problems, and designing new experiments or new research techniques in order to approach these problems,

> b) People: collaborating with numerous people, teamwork, conferences, seminars, academic discussion, academic *Twitter*, mentoring students, teaching courses,
> c) Reading & writing: reading articles, writing articles, blogging, disseminating knowledge, scientific communication,
> d) Actual freedom: the ability to differ your own research problems, the ability to work from wherever you want, job-related travels, conferences in beautiful places, friends all around the world, taking opportunities, flexible hours, no dress code.

PhDs can choose among many industry professions (Bielczyk et al., 2019). Below, I list a number of professions in which PhD graduates often excel, given the options mentioned above. I deliberately start the names of professions with capital letters; in academia, we tend to use capital letters to call our positions: PhD candidate, Postdoc, Assistant Professor... Industry jobs are the same valuable and prestigious! Furthermore, I mark the professions that require a long preparation/training after PhD, or in which there are (financial) barriers to entry, with an asterisk.

➢Research

a) Research Scientist. To put it simply, Research Scientists do research: they propose new hypotheses and test them, or come up with new, original methods for approaching certain problems and demonstrate the added value of these new methods using measurements. For researchers in STEM, this is a natural choice, especially if the process of conducting research projects is what you enjoy the most. If you enjoy research and writing reports summarizing your results, and at the same time, you do not enjoy writing grants and short-term academic contracts, this might be a good solution for you. However, you have to remember that once you decide to work as a researcher in a private company, the goals of all your research projects should be compliant with the goals of the company. Therefore, you might experience a bit more micromanagement and less freedom to choose the scope of your research projects than in academia. Research Scientists typically work in R&D departments. Choosing this career path doesn't necessarily imply that you need to resign from publishing—many R&D departments conduct original research, go for traditional peer review and/or publish preprints in open access.

b) Data Scientist/Machine Learning Engineer. To put it simply, Data Scientists/ Machine Learning Engineers clean, analyze, and interpret datasets. The difference between the two is mostly the nomenclature—in many industries, you need to get familiar with the whole production process to get a deep insight into the properties of the data, hence the "engineer." This is yet another natural direction for PhDs who enjoy the research part of their jobs. There is rapid growth in the amount of data and the associated jobs in industry. Many companies are fully dedicated to analyzing large amounts of data in areas such as, e.g., healthcare, meteorology, marketing, or analysis of the public opinion. Also, most corporations form R&D departments and hire teams of Data Scientists to analyze their own datasets, improve on the production process, prepare better marketing campaigns, and make financial projections for the company. Data science usually doesn't lead to scientific publishing, but rather, it is concentrated on *mining information* from the datasets. If you enjoy research and data analysis but you don't enjoy writing reports summarizing your results, this might be the best solution for you. The data science market is huge; the tools and statistical approaches vary between subdisciplines. Therefore, Data Scientists often specialize in one market sector (e.g., Market Research Analyst, Financial Markets Analyst, or Trading Analyst). If you know the basics of programming and if data science sounds fascinating to you, you can consider taking parts in specialized, intensive boot camps where you can learn all the modern techniques in signal analysis and machine learning techniques—from simple, linear classifiers to deep neuronal networks—within a few weeks. These boot camps are often affiliated with dedicated recruitment programs. Moreover, many PhD graduates successfully launch their data science careers by educating themselves online. Mind that, since data science jobs are currently attractive, the numbers of candidates for junior positions grow very fast, and it can be hard to get into this industry (the statistics depend on the country, of course).

c) Software Developer. Software Developer is currently one of the best-paid professions—especially in the new, developing fields such as the blockchain industry. If you feel that during your research career you developed good programming skills, you might consider this career path. Researchers often undervalue their programming skills—in academia, programming is only a means to reach the goals while conducting research projects. You might discover that your programming skills are strong enough to become a junior software developer in many companies. If you would like to test your programming skills and find out how fluent you are compared to average developers, there are professional recruitment agencies in IT such as *Codility*[15] which can evaluate your current programming skills and give you professional feedback. Many potential employers will also give you test assignments when you apply for jobs as a Software Developer—so you can also directly test your programming skills during the recruitment process.

d) Information and Communications Technology (ICT) Specialist. If you are into programming but you would prefer to stay at the university, you might consider applying for jobs in ICT departments. Furthermore, in most countries there are separate, government-funded institutions oriented at building research infrastructure that provides free data hosting and cloud computing services to universities. There are also startups aiming to improve on the research infrastructure and publishing process on the more fundamental level such as the *Liberate Science*[16] project.

e) Data Curator. Many large institutions and companies create separate units to take care of the collected datasets: create documentation, properly archive the data, monitor who has access to them and whether the data is analyzed as expected. If

---

[15] www.codility.com

[16] www.libscie.org

you have a sweet tooth for handling data and organizing information but you are not as much into creating new software, you might consider this type of job.

f) Lab Manager. Lab Manager is a profession where—given some experience with working in the lab—it should be relatively easy to find employment as an academic. A Lab Manager is supposed to manage the resources of the lab. Lab Managers are usually necessary for labs in which there is a constant demand for ordering new equipment and utilities, e.g., wet labs or ICT labs. This profession requires strong logistic skills, especially when two or more research labs share a Lab Manager.

g) Product Manager. Product Managers have an overview of the product. As a Product Manager, you need to make sure that the end product has good quality, reasonable production costs, and a good product-market fit. Product Manager needs to take care of the quality control during the process of building the prototype on the one hand and of the marketing side on the other side. Marketing involves setting the right price for the product, training the sales team, preparing and managing the marketing campaign, etc. Typically, Product Manager is an individual position but in some cases, multiple Product Managers work in a team as the members of the Product Managing Team. Product Managers need to have in-depth knowledge about the product and understand each step of the production process. Therefore, researchers with an associated background are often desired for this type of position. Furthermore, since technical background is an advantage at this position, for PhDs it's generally easier to land the position of Product Manager than Project Manager (described later in this chapter). However, as this job involves high-level business intelligence, it requires lots of industry experience and an in-depth understanding of the market. Therefore, it's not easy to land such a position as your *first* job after moving out of academia. If you would like to pursue a career in this direction, you should probably look for a position of a Product Owner first (see: below).

h) Product Owner. The name of this position can be misleading as it vaguely relates to the scope of responsibilities associated with it. Product Owners are responsible for a *particular feature* (or features) of the product. They typically work under the supervision of the Product Manager (or the Product Managing Team). Product Owners work in companies where *agile* development is the default way of building projects, primarily in IT. "Agile" means that the development of new solutions is the joint effort of self-managing and collaborative teams and their customers. In this setting, the Product Owner interacts with the development team responsible for a particular feature (or a set of features) and communicates with customers and with the associated Product Manager. The Product Owner needs to make sure that the feature is functional from the technical point of view, well-integrated with other functionalities of the product, and guarantees a positive user experience. For the Product Owner, the position of a Product Manager is the natural path of promotion.

i) Researcher in Marketing, Finance, and other branches of industry. Researchers are invaluable in every corner the job market. For instance, private companies always perform or outsource market research before investing in the development of a new product. Or, they measure and track user experience (UX) both during product development and after it gets released. They also investigate how the general interests and needs of their customers change over time. Investment funds perform equity research to evaluate the value behind companies listed on the stock exchange before investing large amounts of capital in stocks. Governmental institutions hire researchers to investigate whether the projects of new investments hold water and if they will positively influence the economy in the future. I consciously made a distinction between this career path and Research Scientist—while Research Scientists use scientific rigor as we know it, many of these research professions will involve *research* in a very different form. Namely, while in academia, we perform precise laboratory measurements and complex statistical analyses, in some branches of industry, "research" means conducting informational interviews and writing down the reports or googling and putting together simple Excel sheets. Therefore, next to the analytic mind, you might also need strong communication skills and/or writing skills for this type of job.

➢ People
a) Academic/High School Teacher. Teacher is yet another often choice for PhDs. If you enjoy teaching academic courses and if you are fond of observing young people in the process of self-growth, you might also enjoy teaching full time—not only at the universities but also in high schools.
b) Coach/Advisor. Most universities develop career units to advise undergraduate students and researchers career-wise. Graduate schools also hire external coaches/ advisors for their employees. If you enjoy listening and solving career problems, you might consider this type of job. Unlike working as a professional therapist, coaching doesn't formally require any university education, although completing some specialist courses and getting the professional coach certificate wouldn't hurt.
c) Project Manager. Many companies look for fresh, energetic, and well-organized employees to lead projects as managers. In short, a Project Manager is supposed to manage/supervise the team appointed to solve a particular task at every stage of the project, all from the conceptual phase until the output is successfully delivered. Corporate managers are usually expected *not to* get their own hands dirty with executing the project but rather, divide the work, instruct, and motivate team members to successfully conduct the project. Even though in general, it's hard to convince corporations to your management skills as an academic, with a bit of luck—and often, some personal contacts—you'll be able to get a junior position. In public institutions, obtaining the Project Manager position as a PhD is generally a bit easier than in private companies.
d) Business Coach/Business Developer. If you enjoy building projects yet you prefer to play an auxiliary role and assist others, and you enjoy participating in multiple projects at a time, you might consider becoming a Business Coach or a Business Developer. Sometimes, the transition from academic jobs towards business development is not straight forward and requires some additional training—going for MBA studies or an internship at the local startup accelerator. Still, many PhDs

successfully become Business Developers. As such, you can choose to work at a public institution (e.g., at a university), at a startup accelerator, or at a local unemployment office. You can also launch your own consultancy services as a freelance Business Advisor.

e) Study Advisor. Today, most universities hire at least one Study Advisor—and often, they summon a whole team. Study Advisors, as the name suggests, advise early career researchers across a broad range of topics, including mental health, work-life balance, family circumstances, developing transferable skills, or looking for jobs outside academia. Study Advisors also organize courses and career events dedicated to the aforementioned subjects—they either give lectures by themselves or hire external lecturers/coaches for this purpose. If you would like to help academics in their development and make academia a better place, but you're also searching for some stability in your professional life, this might be the right job for you as the position at the university guarantees the working stability.

f) Human Resources (HR) Officer. At some universities, there are majors such as Human Resources, Human Resource Management, or Human Resource & Career Management. However, you don't formally need this type of education to start in this area, and most HR professionals get trained in the process. Therefore, people of all backgrounds can become HR Officers. This job requires learning about the company culture and expectations, empathy, and the ability to foresee how a given individual will fit into the particular team. While some companies use quantitative metrics to evaluate and rank candidates, other companies put more trust in the gut feeling of the recruiter—so in this profession, you might expect a variety of techniques. The recruitment process looks different in every company! In general, this is probably not the most stimulating job since you will need to comply with your employer's needs and expectations. However, if you are a "people's person" and you enjoy reading people, you might consider this career. After all, the HR officer is a highly valued contributor to every company.

g) Scientific Consultant. Consultancy agencies are very popular these days (more information on this topic in chapter 4: *What is My Perfect Working Environment?*). If you get hired in such an agency, you'll be sent to companies and public institutions to assist in their internal projects, e.g., analyze the client's data or consult their R&D departments if necessary. This gives you an opportunity to use your research skills gained during your academic career. At the same time, you have the opportunity to visit multiple companies, work with a lot of people, and get an overview of the whole market sector. Consultancy is especially popular in IT as well as in healthcare where you can find employment as a Healthcare Information Technology Specialist.

h) Medical Science Liaison. A Medical Science Liaison is a consultant with research background, hired within biotech, healthcare, or pharmaceutical company. The main role of a Medical Science Liaison is to develop and maintain relationships between the employer and authorities coming from universities and renowned clinics. This role requires strong expertise in the field as well as strong interpersonal skills and salesmanship. Since making deals is an essential part of this job, it's hard to land a contract without a perfect command of the local language. It is also often the case that *whom* you know is more important than *what* you know. Therefore, Medical Science Liaisons intensively network within their community and attend dedicated conferences.

i) Legislative Analyst. Legislative Analyst reviews new legislative projects to investigate how they will affect employees. As a Legislative Analyst, you can be employed in multiple branches of the job market, from public institutions to private companies. Surprisingly, this job usually doesn't require a degree in law. However, it's required to present strong communication skills since you will need to communicate your findings through reports, presentations, and appearances on the media. In some cases, Legislative Analysts may also play an advisory role in the government and assess new bill proposals. They also communicate with the government, lobbyists, journalists, and representatives of the public opinion who might have questions about the new legislation. There are two main types of Legislative Analyst jobs. On the one hand, this position can be focused almost solely on communication and networking. On the other hand, legislative analysis can be focused on reading about the current legislation and writing reports/articles. As a Legislative Analyst, you can usually choose in which direction you prefer to develop. For this reason, Legislative Analyst as placed on the list twice, under the labels "People" and "Reading/Writing."

j) *Public Speaker. Some PhD graduates declare that *presenting in public* was their favorite part of the PhD program. If you are one of these researchers, and if you have some particular expertise that is of interest to multiple institutions or private companies, you might also consider becoming a public speaker. Professional public speakers often have a fascinating daily life: they travel, constantly meet new people, and they are also usually well-paid (or at least, well-paid per hour while they are standing on stage). Unfortunately, there are some barriers to entry, hence the asterisk: public speaking usually requires building a personal brand in some area, and this can take years. For this reason, it's often the case that becoming a public speaker is not the career goal in itself, but rather, it's a side effect of becoming successful in some area, e.g., as an author, an entrepreneur, or an athlete.

➤ Writing
a) Grant Advisor. During your academic contract, you may have gained some experience with grant writing. If you enjoyed writing personal grants so far and if you are fine with playing an auxiliary role on projects, you might consider grant writing as your next career choice. Grant writing is associated with helping other people to build and improve on their project proposals. It's a bit like becoming a doctor who, instead of stomach flu, heals grant proposals.

b) Patent Officer. In most countries, becoming a Patent Officer doesn't require any additional official qualifications or passing public exams—as in the case of HR Officer, this is a type of job in which you get trained in the process, particularly in the legal and IP aspects. However, some patent offices, e.g., employees of the European Patent Office, have minimum language requirements. If you are keen on new technologies, you might be interested in researching proposals for new patents and in writing patent applications. It's good to keep an eye at innovation in industry and learn to recognize novelty.

c) Publisher/Scientific Editor. Working in an editorial team is quite a natural choice if you enjoy the process of polishing and editing manuscripts. Most researchers are not fans of this part of their job—but if you are, you should give it a try! Today, most journals hire a dedicated editorial personnel rather than appointing full-time researchers to play the Editor's role after working hours.

d) Scientific Communication Officer. A Scientific Communication Officer is a person responsible for disseminating information about recent progress in science —either science in general, a specific branch of science, or research which takes place at some institution. Today, there are multiple channels for scientific communication, from the "traditional" press, through blogs, university websites, to *Twitter* and other social media. Therefore, as a Scientific Communication Officer, you won't be bored! Next to the in-depth understanding of some branch of science, this function usually also requires some interpersonal skills: a genuine interest in people and their achievements, the ability to do interviews, but most importantly, the aptitude to distill technical-scientific content into a format that the public can understand and write engagingly. Science communicators are wanted not only in the Public Relations offices at universities but also in private companies—especially in fields where companies base their new products and services on R&D, such as the pharmaceutical industry or IT. If a company has a blog where they post news about their recent developments, they might employ people specifically for this purpose. Finding a good, versatile writer with technical expertise is not as easy! Many companies struggle to persuade their employees to write for the company blog and to represent the company on social media—which is true especially for startups in the early phase of development when they only hire specialists. So, if you send your resume to such a company, they might get interested!

e) Writer/Content Writer/Copywriter. As a PhD graduate, you have proven your technical writing abilities. This skill will be highly valued multiple branches of industry—especially if you channel your writing in a specific direction, e.g., copyrighting, writing white papers, scientific grant writing, medical communications, or writing technology essays. As a writer, you can cooperate with a news agency, an (online) newspaper, a public institution, or a private company.

f) Legislative Analyst. As mentioned above, a Legislative Analyst reviews new legislative projects to investigate how they will influence employees, and then communicates their findings through reports, presentations, and appearances in the media. If you have affinity to reading and writing, you can become a Legislative Analyst specialized in interpreting new regulations and preparing reports.

g) *Author. You could also consider writing books. If you have a sweet tooth for writing, enough time for writing a full-length book, some important message to convey, or an idea for a story to tell, this might be worth to try. This job is only possible under certain conditions (hence the asterisk), i.e., when you have enough savings or some other sources of income that will allow you for writing books without worrying about tomorrow.

➢ Freedom
a) Entrepreneur. If you like to think big and choose your own working schedule, collaborators, and projects, you might consider becoming an entrepreneur. Of course, being an entrepreneur requires not only the desire to become one but also a specific personality and a high ability to adapt (more information on this topic in chapter 4: *What is My Perfect Working Environment?*).
b) Freelance Coach/Advisor. If you enjoy freedom above all, you might also consider running a sole proprietorship as a Coach (more information on freelancing in chapter 4: *What is My Perfect Working Environment?*).
c) Freelance Data Scientist/Software Developer. You might also consider yet another popular form of freelancing, i.e., take on freelance data science and/or software development projects. Currently, there is a huge market for these types of services and you can count on a very good payoff.
d) Freelance Writer/Copywriter. You can also consider writing as a self-employed person. Many companies (e.g., in IT) delegate creating content—from writing business plans and white papers, through the web content, to campaign ads—to freelancers.
e) *Angel Investor/Venture Capitalist. In this case, you'll need a lot of accumulated capital for the start, hence the asterisk. An Angel Investor is a person who supports entrepreneurs in the early stage with (typically, seed) capital and business experience in an exchange for equity. A Venture Capitalist operates according to similar rules but on a larger scale: invests a higher amount of capital than a typical Angel Investor, and mitigates risks by investing in companies at more advanced stages of development. As a rule of thumb, an Angel Investor is a person with at least a million dollars to invest while a Venture Capitalist works with a budget of ten million dollars and more. Because of this high barrier to entry, Venture Capitalists are usually companies rather than individuals. As in the case of Business Developer, you don't need to have an MBA title to be successful in this profession; the hands-on experience gained through building startups is much more important.

Additionally, you can also explore the O * NET Online[17] database where you will find descriptions of thousands of professions.

External resources and aptitude tests

If you still feel unsure about the scope of your strengths and interests, you might consider using one of the following tools:

---

[17] www.onetonline.org

a) *Gallup StrengthsFinder*[18]. It is a commercial aptitude test that aims to explore your five main talents. The StrengthFinder was first proposed by Rath in 2007. It assumes that your performance at work can be positively influenced by 34 common "professional" talents (e.g., being a good listener, creativity, the ability to finish projects, a talent for motivating people, etc.). This tool won't necessarily focus on the strengths that you use at the moment but rather, it gives an insight into your *potential* strengths. After the test, you will also receive tips on how to better use your potential at the workplace so that you get better results at work. This tool could help you to better understand yourself, be more self-aware, and avoid certain patterns of behavior that can lower your performance at work.

b) *My Individual Development Plan (myIDP)* by Science Careers[19]. It is a free self-management tool that helps in monitoring your progress in executing your career goals. The platform also coffers a free aptitude test that will give you insights into your strongest soft skills. The test will indicate which of the twenty career paths in industry popular among researchers might suit you best. This tool is tailored for researchers and focuses on the scope of careers often chosen by PhDs.

c) *16 Personalities*[20] test. Personality tests have always been controversial (Lilienfeld et al., 2014), for two main reasons. Firstly, they often contain questions burdened with social approval, therefore, the results might be subjective. Secondly, as a subject, you can experience the so-called Barnum effect (a.k.a. Forer effect, Vohs, 2018). This means that you tend to justify and corroborate any results you get out of personality test and perceive the results as much more personal and specific than they are. Despite these caveats, it might still be beneficial to look into classic tests such as the Myers-Briggs Type Indicator® (MBTI®, Briggs-Myers & Myers, 1995) based on the personality theory by Carl Gustav Jung as implemented in the *16 Personalities*. The test is one of the most standard psychometric tools and is used as an assessment tool in multiple areas of industry. Even if you don't get any clues about your dream job from this test, it might help you discover some of your personal strengths. The test is free of charge and only takes 12 minutes to fill in, thus, it's definitely worth to try.

Lastly, as mentioned earlier in this chapter, it is hard to assess your talents all by yourself as you might underestimate some of your strengths. Therefore, it's a good exercise to collect 360-degree feedback on your talents from your environment. People who know you for some time might be much better at spotting your strengths and weaknesses than you! And you might be surprised by how much input you can get out of this exercise.

Hence, the homework:

---

[18] www.gallup.com/cliftonstrengths/en/254033/strengthsfinder.aspx

[19] www.myidp.sciencecareers.org

[20] www.16personalities.com

Go down the memory line and look for patterns

It's also beneficial to go down the memory lane in search of your core competencies. While doing so, you can think about all the things that went *wrong* in your projects so far. If you are slowly coming to the end of your PhD, then you probably have experience with several research projects, internships, summer school projects, and/or hackathons. Were there any recurring difficulties, coming back over and over again? For instance, if you had conflicts will all your previous bosses, this might be a matter of your independent personality rather than the result of whom you encountered on your way. In the case, perhaps you should consider choosing the path of "personal freedom"?

So, what went wrong? Maybe writing manuscripts was always killing all your steam and enthusiasm because writing is just not your thing? Maybe every time you were coming back from an international conference, you felt exhausted and frustrated because the crowd drains all your energy? Maybe there is one pejorative expression—e.g., a "control freak/perfectionist," a "maverick/loose cannon," or "unfocused/distractible"—which you heard under your address many times over the years? If there was such an expression, you might now use it to your advantage. Just consider what personality traits this expression implies, and in what professions these personality traits are desired—you will certainly find a number of options. For instance, while in most professions it's hard to work with perfectionists, no one would mind if a sapper, or a surgeon, were perfectionists after all.

41

The take-home message

1. There are multiple approaches to the job search:
a) What is my passion? What gives me the most energy?
b) What type of activity is the most comfortable for me/induces the least stress?
c) What am I best at?
d) Where do I produce the most value for other people?
e) Where do I get the best benefits?
f) What would I do with myself if I had just one year left to live?

2. You have hundreds of career options. The optimal choice of the profession will depend on the aspect of academic life which you enjoyed the most, and in which your core competencies are accumulated:
a) Research,
b) People,
c) Writing,
d) Personal freedom.

3. It's often hard to assess your core competencies all by yourself. If you are not sure, you can do the following:
a) Think of all your strengths at work and the activities you most *enjoy*,
b) Try online aptitude tests if you have doubts (but still make your own choices),
c) Collect 360-degree feedback from your environment,
d) Think of what went wrong in your previous projects.

PART II

How to spot and land your dream job

CHAPTER 4

WHAT IS MY PERFECT
WORKING ENVIRONMENT?

Those overlooked dimensions

In this book, I assume you are either a PhD candidate or graduate. This means that you were looking for a job *at least once* before. Please take a look at the following question, then *take a break from reading for a few minutes and deliberate on this question on your own before you come back to reading.*

> What factors do you consider while reading a description of a research position you might potentially apply for?

What most people usually focus on when approaching this question are the following aspects:

a) What is the scope of the lab (what is the company known for)? Would I click with this PI (i.e., my potential boss)?
b) What is the topic of this project? How does this topic fit into my project portfolio?
c) Given my skill set and working experience, am I capable of pursuing this project?
d) What is the salary?
e) Would I need to relocate? Would I need to commute?
f) How long is this contract?

Mind that many of these questions relate to your skills and prior professional experience but none of these questions concerns your *personality traits* and whether you'll mentally fit your next environment.

It is natural: as you have lived the academic life before, you know what to expect in your next *academic* job. Of course, some habits might differ between labs. For instance, in one lab, the PI will check if you are OK and ask where you have been if they don't see you in the office regularly, while another PI will never look after you. In one lab, you will have an informal obligation to join the group lunch daily, while in another lab, there will be no group gatherings other than the weekly progress lab meetings. In one lab, you'll need to give a notice a month ahead if you are planning to take a vacation, while in another lab, your boss will let you go on vacation whenever you wish. Regardless of these little inter-lab differences, you can still have a fairly clear picture of what tribal behaviors you can expect in your next academic job and what level of engagement will be required. For instance, you can expect that the more good quality articles you publish and the more collaborations you set, the more valued you will be. Or that in general, the quality of your work will be the essential ingredient in your assessment, while your working style and your choice of working hours will have a minor contribution to this assessment. We treat these basic rules as fundamental aspects of a job—almost like axioms.

However, when it comes to looking for jobs in the open job market, there is much more variety in working styles and tribal behaviors. If you choose a job only based on merit, and you disregard the nature of the working environment that you are getting into, you might find yourself in a miserable place. It is because the free market consists of multiple tribes that live according to very different rules. And, many of the tribes function according to the rules that substantially differ from the rules you are used to.

In this chapter, I present an overview of the main classes of tribes that you can encounter in the job market as a PhD and their main characteristics. But first, please take a look at the following question, then *take a break from reading for a few minutes and deliberate on this question on your own, before you come back to reading.*

> What are your three most favorite, and three least favorite aspects of your job? You can think of anything.

The point of this exercise is to get in insight into activities and mind states that you enjoy the most and those that you should try to avoid in the future. If you answer the above question to yourself first, then go through the following chapter and read the characteristics of the various working environments, you might get a picture of which tribe fits you best.

How you relate to other people

Just as mentioned before, even though we live in the 21st century, we still live in tribes—we join tribes, both in our private and professional lives. Tribal affiliation gives us a sense of belonging and identity and helps us develop a sense of purpose (Godin, 2020). Therefore, before starting your journey in the open job market, it's good to explore its tribal culture!

In every working environment, there is a (either written or unwritten) hierarchy and some rules of cohabitation. As a new member of the tribe, you feel like a new kid on the block, and you attempt to learn these rules as fast as you can. You naturally aim to develop healthy relationships with all the other members of the tribe and to gain some level of respect and appreciation for your work—and you as a person. Although you get rewards for your work in the form of a salary, the vast majority of your job satisfaction comes from the non-material aspects of the job. Fitting to your new tribe is an integral part of it.

Before we get down to visualize the whole job market as a cluster of tribes, let's go down memory lane for a moment. Please take a look at the following question, then *take a break from reading for a few minutes and deliberate on this question on your own before you come back to reading.*

Think of your sweet high school times, paying special attention to your social life back then. Furthermore, think about the times of your undergraduate studies.

So, in high school/undergraduate studies, you were the student who:
a) Was the heart and soul of every party. You used to come up with (crazy) ideas and everyone else followed,
b) Belonged to a group of friends led by someone else, and you were happy with this arrangement,
c) Did not belong to any particular group but you talked to everyone, and you were welcome to join all the parties,
d) Were rather aloof and didn't go out with your classmates too often.

None of these answers is good or bad—there is nothing wrong with not belonging to any group or with being introverted. Furthermore, most people change their behavior over time and today, ten or twenty years later, they no longer resemble themselves from the pre-study times.

I asked this question because the times of school and undergraduate studies were the last time when you co-habited with a group of people (your classmates), and no one imposed any rules on this little tribe from the outside—so the tribe could form on its own. Therefore, the way you related to other people back then might now give you a clue for what your natural way of relating to other people is. Again, this self-awareness can help you in choosing the right tribe in the job market.

The tribes of today

Before reviewing the most common types of working environments, a.k.a., tribes, one last question! Please take a look at the following question, then *take a break from reading for a few minutes and deliberate on this question on your own before you come back to reading.*

> Which of the following factors correlates with personal freedom at work the most?
> a) Stability at work/working benefits,
> b) Salary,
> c) Satisfaction from work,
> d) Opportunities for promotion.
> By personal freedom at work, I mean the opportunity to define your projects, collaborators, working style, and the freedom to choose the direction in your career path.

All these factors correlate with personal freedom at work to some extent. People who have more personal freedom, usually have better-paid jobs that give more room for growth and promotion. It can also bring you more satisfaction from work, although at the same time, it also implies responsibility, and this can yield stress as well—so this relation is not as simple.

But first and foremost, personal freedom at work is strongly correlated with *stability at work*—and it is a strong *negative* correlation. Stability means that you can feel relatively safe about the continuity of income, and you can enjoy good working benefits. Moreover, you also don't suffer from constant pressure to outperform other professionals or yourself, and you don't need to face direct competition that might jeopardize the market position of your employer.

So, the more freedom you have concerning your projects and your ultimate goals, the more you need to give up on the working benefits and certainty about the future (Fig. 3[21]). It is hard to have both at a time. Therefore, you'll need to choose which of the two qualities is more important for you.

As PhDs, we can choose to join various working environments with our skill sets. So, let's assume that you are good at programming and statistics. You go to the professional recruitment agency, and you hear: "Great! We have a Data Scientist position for you! The job pays this and that. Are you interested?" But hey, what kind of working environment is this? What type of relationship with other people will you develop in this environment? These details are often overlooked in the recruitment process. You might be a free spirit who cannot be happy while working for someone else and who would choose to spread wings as a freelancing Data Scientist. Or, you might be happier in a huge corporation where you do the same type of data analysis but in a safe, steady, predictable environment. What matters for your overall job satisfaction, is not only *what you do*, but also, the environment, or rather, *the tribe* that you belong to.

Various working environments are associated with various career trajectories in this two-dimensional "personal freedom" versus "stability at work" space (Fig. 3 A). While entering an academic career, you are usually given some level of security and (ideally also) autonomy for the initial few years during your PhD program. Sometimes, the amount of freedom is even higher than you would wish as your

---

[21] Fig. 3 can be downloaded from
www.welcome-solutions.com/index.php/bielczyk2020-what-is-out-there-for-me-fig3
and reproduced for non-commercial purposes (with a citation).

supervisor is hard to catch! This situation usually gets worse during the post-doctoral years: contracts get shorter, the numbers of stakeholders in your projects grow, and you need to marry writing new manuscripts with supervising students and grant writing. However, if you successfully make it through during that phase and achieve a tenured position, you can enjoy a (relatively) stable working life, and a high amount of personal freedom.

If you choose to go to the public sector, you usually score high in terms of working stability from the very beginning of your career till the very end. However, this happens at the cost of relatively low amounts of personal freedom—you work in huge, inert organizations, and every new initiative needs to go through a lot of bureaucratic procedures. If you choose to work for the private sector—either a startup, a consultancy company or a corporation—as a freshman, you will need to start from a relatively low amount of freedom and stability. Many companies only accept new employees for traineeships or sign contracts only with the trial period clause. They also typically don't offer too high starting salaries and start investing in you for real only after you prove yourself in the first one or two years of your employment. However, if you work well, your status in the company will gradually improve together with working experience. You will get a higher salary, more professional courses and certificates, and travel opportunities, more trust, more responsible projects, more autonomy to propose new initiatives. As a rule of thumb, jobs in large companies—corporations and large consultancy companies—are more secure but also offer less room for creativity and less flexible working schedule than jobs in small companies (including small consultancy companies) and startups.

In entrepreneurship and freelancing, you also start your career path from low levels of working stability. However, high amounts of personal freedom compensate for this uncertainty. In entrepreneurship, the amount of freedom drops with time while you get more and more stakeholders on board. In both these environments, the level of stability gradually grows with time. As a freelancer, you develop your brand and acquire returning customers, which increases your stability. As an entrepreneur, you find a market niche, build a base of customers, and gradually increase the value of the company—which also increases your stability.

Fig. 3 B presents a simplified landscape that summarizes all these working environments while taking into account the *probabilities* of different scenarios to play out. E.g., in an academic career, you *can* eventually achieve both stability and personal freedom. However, it will only happen when at least one of your projects becomes so impactful on the academic market that you will successfully land a tenured position—for many academics, this dream will never come true.

Of course, this landscape is simplistic. For instance, in some countries such as Switzerland, government jobs offer much more flexibility than in most other countries —so, in Switzerland, Fig. 3 would look different. Also, whether entrepreneurship is associated with more freedom than freelancing depends on the market sector; in many cases, freelancers are more independent and freer than entrepreneurs, especially if they can generate passive income from their work.

But one thing you can take for granted. In the whole job market, there is no El Dorado where you can get wealthy without any specialistic skills or working had—a place where you are safe and sound from day one, and you can get anything you want from your job. If such an El Dorado existed, there would be a long queue to get in! So, wherever you go, you'll need to face some inconveniences and some sources of stress. For these reasons, it is essential to find an environment that best fits your strengths and is associated with types of stress that you can handle. For instance, you might be good at coping with the stress related to the fact that your boss is demanding or inconsistent, but at the same time, weak at handling financial instability—or vice versa. Everyone has different susceptibility to stress.

Also, please remember that you don't need to resign from developing a *career* while moving to industry. In every single one of them, you *can* develop a career—both on the left and the right side of the landscape chart! In some areas of the market, high professional status is sealed by acquiring a specific title such as Full Professor in academia, Principal Consultant in consultancy, or CEO in private companies. In other areas of the market such as in freelancing, there is no such hierarchy and no such entitlement. However, while you are becoming proficient in what you do, your perceived value, recognition in the field, and subsequently also your income will gradually grow regardless of what you do. Therefore, please do not think about choosing a job in terms of whether you are willing to develop a career. Being a world-class professional *is* a career.

In this chapter, I will provide a brief characteristic of all the tribes presented above, together with tips on how to get there as a PhD. I will characterize the academic careers in the same way as other paths as I aim to provide an objective view of the job market. I feel that the academic career is *neither a better nor worse* option than other possible paths—it's a matter of personal preferences for the lifestyle that a given working environment implies. After reading the book, you might still conclude that an academic career is best for you!

1 Working for the public sector: Government-funded organizations and NGOs

Most public institutions welcome PhDs. Among such institutions, one can name government-funded organizations, e.g., the Ministry of Education, the Chamber of Commerce, national grant agencies, data centers funded by the government, think tanks summoned by the government, and non-profits. Some non-profits don't get funding from the government per se; they need to acquire financial resources independently through grants, crowdfunding, public tax benefits, and donations. Such organizations are often referred to as *non-governmental organizations* (NGOs). NGO space covers a broad range of societal problems, from the environment to social equality.

Since both governmental institutions and NGOs are non-profit and share some characteristics, I placed them in the same category.

THE GENERAL STRUCTURE OF THE WORKING ENVIRONMENT

➢ Unlike private companies, all governmental institutions and NGOs run on public funds or donations, which influences their structure. Any private company has a primary objective to produce new products and services and sell them with profits. The company also needs to stay ahead of the competition to keep afloat. Thus,

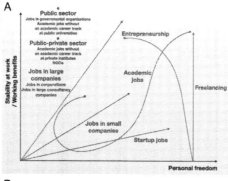

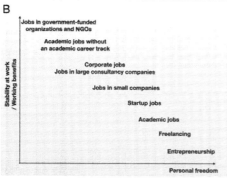

Figure 3 The tribes of today. **A**: The dynamic landscape, presenting the evolution of personal freedom and working stability over time in various tribes in the job market that PhDs often choose to join.

Jobs in the public organizations offer the most static and stable but the least flexible careers. On the other hand, jobs that involve setting a business are on the other end of the spectrum. This dynamic landscape represents the *ideal* trajectories, and thus, the *optimistic* scenario. Reprint adapted from Bielczyk & Bonet-Carne (2020).

B: The static, simplified landscape that takes into account the *probabilities* of success, thus, it is the more *realistic* case. Academic careers are towards the right-hand side in this landscape—yet still, some jobs offer an even higher degree of personal freedom and lower stability. It is a simplified landscape as every company and every institution has its own culture. This landscape could also slightly vary between countries.

private companies need effective and dynamic management systems. Management is like a *backbone* to the company: it's compulsory to coordinate and move forward. On the contrary, In public institutions the situation is different: the stream of public money will never dry out regardless of how efficient the management is. Therefore, the management layer is often smaller and less involved in the daily operations of single teams than in private companies. In many public institutions, specialists need to effectively self-manage. It is why chaos often happens whenever there is any change in the law or extenuating circumstances such as the corona crisis.

➤ While all private companies focus on generating profits, public institutions have a variety of goals. Some institutions distribute funds to other institutions. Some of them care about residents who are in a difficult personal situation, e.g., unemployed, disabled, elderly, or poor. Others aim to heal people or build an infrastructure, e.g., public servers, voting systems, roads, schools. Since every institution has a different set of goals, it also has a different structure.

➤ As mentioned above, the structure in the public institutions and NGOs is hard to generalize. However, typically, it is closer to a corporation than to academia: departments are composed of teams, and one central Human Resources (HR) department manages salaries for all employees.

➤In most public institutions, the workflow is project-oriented. Therefore, you'll most likely be a team member on many projects in parallel—in some of them, you might have a leading role while in others, you will be a minor contributor.

WHAT DAILY LIFE IS LIKE

➤Typically, you need to attend a lot of meetings as you take part in multiple projects at a time. Also, there is a large body of additional work associated with handling the meetings: either preparing for the incoming meetings or producing/reading minutes from the previous meetings. You might also go on many business travels—most of the public institutions collaborate with units abroad, or in a different part of the country, and present themselves at conferences.

➤Usually, the working benefits are very attractive: typically, more paid vacation days compared to private companies, plus additional benefits such as childcare and pension plans. Furthermore, there is no pressure to work longer than for the number of hours you are contracted for. However, mind that in some institutions, there are certain hectic periods throughout the year. E.g., in grant agencies, the evaluation period right after the deadlines for major public grant calls is usually very busy. In such cases, it is often the case that you need to work long hours for a period of few days to a few weeks. Usually, employees are compensated for that—it is possible to work fewer hours for a period of time when the hectic period is over. So eventually, you don't need to put on extra hours with respect to what you are paid for.

YOUR OPPORTUNITIES

➤As mentioned before, even though this is not an academic track, you can still develop a career here. With time, you will gain more experience and move towards more senior and better-paid positions where you have more room to propose new initiatives and supervise/manage junior members of your team.

➤Usually, professionals with academic titles get some respect from day one. They not only get higher starting salaries but also, their opinion is valued. In that sense, once you join such an institution as the new kid on the block, you don't need to work on your authority as much—you have it at "Hello." And all you need to do to keep this high status is to be very kind and respectful to people around you and cut your tongue whenever they make mistakes. That's pretty much it—as long as you don't evoke any conflicts, you will be considered a valuable team member.

➤Working for the public sector is typically associated with high social approval: you work on behalf of society as you create a new infrastructure or services that aim to serve to everyone. It can also become a source of job satisfaction!

➤As mentioned above, with a PhD title, you are usually offered an attractive starting salary. In the public sector, salaries are regulated by the local collective labor agreement. This implies that you typically don't need to negotiate the salary at the job interview and fight for every penny. If negotiating salary is that aspect of the recruitment process that stresses you the most, this is one way to go around it.

➤You can enjoy the feeling of *closure*: when the project is done, it's *really* done! Some projects can last for months but at some point, the team summons for the final meeting—after that, you can erase the project from the back of your head. It is much healthier for your mental health than conducting research projects that last for years.

➢You can enjoy a very high level of stability at work. If you work at a large governmental institution, it is very improbable that it will get closed at any time during your professional career. And, if you enjoy the job, you can stay for as long as you wish—even for the rest of your professional career. Most likely, you'll also be able to avoid the pressure to "gain international experience" by relocating to another country. Thus, you can settle down and enjoy your life without worrying about what happens tomorrow.

➢A public institution or an NGO will not only take care of you while you work there but also later on. In developed countries, many institutions allocate special budgets for employees who are willing to requalify and find jobs elsewhere. These budgets are dedicated to external coaching, professional courses, and giving the employee some financial buffer to peacefully find a new job. It would be unthinkable in a private company!—no boss would ever pay for a dedicated training with the intention that you successfully land another job and say, "Goodbye!" to them. Yet, a public institution might go for it. It's just easy for them to spend the tax-payers money on such luxuries!

➢This working stability also permeates to interpersonal relations: since everyone feels safe and there are enough resources for everyone, the overall atmosphere is positive, and there are no tensions between people. It's just pleasant to jump out of bed and go to work in the morning. It is also easier to achieve a good work-life balance here compared to academia and the private sector. No wonder that the employees of the public sector are the group that declares *higher* levels of job satisfaction than employees of the private sector (Witters, 2011).

WHAT YOU WILL NEED TO ACCEPT IN THIS WORKING ENVIRONMENT

➢Your impact stays within the organization. This environment offers a different type of career than academia: you will not be acknowledged for your projects in public as an individual. In a sense, by working here, you need to give up on your individuality to some extent. While working for the public sector, you become a part of a cloud, and mostly the people within this cloud will recognize your expertise and personal achievements. If your management does a good job, you will still feel valued and accomplished though!

➢Meetings, meetings, meetings! Public institutions share some features with corporations: procedures, delays, and overflow of meetings/workshops to attend. Also, since this is a public sector, some of the projects might not be as efficient and goal-oriented as you would wish.

➢Double agenda. Even though officially, public institutions promote innovation and technological progress, they are most interested in keeping the status quo. Behind the curtains, employees of the public institutions often fear from technologies that might disrupt their field and take their jobs. For instance, governments and the structures that represent these governments, such as the Chambers of Commerce, are often reluctant to facilitate blockchain projects. It is because the whole idea behind blockchain is to replace centrally governed structures in the society with decentralized systems—and this is not in line with the interests of the public institutions and the decisional people therein. Therefore, you might get frustrated by working in the public think tanks focused on technological innovation—you will not

have any power to implement any new solutions. It means that if you wish to work on the application of any disruptive technologies, you need to go elsewhere.
- ➤Kind faces get promoted first. In a public institution, a kind face can matter more than being competent or efficient. People who get promoted in public institutions the fastest are those who are polite, patient, can find a common tongue with everyone, always find time for a little chit chat by the coffee machine, and don't impose any stress on anyone around them. Therefore, if you are the type of person who gets annoyed by incompetence and prefers to speak out their thoughts, you might get frustrated here. Most probably, you won't be valued as high as diplomats even if you are the best specialist on the block.
- ➤Farewells. You may work with the same people for many, many years, and you effectively become a family. If they retire or change the job, it can feel almost like losing a family member. You'll sincerely miss your former colleagues, and you might get a deep feeling of abandonment every time someone says, "Goodbye."

BEST ACCESS ROUTES FOR PHDS
- ➤Jobs in the public sector are usually offered openly through job listing platforms and social networks. Agencies specialized in hiring PhDs are typically also informed about the open positions in governmental institutions and NGOs—so if you indicate this type of job as your preference, they should be able to find job offers for you.

OFTEN-ENCOUNTERED TRIBAL BEHAVIORS YOU SHOULD KNOW ABOUT
- ➤Little celebrations. Birthdays, baby showers, job anniversaries—almost every day, there is yet another reason to have coffee and cake.
- ➤Many people prefer to work from home as often as they can. Therefore, sometimes it happens that you bring your delicious cake to the office and find out that there is no one around to celebrate with!
- ➤Baby-talk. Since, as mentioned above, the work-life balance is typically pretty good at public institutions, you can expect that talking about kids will be one of the top talking points at lunch. So, if you are not that much into kids, brace yourself!

2 Working for the public sector: Academic job without an academic career track (at universities and private research institutes)

By academic job without an academic career path, I mean working in a research institution, but on a position that is not associated with research: as a Grant Advisor, Lab Manager, departmental Administrative Manager, Legislative Analyst, Human Resources Officer, Science Policy Advisor, etc.

THE GENERAL STRUCTURE OF THE WORKING ENVIRONMENT
- ➤The structure is the same as in an academic career. However, your salary will be covered by the budget of the department/institution rather than by a particular lab. You will also likely enjoy a more stable working scheme.

WHAT DAILY LIFE IS LIKE
- ➤You will likely have a more stable working pattern than active researchers: for the most part, it will be possible for you to close the door behind at 5 pm and disconnect from work. Logistic jobs around academia are associated with a lot of meetings, so

you should mentally prepare for that. However, the level of working stability will depend on your employer. In some countries (e.g., in Spain), there is a class of research institutes beyond universities. The government doesn't fully cover their budgets. Thus, they are either partially or fully funded by public grants and the private sector. The level of working stability in such institutes is much lower than at universities, and contracts are often short.

YOUR OPPORTUNITIES

➤ On this path, you can also develop a career! For instance, a professional Grant Advisor with a high success rate, can be well-paid, and get a team of junior employees to work under their wings. You can also get promoted from a small institute to a large institute with many more employees, and a much more complex structure. Also, if you work in the policy space, you can get promoted towards advisory bodies around the government—which is a very prestigious career path.

➤ As in governmental institutions, you can enjoy a very high level of stability at work: it is very improbable that the institute you are working for, will get closed at any time during your professional career. And, if you enjoy the job, you can stay for as long as you wish, even for the rest of your professional career—and, you can settle down where you are.

➤ No more need to race. You can just focus on doing your job well, and on your other priorities without the constant need to worry about how strong your resume is, and what the competition is doing.

➤ If this matters to you, one advantage could be that you can get a job in an environment which you already know very well. This is a form of a *soft* transition to industry: you can change position within the institution where you used to work before; just jump from a research position to a position without an academic career track. It's also often easy to find non-academic positions this way: since you already know the management of your research institute, you will be well informed when the new administrative positions are coming out.

WHAT YOU WILL NEED TO ACCEPT IN THIS WORKING ENVIRONMENT

➤ Auxiliary role. You'll need to accept that from now on, you'll watch and support people building their research careers from the sidelines. If you have a high level of empathy, this might also be a plus! But, before you decide to take this type of job, you have to seriously ask yourself: did I get over my desires to pursue an academic career? If deep inside, you are not done with the wish to become a PI, you'll suffer watching other people pursue their academic careers next to you.

➤ Influence of the working environment. Academia is a place where burnout and depression rates are still very high, and this can permeate onto your level of satisfaction from work as well—even if you are happy about your job, working around frustrated people can have negative consequences on your mental health.

➤ Capitalism. Capitalism is also slowly crawling into this space. Even though you might technically stay in one place for long years, or even for the whole professional career, there is some peer pressure to build a resume by changing jobs every few years. It's often hard to get promoted within the same institution because there is only one employee over you, and that person is not going anywhere. For this reason, employees working in this space often go for *diagonal promotion* instead: they climb the ladder by finding an open position one step higher in another institution. Especially in the US, many employees working in this sector change jobs even more often than academics, and travel around from one institution to another to build their portfolio and climb up the ladder.

BEST ACCESS ROUTES FOR PHDS

➤This type of job is usually announced online, through *Academic Transfer*[22], social networks, job boards, *Twitter*, and other public channels. Of course, it is good to use your contacts in this case: the easiest way of getting this type of job is to ask around about the incoming vacancies at your current institution.

OFTEN-ENCOUNTERED TRIBAL BEHAVIORS YOU SHOULD KNOW ABOUT

➤No specific tribal habits. Actually, in this type of job, you usually need to find your place as a lonely wolf among other tribes. It can be quite an isolating feeling.

3 Corporate job

Corporate jobs are positions within large companies (hiring more than 250 employees). People who have never worked in a corporation usually have a picture of how such a job could look like—there are lots of urban legends and stereotypes about corporations spread by Hollywood. In the movie world, a corporation is always an evil institution. Some examples: movies such as *Office Space* (1999), *WALL-E* (2008), *The Jurassic Park* series (1993-2015), *The Terminator* series (1984-2015), or *Resident Evil* series (2002-2016), TV series such as *The Simpsons* (1989-), *Futurama* (1999-2013), or *Mr. Robot* (2015-), and documentaries such as *The Corporation* (2003) and *Enron: The Smartest Guys in the Room* (2005).

THE GENERAL STRUCTURE OF THE WORKING ENVIRONMENT

➤In international corporations, there are multiple management levels: Managers of Plant, Managers of Branches, Managers of Europe/Asia/America Associations, Managers of Headquarters. Typically, you have a boss, and he/she still has a few bosses over them.

➤In most corporations, the organizational structure is a *matrix*. So, you typically encounter the following: a) Direct Manager who accounts for your presence at work, fluent communication with other team members, and monitoring the results of the whole team; b) Human Resource Manager who manages employee development and decides about their fate (or, their career if that's what you prefer to call it); c) Dotted-Line (executive) Manager who works with you on substantive tasks; d) Heads of various specific projects (because you are participating in their teams as a specialist). In all this, you can also be a leader (or a boss) to someone else, e.g., next to being a team member of five projects, you can also be a leader of three other projects—which makes you a member of another three teams.

➤The way management is structured depends on the sector of the market. In large engineering companies, in most departments, the management is still old-school: managers just manage (and usually come from management-related backgrounds)

---

[22] www.academictransfer.com

56

while specialists in their teams create products and solve problems. Only in the R&D department, it's often the case that the management structure resembles the academic system: you work closely with your direct boss, who is a specialist in your field as well. In IT, on the contrary, most companies prefer to promote specialists to managers within the company. In that fashion, managers always have some degree of specialistic knowledge as well.

WHAT DAILY LIFE IS LIKE

➤Typically, there is a clear division between managers and specialists. Some companies promote their senior specialists to managers while other companies focus on expertise in leadership and hire external managers. In either case, managers and specialists have a well-delineated scope of duties. A manager is there to manage and motivate people—the team members should focus on executing projects. A specialist should work on the projects and come up with creative solutions rather than to steer the projects. A manager's goal is to get to a higher level of management. A specialist's goal is to become the "to-go-to" person regarding come class of problems within the company. There are just two different career tracks, and you should decide early on which one of them interests you more.

➤Your daily schedule depends on your function of course. However, your Outlook Calendar tends to get overloaded with various corporate appointments— the corporate executives want to broadcast their vision to all plants regularly. It often happens that multiple meetings of the teams you participate in are arranged at the same time, and you need to find your way between them. Besides, there are meetings arranged by all the managers mentioned above. Additionally, if you want to set up meetings for the teams you lead, you need to invite your lab members according to their availability. Your team members might be already booked for other meetings so you need to find the first spot that suits everyone—which can be weeks ahead.

➤It's hard to determine what daily life will be in every detail, as every company has its own company culture. One company will enforce you to come in and leave at precise hours, while another company will give you much more flexibility. One company will allow you to take work (including the company documents) home, and another company won't. One company will be liberal about the topics you can or cannot touch on at lunch, while another company will strictly forbid talking about politics or religion. Usually, the culture of the company develops from the seed of the first twenty people who were working there when the company was still a baby. These people, and the communication between them, strongly influence the spirit in the company while it develops. This is why it's better not to take too much for granted, and ask a lot of questions once you start working to make sure that you are familiar with the local (written and unwritten) rules.

YOUR OPPORTUNITIES

➤You have access to almost unlimited know-how. Employees have access to multiple electronic systems and applications regarding technical and technological solutions, also organizational models and various personnel management projects. So, if you want to learn, there is an ocean of possibilities! There are also both facultative, and obligatory online and on-site classes to attend.

➤You can enjoy a very decent payment, usually accompanied by a large selection of corporate working benefits. Usually, there are also team- and individual bonus programs for various sorts of achievements. Bonuses are usually announced at various company meetings and celebrations.

➤Travel opportunities. Large corporations often have offices spread all around the world, which allows you to visit distant, exotic places—and even get paid extra for that! During the application procedure, you might be asked whether you are ready to travel and to what capacity. There are three groups of traveling employees: a) young employees who are supposed to develop within the company and go through multi-site training programs; b) experienced, highly qualified specialists who need to troubleshoot problems in different plants; c) managers who need to examine the progress in other plants.

➤You are a free person, in a sense that you can make decisions that support your career. For instance, if you believe that your opportunities for self-growth have dried out in your current place, you are free to search for another corporation in the field. And, unlike in academia, you probably won't be asked for reference letters while applying. Why would anyone ask you for references from a company you are just leaving? This is an obvious conflict of interest. So, you can peacefully apply for a new job, and only your skill set and the general employment history (as opposed to, e.g., the opinion of your previous boss) will decide about the outcome of this process.

➤Many corporations experiment with modern management practices that were traditionally the domain of startups. If you are looking for innovative and dynamic working environment in which new products are created using scrum and/or agile development, many corporations—especially in IT—give that opportunity today. Furthermore, corporations also learn to outsource many positions that were traditionally seen as the backbone of the company structure. For instance, it becomes an often practice to outsource project management to managers based abroad, e.g., in countries where labor is much cheaper. This practice was unthinkable just a decade or two decades ago because of the common belief that you need in-person meetings to develop trust in the team. Today, it's becoming obvious that you can work in teams and develop a team spirit online, and be as productive as in the traditional, office setting. This also means that it is possible to work for more than one employer remotely and from anywhere you wish.

WHAT YOU WILL NEED TO ACCEPT IN THIS WORKING ENVIRONMENT

➤Star qualities. In every competitive field, you need some *star quality* to thrive—the only question is, what does star quality mean? In corporations, professionals who usually are the most valued and get promoted the fastest, are those who are perceived as creative, productive, well organized, communicative, easy going, and well-connected within the company. Of course, there is a difference between how you are perceived and how you are. The fact that other employees notice what you do for the company and they *believe* that you are very busy and irreplaceable, is often much more important than how much you do in reality. Thus, building self-image is everything in a corporation.

➤Individuality. Related to the previous point, in a corporation, everyone cares about their career path. In that sense, this environment is highly individualistic. Therefore, you'll need to optimally manage your time between doing the actual work and self-promotion: showcasing everything you did, even if it was the smallest solution to the smallest problem. Just tell everyone, "Look at this cool solution!"—which means, "Look at how cool I am!" This very much resembles primary school: you need to raise your hand every time you have anything to say so that the teacher notices your engagement and lets you speak. As mentioned before, to get promoted, it is not enough to be hard-working—you also need to be noticeable. For the same reason, in case you have a good idea for a new project or a new solution, it's generally better for you to walk straight to your boss' office and present it, rather than discuss with your colleagues by a coffee. In corporations, there is less respect to the authorship of ideas and people are less ethically oriented than in academia. Thus, if you don't arrive at your boss' door early enough, someone else could be first.

➤Lack of competencies. Most often, people who are the loudest and most noticeable are getting promoted. Some of them come from outside the company to take specific positions (i.e., the diagonal promotion). They often suffer from a lack of competence but HR cannot see it, and their current bosses need to limit the losses and teach them. The incompetent people are rarely laid off. They are usually shifted around to other departments—so that the rotation within the company is high. And, so it goes on. Since those incompetent employees move around the departments a lot, they always have time to start over. In general, you need to be prepared that your boss will likely know less about the subject-matter of the project than you, and some boss might also be mediocre managers. You need to develop sacred patience for your bosses in corporations, as in that case, the best coping strategy is to just wait until that person moves to another department (or, swap seats by yourself).

➤Focus on revenue. It's not a secret that corporations are capitalistic monsters fueled by profits. Once you work there, you will feel this fixation on numbers daily: your team will be given yearly targets to meet, and you can expect regular audits and discussions about what you can do to further increase the company income (or, to decrease the costs which is equivalent when you think about it). If this aspect of the job is repulsive for you, you should focus on applying to the departments that are away from production and sales—those that are more concentrated on providing professional training to employees and R&D. These departments are treated by companies as *investments*, so there is no expectation that your work there will yield any direct revenue.

➤Chaos. The agenda constantly changes throughout the day. At a corporation, no one knows what will happen today. Usually, the agenda for the day falls in ruins because the urgent, unexpected tasks need to be completed. But it's up to you to decide what to do first as a priority. Everyone is polite, and if you tell them, "I didn't do this yesterday because my nose itched," they would just answer, "No problem, please recover and do this whenever you can."

➤Even more chaos. In developed countries, the costs associated with laying off an employee are often astronomical. For this reason, many large companies mitigate the risks of baring such costs by hiring employees through external hiring agencies.

The mechanism is simple: the employee is hired by an external agency and the company pays a commission to the agency. The commission includes some amount on top of the salary. The agency makes profits on the commission while the company has the right to dispose of the employee at any point in time with additional costs. This policy often has consequences for the efficiency of the company: people come for a specific project, then leave, and another person needs to pick up the project after the employee who just left. This turnover can lead to even more chaos and the feeling of working in vain: people around you are coming and going, and projects are getting abandoned.

➤Eeeven more chaos. When the company grows big, its departments might get detached from each other. If the company is a player in a very competitive market such as IT, the central management typically has a good grasp on all the projects going on in different departments. However, what happens when the company becomes a market leader in a sector where you can protect your IP with patents (such as engineering), and doesn't need to compete anymore? Well, in such case the efficiency might go down, and the departments stop communicating with each other. It might be frustrating to discover that the project you are working on since six months or so, is being executed independently in another department. Such stories happen quite often.

➤Meetings, meetings, meetings! You will likely spend over 50% of your working time on meetings. Sometimes even 100%. It is not a joke; the movie scenes in which corporate employees spill coffee on their impeccable white shirts while running from one office to another in panic are not far from reality. On the bright side of things, you might get fit from just running from one meeting to another for the whole day.

➤Tyranny of morning larks. If you happen to be a night owl, a.k.a. a nocturnal person or a B-person, you will have a hard life in a corporation (unless you happen to work in the evening shift). Chronotype is a term to summarize all behaviors related to circadian rhythms. The fact that individuals have a distribution of chronotypes and a preference to sleep at different times has a deep biological meaning. In the old days, this interpersonal variability allowed small tribes to stay vigilant to potential dangers overnight. Thus, morningness-eveningness in the population follows a normal distribution (Roenneberg et al., 2007). This trait is probably at least partly genetically determined (Pegoraro et al., 2015), and we cannot influence it. Yet, corporations are under the dictatorship of morning larks: in a typical working scheme, employees should appear in the office in the early morning.

➤Procedures. Not following the company procedures closely enough is the easiest way to get fired from a corporation. And, there is a wide range of rules to follow. Firstly, you'll encounter a multitude of procedures listing the requirements in terms of financials, personnel policy, quality, environmental protection, security, code of conduct, etc. These documents are usually sent out to everyone in the corporation by *Outlook*. For worse, the rules change all the time. It's hard to even keep up with reading them! Secondly, you'll also need to follow a multitude of procedures arising from the applicable law in the market sector the company operates in—e.g., the aviation law for aircraft, the health protection law for drug manufacturing companies, the employee protection law for all companies. These procedures are there to make sure that employees comply with legal requirements and that they record all the details on the manufacturing process or laboratory tests. All the data is usually saved and archived for another 20 years or more.

➢Political correctness. Touching on some particular topics might not be welcome. In academia, we are used to the freedom of speech. At lunch, we use to chat about almost anything, from politics to diapers. Discussing even the most sensitive topics with coworkers in a coffee break (such as e.g., the progress in our mental health) is often acceptable in academia. In a corporation, it is often different: there are strict rules on what is or is not allowed as a subject of a public discussion. For instance, many corporations aim to be apolitical, and discussing politics at work is not appreciated. Related to this point, most of today's corporations also educate their employees on how to be politically correct. Thus, you can expect hundreds of compulsory courses on inclusivity, diversity, responsible leadership, etc. Nothing wrong with such training—but you might get overwhelmed with the amount.

➢Subjective way of assessing your performance and awarding bonuses. The vast majority of private companies perform the annual assessment of all their employees' performance. During such a judgment day, you not only have a progress meeting with your superiors, but you also get a grade, typically on a scale of A-F or 1-5. It can feel like getting back to primary school when your teachers were grading your school tests and behavior. Whether you'll receive a yearly personal bonus depends on that grade. Christmas parties at corporations very often resemble Oscar ceremonies: all those who believe they should have received a yearly bonus, but they didn't cry together in the restroom.

➢Cult-like strategies. The corporation pays for your time but would appreciate getting your soul too. Be prepared for the fact that the number of projects going on in parallel, emergency dinners with guests from other plants, business travels, and the necessity to showcase your work all the time, can drain you from all your energy in the long run. This lifestyle can also cause intrusive thoughts about work, even when you are supposed to rest. You need to demonstrate a lot of assertiveness and self-control to be able to push these thoughts away. Corporations can also be very manipulative in their strategies to make you obsessed. Rather than threatening employees with a vision of unemployment, they stimulate an informal competition for the status of the most engaged, the most dedicated, and the most experienced person in the company. For this purpose, companies organize lots of extracurricular events such as open days or internal conferences. They "stimulate the company culture" by developing some internal communication platforms such as company-wide blogs and newsletters. They also invite you to take a lot of compulsory and/or optional courses. In the end, in pursuit of becoming the most engaged employee, you hectically jump between all these activities: social events, writing blogs and essays about the progress within the company and/or developments in the field, completing dozens of leadership and management courses, and your *actual projects* —until you reach the level of utter exhaustion.

BEST ACCESS ROUTES FOR PHDS

➢Specialist in the R&D department. These are usually densely populated by PhDs.

➤Product Owner/Product Manager positions. As mentioned in chapter 3: *What Are My Options? What Types of Jobs Suit Me?*, it's hard to get these positions without prior managing experience, but it is still possible—especially if you have any personal connections within the company. Product Owner is usually a good entry point. *Project* Manager positions are also possible to get with a PhD, but it's harder to land such a position as the first job after leaving academia.

➤Most corporations have the policy to refresh their staff with new blood regularly so getting into a corporation without personal contacts is usually possible. Corporate jobs are announced through professional social networks (e.g., *LinkedIn*) and job boards (e.g., *Indeed*). Specialized agencies hiring PhDs usually also collaborate with corporations.

OFTEN-ENCOUNTERED TRIBAL BEHAVIORS YOU SHOULD KNOW ABOUT

➤Corporate lunches and Open/Family Days are *not optional*. You are expected to demonstrate your devotion to the company by "choosing" to join these—officially facultative—events.

➤Every corporation is a bit like separate, small academia—a small universe with its own laws of physics. Most employees attempt to find their path up the ladder, get promoted, and build a career within the company. A corporation is *not* a safe harbor; it is a populated, vibrant marketplace where you need to sell yourself, and keep on demonstrating how indispensable you are (Godin, 2010).

4 Startup job

A startup is a company in the early stages of development (hence the name). Yet, from the very start, the aim of the company's founders is to scale the operations and grow. Startup culture also earned a lot of stereotypes spread via movies such as, e.g., *The Social Network* (2010), *The Inventor: Out for Blood in Silicon Valley* (2019), or *Ingenious* (2012). According to Hollywood, a proper startup is created in someone's garage, preferably by some Ivy League dropout who decides to go on a personal crusade to change the world. Or, by a bunch of underachievers who get together and accidentally get rich. And of course, startups are populated by long-haired hipsters who are not fond of the shower and spend evenings alone in the office by pizza and beer. Well, needless to say, these stereotypes are (usually…) far from reality.

THE GENERAL STRUCTURE OF THE WORKING ENVIRONMENT

➤Startups usually have a much flatter structure than corporations. Of course, this is a professional environment in which you sell your time to execute your boss' projects. Yet still, your employers do their best to give you the impression that you are a team member, everyone in the team is equal, and you can step forward with your ideas. Indeed, in many startups, this is true: you are more than welcome to be creative and propose your solutions as they become the IP of the company and can help with winning the race against the competition in the market.

➤While a corporation is like an army, a startup is like a band. Namely, it is a group of people who need to synchronize their actions and play together. Since there are only a few people in the startup, it's usually welcome if you have more than one core competence, and you can share or swap roles with other team members if necessary.

For instance, let's assume that you are a software developer in a startup. Your boss is on a business trip, and the secretary just got sick. The phone in the secretary's office is ringing. Will you ignore it, or will you storm into the secretary's office and pick it up? In a corporation, getting into someone else's office when they are absent (without the authorization to do so) would be seen as a violation of the corporate rules and could have serious consequences. In a startup, proactive behavior will be treated as a sign of team spirit rather than as a problem—as it can save the business deal for the company. In the startup, every time you get out of your role to help someone else or think out of the box, you'll score points.

WHAT DAILY LIFE IS LIKE

➤You can expect even more chaotic working dynamics than in a corporation. A little startup is usually dependent on a few core clients—and sometimes, even on a single client. It means that the dynamics within the company is hardly ever stable, and usually, life accelerates before every deadline as *the client is the king*. You can also expect that investors and other stakeholders might interfere with the roadmap, and the development plans might rapidly change in the process.

➤At the same time, you can also expect more flexible working hours. While most corporations control the working hours of their employees with the use of chip cards, most startups do not do that. If all of a sudden you disappear for half a day because you have got an appointment with a doctor and work in the evening on that day, no one will perceive this as a problem—at least, as long as your absence will not make the job of other team members harder. While in a corporation, your diligence and presence are closely watched, in a startup, everything boils down to your results. If you make money for the company, you are a valuable asset, and no one will care if your work for ten hours a day or you leave early every day. Other than corporations, startups concentrate on being *effective* rather than *efficient*. Namely, in a startup, the ultimate *impact* of your actions on the production and sales matters more than *how fast* you can work, for how many hours you can hold your attention, and how many tasks you can complete per day. Startups are also more welcoming to the idea of working from home than corporations—today, many startups *only* work remotely. Since in some startups, employees work remotely from all around the world, they don't even have a stationary office. In that sense, startup jobs are closer to academic jobs than to corporate jobs.

➤The extent to which startup life is unstable depends on *where* in the world you are based. If you find yourself in one of the sacred temples of entrepreneurship such as the Silicon Valley in the US, or Bangalore in India, you can expect a higher tempo than when you work, say, in Western Europe. In those epicenters of startup culture, there are herds of dreamers who are obsessed with the idea to create something bigger than life that will change the world—so they won't treat your time with too much respect.

YOUR OPPORTUNITIES

➤As mentioned in chapter 1: *Should I Stay, or Should I Go?*, academia is a dysfunctional system. Namely, you need to work in teams yet still, at the end of the day, all the "team members" need to prioritize building their academic CV over the common goals of the group. If you feel a strong desire to improve on your teamwork experience, a startup job might be a solution for you. Any startup team indeed has just one, well-defined goal: to develop the best product and to rock the market. Your colleagues' success automatically becomes your success and vice versa. There is no gradation of contribution within the team: you win together, or you lose together, no author list included. The most common comment from PhDs who went to startups is that they enjoy the quality of teamwork, they feel supported, and the sense that the other team members root for them.

➤If you join the startup early on, you can the company share certificates next to your salary. These shares are usually vested for a period of a few years, and their purpose is to motivate you, even more, to work on behalf of the startup and stay with the company. I think that this is a *good* way of motivating people: instead of motivating you negatively as in academia ("If you are not good enough, your contract will expire and you'll become jobless"), this gives you a positive motivation: if you do a great job and the company gains in value, your assets grow together with it.

➤In many countries, startup jobs are paid better than corporate jobs. This is a form of compensation for the higher level of insecurity associated with working for a startup. This is not true worldwide though—and especially, not in the developing branches of industry where most new projects struggle with the cash flow. For instance, in 2018-19 a major bear market came to the blockchain industry, and blockchain startups were paying very modest salaries compared to the "traditional" IT startups.

➤Growth together with the company. If you join the core team early in the process and the company grows from that point, this will bring you lots of benefits. Your amount of responsibility and your status in the hierarchy will go up. Typically, the members of the core team are further appointed as heads of the departments and have a say when it comes to making decisions about the shape of the whole company. Most likely, new employees will get hired under your lead—so, if you stay within the company, one day, you might become the head of a large department.

➤Learning experience. Many entrepreneurs started their careers by working in startups where they learned from their bosses' mistakes. Before you start your own business, it's good to see how to run and how *not to run* a startup. Thus, an opportunity to closely watch an entrepreneur at work is an invaluable experience if you are thinking of ever starting a company on your own. And, you will receive a lavish salary for this hands-on business training!

➤Results matter the most—which is usually good news for PhDs. Let us imagine that you are the type of person who doesn't hesitate to speak out whenever some solution is suboptimal, something doesn't make sense, or needs to be radically improved. If you are such a person, and if you tend to react in situations when someone around you misbehaves, startups will value you. And, they will appreciate your input much more than public institutions or corporations where keeping the status quo has a higher priority than doing things right. So, if the freedom to speak out about what you think is important to you, the startup culture might be the place to go.

WHAT YOU WILL NEED TO ACCEPT IN THIS WORKING ENVIRONMENT

➤Focus on quick results. The focus on productivity and sales also has a dark side.

Namely, while in public institutions and corporations, you will likely be treated with more respect because of your academic background, in a startup, you need to prove yourself every day. The owners of the company are entrepreneurs; they are down to earth and practical. They will look at your results and the direct influence of these results on their business. And, they will value your opinion based on that. If you theorize, pay attention to every detail, and focus too much on making the perfect product rather than concentrating on shrinking the time to market to the minimum, the startup's owners might treat this as counterproductive and detrimental to the company. Many PhDs have issues with adapting to the culture in which you often push a half-baked product out to the market and start selling as soon as you can, even knowing that the quality is way below what you would be happy about. Startups often do so: they first sell a beta-version of the product, and then bootstrap, i.e., improve the product using the funds acquired from sales. This practice is called a *lean startup* (Ries, 2011).

➢ Dependence. Since the team is small, you will be highly dependent on your direct boss and your colleagues. If you do not click with your boss or any of your teammates, it might influence your level of job satisfaction. For instance, let us assume that you have a different outlook on life than that of your close colleague. You find that guy's views ridiculous—to such an extent that after some time, every conversation with them is uncomfortable, even if you are talking about the weather. Yet, when it comes to lunchtime, you have to spend an hour at lunch together every day; you have no choice as there is only one table and all the team members sit together. It is even worse if you have a different approach to every possible problem than your boss: you can feel like your every initiative gets killed, and your wings get clipped. Since the company is small, there will be no room in the company to shift you around to another team. Therefore, if you find yourself in such a situation, you either need to learn how to accept reality, or you'll effectively need to change your job.

➢ Sync. In a startup, you need to synchronize your actions with your colleagues. If your colleagues are taking vacations, you often have to take over part of their job. Since the team is small, it is often the case that one person is responsible for one particular role—and if that person is away, the company operations are in danger of freezing. Therefore, you need to be very flexible with taking up tasks, and often, take one for the team: stop your work, and take over someone else's responsibilities when they are away. It can be quite distracting and frustrating. It might also happen that you cannot effectively take vacations while other people are gone because someone needs to stay around.

➢ External risk incorporated. You might suddenly lose your job if the whole startup flops in the market. A startup can lose competition on the market for many different reasons: the lack of cash flow, bad timing, a competitive project that takes over the whole market sector, disagreement between the founders, etc. Even if you are the best, the most dedicated employee, you suddenly end up on the street just because the whole company sinks.

➢ Not your dream. By working in a startup, you work on fulfilling someone else's dreams—although the founders of the company might make a lot of effort to plug this thought in your mind that you share their vision (by the inception of sorts). Even if you get company shares for working on behalf of the startup, it is still a small portion of the cake, while the vast majority and the voting power stays on the founders' and investors' side. Therefore, while contributing to building the company, you are effectively making someone else rich. If the startup will grow and get sold at some point, all the major shareholders will become millionaires, while you will get some little bonus—even though you were with the company from the very beginning. Most founders deliberately choose to hire professionals who are *better experts* than them. Therefore, you might discover that you are more hard-working, more qualified, and more competent than your boss. Yet still, that person will eventually get rich, not you.

➢ Your reality can change. Every startup aims to grow by design, and in principle, it can become a corporation one day. Thus, you might join a startup and wake up in a corporation several years later. Usually, once the population of employees exceeds 20 people, the first corporate structures start forming. With the further growth of the company, the percentage of managers and administration within the company gradually grows while the percentage of specialists drops. The atmosphere in the team slowly morphs from casual to more formal. In the process, you might discover that you do not like this cultural change. Thus, it often happens that employees leave startups at the point when first corporate structures appear.

➢ Hypocrisy. Many new startup employees experience a mental dip a few months after joining a startup. Namely, right after they join the team, they feel like on a honeymoon. However, after some time, their initial enthusiasm fades away, and they fall into a deep depression. The main reason is that many startup owners are typical salesmen who can pitch their companies as oriented at the Sustainable Development Goals (SDGs)—ethical and good for humanity. They know how to lure a new person. At the job interview, they will focus on telling you the story of their passion, explaining the particular (societal) problem they are solving, telling you about the team that they have built, and praising the team spirit in the company. Many PhDs are thirsty for doing team projects that are good for society, and they quickly fall for these stories. Then, after a few months of hard work, they discover that the startup owners are, in fact, aggressive capitalists who focus on the profits under the excuse of conducting environment- or society-friendly projects. It can lead to a lot of frustration. In my mind, the best solution to this problem is to be realistic. It's better to mentally prepare that every project developed by a private company is commercial to some extent and that the interest in revenue will always be there, regardless of what the company owners will tell you at the start.

➢ Peer pressure. Even though the company owners typically attempt to create an atmosphere of brotherhood and encourage employees to treat each other as partners, you will also bump into rats obsessed with building their careers here. Many professionals who have prior working experience with both corporations and startups declare that—against the stereotypes—there are more career-oriented people in startups than in corporations. The overall amount of tension and peer pressure is also higher here. It is because in a startup, almost every employee is a specialist, and everyone contributes. Once you work there, your results are explicit and directly comparable with other employees' results. For instance, if someone else codes ten times faster than you, this will not get unnoticed. It can feel a bit like a travel back in time to the times of high school. Back then, you used to get the same tests as your classmates, and every single time, you prayed that you wouldn't come last on the classroom leaderboard. Now, once you work in a startup, you don't want to feel like an underachiever, so you struggle to be at least average in the team. And since all your teammates think the same, the peer competition naturally emerges. In a corporation, on the contrary, there are lots of employees around who are just talking heads: attend meetings, sort out logistics, instruct other people, discuss concepts, write reports, drink coffee with everyone. In such a working environment, you can feel special as a specialist from the start, even if you work in a team with other specialists. Thus, the amount of perceived pressure is much lower in corporations.

➤Not as equal as it seems. As mentioned before, people who joined the startup early on, as cofounders and first employees have the shares and the voting power within the company. Moreover, they are important and trusted just because of their history with the company. These people are often respected for what they say and can decide about the course of the company. They are listened to even if they know less about a particular subject than you and if they are wrong about their assessment of the situation. This informal structure is typically not visible when the startup is very tiny (e.g., ten employees) but becomes explicit when the company grows to 30-100 people. Many PhDs who enter startups get frustrated after they discover that the structure of the startup is some form of oligarchy (often referred to as "a clique")— regardless of how competent and productive they are, they can't get promoted in this system.

➤Subjective way of assessing your performance and awarding bonuses. Just as corporations, many startups perform the annual assessment of all their employees' performance that concludes with a grade—and possibly, also a personal bonus. It's not a rule here, though.

BEST ACCESS ROUTES FOR PHDS

➤The good news is: most startups need smart, flexible, self-disciplined, and creative people—a type of a "hacker". Therefore, they typically welcome PhDs. The best way to get a startup job is through networking—since startups are small, it usually needs time to develop some trust before the contract is signed. Friends who already work in startups might help you here, or otherwise, you could consider going to meetups and small industry conferences/hackathons in your area. Some startup jobs appear on social media such as *LinkedIn*. Agencies specialized in hiring PhDs, are often also in touch with startups; if you indicate a startup job as your preference, they should be able to find a suitable position for you.

OFTEN-ENCOUNTERED TRIBAL BEHAVIORS YOU SHOULD KNOW ABOUT

➤"We." If you ask someone at a party about their job, and they say, "We do this, we do that," and the "we" keyword comes back in every sentence, this might be a sign that they work for a startup. In the startup culture, a team is supposed to be like a fist, and people naturally identify themselves as members of the tribe.

➢ Cheering. Early phase startups are always balancing on the edge. Therefore, every little success is cheered. A new client? A good reason for a party. A new employee? A good reason for a party. A visit from a business partner? A good reason for a party. A new fern tree in the office? Why not a party!

➢ Positivity matters. Since, as mentioned above, early phase startups are in constant trouble, it is essential to keep a positive atmosphere in the team. Complaining and crying over yourself are not welcome. And, people who have average competencies but are optimistic by nature, have a good sense of humor, and can lift the mood of other people around them, are often more successful and get further in the startup culture than grumpy geniuses.

➢ Playing it cool. For the same reason, namely because of balancing on the edge, image is everything. If a client or an investor is just knocking at the door, everyone needs to immediately put themselves together and pretend that you are the most successful startup on planet Earth. Even if five minutes before the visit you had a major argument in the team and you almost said, "Goodbye!" to each other, you still need to smile and play it cool. And that's how entrepreneurs are; no matter how bad the financials are, and no matter how little sleep they got over the last few days, your boss will instantly jump on their feet and play it cool whenever the situation requires. It is a sort of a game—and if you work in a startup, you better learn to play this game along with everyone else.

5 Consulting

In this context, consulting means project-based work in some area of expertise. As a consultant, you work under the umbrella of an agency which assigns you to projects (although in some agencies, consultants are hired as subcontractors and paid per hour indeed), and gets commission on your work. Consultancy is a very broad term; consultants work in multiple areas: data science, biotechnology, technical assistance, business management, general management, education, conflict resolution, planning the public infrastructure, professional trainings, etc.

THE GENERAL STRUCTURE OF THE WORKING ENVIRONMENT

➢ There are two main types of consultancy companies. Large, international players such as "The Big Four" (i.e., *Deloitte*, *Ernst & Young*, *PricewaterhouseCoopers,* and *KPMG*), have a multi-layer structure that resembles a corporation. They have very broad coverage of the market, offering consultancy in many areas of industry. The smaller, local consultancy companies can be even as small as a few employees and are usually specialized in one area of expertise.

WHAT DAILY LIFE IS LIKE

➢ Typically, you'll have one employer and multiple clients. However, your daily life strongly depends on the type of consultancy company you are working for. Large, international consultancy companies typically orient themselves on short-term projects and summon the team to execute every project within the company. They have multiple plants in different countries so it's often the case that they summon a team in a plant closest to the client or send some people to that plant. Small, local companies typically choose long-term projects and send their employees to the client's side so that they execute the project hand in hand with the client's employees. In that case, you might work from a stationary office of your client, or be based at home and commute to clients from there—this depends on your employer and on the client.

YOUR OPPORTUNITIES

➤Just as in other environments, you can build a career here. In consultancy companies, consultants are assigned with various ranks based on their experience and scope of duties. The common model—ordered from the lowest to the highest rank—is as follows: Associate Consultant, Senior Associate Consultant, Consultant, Managing Consultant, Principal Consultant, Partner (the detailed structure varies between companies). While becoming a senior consultant, you will be given more and more freedom to look for new clients and projects on your own.

➤Good financial benefits. Large companies usually pay centrally-regulated salaries, but you can also be offered some shares in the company when you become a Partner. In smaller companies, you might be paid at a fixed salary (and this is usually the case), or alternatively, as a percentage of the value of the deal, or a fixed rate per hour. In the process, you can become a very well-paid independent professional. In data science, pharma, biotech, business development, and many other disciplines, independent consultants can charge rates of $100-200 per hour or more (at least, this is the case in the US and Western Europe).

➤Starting in consultancy will quickly provide a lot of industry experience. On the one hand, you will gain a lot of experience with working in dynamic teams, and on the other hand, you will learn about the working culture in multiple companies. Moreover, you will receive intensive training on soft skills, which are often lacking in PhD programs. Therefore, if you are pondering options for the first job in industry, you might consider a consultancy job. With 1-2 years of experience in consulting under your belt, you will be a very competitive candidate for positions in almost any branch of private and public sector.

➤If you choose for a large, international consultancy company, you can travel the world! No one will stop you from applying to a project in another corner of the world every single time. And, fixed working hours will leave you with a lot of extra time for sightseeing!

➤If you choose to work for a small consultancy company, you can visit many companies as an outsider and learn a lot about their company culture. Most professionals never get that opportunity! Who knows, maybe you will get to like one of these places enough to stay there as an employee. Many companies recruit employees this way: they first create projects, hire external consultants, and then offer contracts to consultants who did well on the project and pay the recruitment fee to the consultancy agency. Such a transfer is a good option whenever you encounter a client with a good working culture and interesting projects.

➤If after a few years of working for someone else, you get confident about your hard and soft skills, develop a broad personal network, and get to know your market sector well enough, this gives you an option of setting your own business. Many entrepreneurs working in consultancy begin their journey as employees. At some point, they resign from their job and take over some clients from their last employer.

By working for your current employer, you can also learn first-hand about how this business is done.

➢ If you are thinking about possibly becoming a freelancer in the future, but you would prefer to start from a safer option, this might be a solution for you. You might slowly grow your network and competencies, and detach from your employer at the point when you feel confident about your perspectives to get your first clients.

WHAT YOU WILL NEED TO ACCEPT IN THIS WORKING ENVIRONMENT

➢ Star qualities. To thrive as a consultant, you'll need to effect your analytic thinking. You will also need to remember *who pays you*: if you work for one of the companies that send you to projects on the client's side, it's not the client but rather, your manager at your maternal company who decides about your promotion. Therefore, you should make sure that you stay in touch with the right people, and that these people notice your progress. Other factors for success are similar as in corporations: you'll need to be likable and good with people, and demonstrate very strong communication skills—both verbal and non-verbal. Communication also involves the ability to present your results to the client in a way that will impress them.

➢ Constant assessment. You are in contact with the clients, and most employers will ask for feedback about the quality of your work. You can prepare to be evaluated in some way at every project, whenever you want it or not.

➢ Strong individuality. Similarly as in corporations, in consultancy companies you are left on your own. Officially, you are dependent on some manager but it's up to you whether or not you will get any career opportunities. Since a new team is summoned for every project, you need to focus on your project portfolio more than on making bonds with your teammates. And, to get promoted, you need to score points in your manager's books. It means that you not only need to be good at work but also, sell yourself well during the group projects and get noticed.

➢ Many stressors. In most jobs, you either have a boss, or a client—and these are substantially different sources of stress. However, once you work as a consultant, you experience both these stressors at a time: you need to make your way between your boss and your clients and try to make everyone happy. This can be a huge physical and mental burden, and lead to burnouts. The career path is a bit different between small and large consultancy companies. In small companies, you have contact with the clients from the very start, while in large companies, as a junior employee, you are typically under the wings of your managers and work on the company's side for the first few years. Within this period, you might present the results of the project to the clients, but you are not decisional about the course of the project, and you don't have that much responsibility; your amount of contact with clients will increase only after you get promoted and reach a certain position.

➢ Salesmanship skills are necessary in this job—both in small and large consultancy companies. You need to keep close contact with clients; the ability to communicate with them and sell them your work is part of the game. If you are a type of a specialist who enjoys doing the actual work, but not necessarily the sales part, this might be a barrier to entry for you. Furthermore, convincing your client to launch another project with you (e.g., a follow-up to the current project) will be appreciated by your Business Manager and awarded with a bonus in the next paycheck or in promotion points. So, proactivity in sales is an appreciated quality in consultancy companies and leads to promotions.

➤ You can never really get the sense of attachment. In a large consultancy company, you change your coworkers every few weeks. In a small consultancy company, you work on your client's ground. When you are on the client's side, you know you are an outsider. When you are back to your office, you don't feel like belonging to a team neither—you are, effectively, compared with each other all the time. This is also why for many consultants, this type of job is only one stage in their career.

➤ Hectic environment. In small consultancy companies, the first few years of work can be stressful as you'll be working with multiple clients. Every client will obviously believe to be the key client, and they will expect their project to be your priority. In other words, they expect the project to be completed as fast as possible, as well as possible, and as cheap as possible. You might find yourself under time pressure, as you will need to share time between multiple projects, and start new projects before some other projects are finished. Fortunately, in most consultancy companies, after ~2-4 years of working on projects consultants get promoted to junior managers. As such, they do less hands-on work at the client's site and spend more time networking and looking after their team. The management positions are usually less stressful than junior consultancy jobs. In large consultancy companies, projects are typically team projects. Every project is timed, and the whole team is pressed to finish before the deadline.

➤ Predatory consultancy companies. If you are interested in a particular consultancy company, try to get information about the turnover rate of their staff. Some consultancy companies let their employees keep a healthy work-life balance, and the turnover rate can be higher than 10 years. If turnover rate is very low (1-2 years), it might mean that they just exploit their consultants as much as they can (hopefully rewarding them with an appropriate salary), or their business strategy is based on "selling" consultants to the clients. The first scenario is more often encountered than the latter, so get ready for a couple of incredibly hectic years (e.g., forget about finishing your PhD Thesis on the weekends while working there). After those years, however, you'll probably acquire enough experience for the dream job you want but for which you might not have enough working experience right now. You should treat this as an investment.

➤ Subjective way of assessing your performance and awarding bonuses. Similarly as corporations and startups, most consultancy companies perform the annual assessment of their employees' performance and award personal bonuses depending on the outcome.

➤ Hard to get in. In some consultancy companies, especially in the international giants such as "The Big Four," the barriers to entry are very high. These companies often have an acceptance rate of less than 1%. Therefore, the candidates spend long months on preparations for the interviews. There are tons of specialized courses and online resources solely dedicated to this topic. The upside is that, given the strict selection of candidates, in a place like this you will work with the best. However, you'll first need to put a ton of work into your application, and you are not guaranteed to succeed.

➢In some consultancy companies, high mobility is preferred. In smaller companies, you will be often sent to the client's office to conduct projects. This effectively means commuting to a different office every time you are assigned to a new project. If the client is too far, this sometimes means spending two weeks in a hotel, or a necessity to commute to fancy offices far in the countryside (so, commuting by a car might be required). Working from home is not often practiced.

➢In some consultancy companies, you will be timed. Larger consultancy companies work in a system in which they price the whole project. In a place like this, e.g. in *Boston Consulting Group* or *McKinsey*, it's taken for granted that you work on your project to the best of your abilities and that you spend all your working time on it. However, smaller companies often require clients to pay per hour of their consultants' time. If the latter scenario is the case, you will need to report how you spend your working time. You will often work on more than one project at a time, therefore, you will need to book every single hour of your working time for particular projects, and stick to the schedule. Of course, this system much differs from the academic system where we typically have no external control over our working hours. It might take you some time to rewire your brain to make it highly productive for 8 hours of uninterrupted, deep work—rather than leaving your office after 12 hours of work mixed with self-administered (coffee) breaks as we often do in academia.

BEST ACCESS ROUTES FOR PHDS

➢Consultancy jobs are often announced online through social networking platforms and job boards. Professional recruitment agencies specialized in hiring PhDs are also in touch with consultancy companies. If you are interested in this type of job, you might also be willing to search for interesting consultancy companies in your area online: they usually post vacancies on their home websites.

OFTEN-ENCOUNTERED TRIBAL BEHAVIORS YOU SHOULD KNOW ABOUT

➢No particular tribal behaviors; it's a kind of a "tribe-no tribe" setting.

6 The academic career path

We all know what an academic career generally looks like. But to be scrupulous, I decided to describe this tribe just like any other. By an academic career, I understand a combined research/teaching position within an academic institution (as opposed to, e.g., an R&D department in a company) with an intention to spend the majority/the rest of the professional life as an active researcher (rather than, e.g., a Lab Manager, or a professional Grant Writer). This typically implies a necessity to get promoted to a PI at some point—although, in some countries, there are also other possibilities such as becoming a Senior Postdoctoral Researcher.

THE GENERAL STRUCTURE OF THE WORKING ENVIRONMENT

➢Modular. Every department is divided into labs/research groups, which are effectively little companies with their own budgets, and their own problems. In some countries such as the United States, PhD students belong to the *common cloud*: they are granted a *fellowship* and belong to the graduate school which spans across labs. In other countries such as the Netherlands, PhD students are effectively employees of the labs they belong to, and they are fully dependent on the lab PIs.

➤"Understream." When you enter an institute, you need to learn the net of connections and interdependencies between people who are already employed there —as they are much more dependent on each other than you would think at first. Some PIs have not spoken to each other for many years because of some disagreement they once had. Some people owe each other some favors from previous projects, and you can painfully learn about it during your project—for instance when you find out that a few authors have been added to the author list on your paper for no apparent reason. The distribution of power also dynamically changes over time, and only a few people understand the situation. You can only be certain about one thing: if you are of lower rank then someone else, you are never right.

WHAT DAILY LIFE IS LIKE

➤For most people in academia, the daily life is an artistic mess: juggling projects, struggling with an overflow of emails, running to way too many meetings, trying to keep up with the recent findings in the field, applying to grant calls, sending conference abstracts, promoting research through social media... And, next to all this, trying to come up with some content that is fresh, creative, and useful for humanity. There is also a peaceful minority: researchers who have a peaceful office, predictable weekly schedule, and one, individual, well-defined project. This setting works for some people, while others experience a deep feeling of isolation and a low level of satisfaction from work in such conditions (Tomasello, 2019).

➤Even though you work in an international environment and have collaborators abroad, for some weird reason, there is still an expectation that you should gain an "international experience" by traveling abroad during your career. Or that you should at least swap institutions around the country a few times to broaden your perspective.

YOUR OPPORTUNITIES

➤If you combine a deep level of knowledge in a particular discipline of science with good networking skills, with a little bit of luck, you can climb up to a faculty position. It will secure you a permanent contract, which can (almost) never get terminated. And the permanent contract allows for, among others: high salary, high sense of security, working with intelligent people, the opportunity to define research problems all by yourself, plus a stream of young labor to put your ideas to life, numerous travels to the most beautiful places, and a high level of social approval. And that's a (busy but) happy life!

➤Working with friends. When you become a senior researcher, you are free to come up with any collaborators for your projects you wish. In particular, you can choose your close friends! It is a rare opportunity in the job market, and this can make working life a real blast.

➤A research career effectively means that you earn on your self-development. In no other working environment, this is the case! You get a salary for learning for a lifetime and becoming a better version of yourself. If you treat life as a journey, academia might be the place for you.

➢You are encouraged to share your know-how. In the private sector, companies protect their know-how by Non-Disclosure Agreements, and anyone who breaks the rules will need to face serious consequences. Companies don't organize international conferences so that everyone can present to the other companies' representatives how they executed their projects in every detail. No one shares their pipelines so that it can be reproduced. So, if sharing your results with the public matters to you, academia is the place to go.

➢You put your name on your work. It might sound like detail at first. However, for many academics switching to industry, it's a disappointing experience that they are no longer publicly recognized as authors of their work. When you are in academia, you put your own name on every single research paper, and then it becomes visible to everyone around the globe. In industry, on the other hand, the whole team produces a new product or a document under the brand of the company, and the public opinion doesn't know what your exact input was. Of course, a good manager will make sure that you are recognized for your achievements within the team—yet still, your name won't be mentioned in the history books even if you did something truly groundbreaking. So, if it's important for you to be recognized for your work, academia is one of the few places where you are guaranteed to get this recognition.

➢If it matters to you how you will be remembered, your research will not only be published under your name but it will also become a part of the world heritage for as long as humanity exists. Who knows—maybe a hundred years after you pass away, your research results will lead to a solution to some big problem related to the society or environment. Such scenarios happened on many occasions before.

WHAT YOU WILL NEED TO ACCEPT IN THIS WORKING ENVIRONMENT

➢Hypocrisy. As mentioned before, in every competitive field, you need *star quality* to get far. In academia, people who get tenure positions are usually those who have some aura of grace and wisdom, which earns them respect, allows them to impose their concepts and opinions onto others, and creates "impact." Also, successful academics are often those who manage to create a *persona*: those who appear to be so smart and talented that everything comes to them effortlessly—even though it's not true. More senior academics and grant agencies are willing to invest time and money in such people as they smell potential for an impactful professor. The latter trend has recently started to change because of *Twitter* where it's encouraged to share personal failure and hardship (Cheplygina, 2020). Yet still, a person who seems to be a happy and flawless paper-producing machine stands higher chances of success than individuals who are honest about the amount of failure that they experience daily.

➢Poor teamwork. This is still a bit of a taboo in academia, but many teams exist *on paper*—at the end of the day, everyone needs to take care of their own resume anyway. The way of incentivizing people to contribute to academic projects does not promote teamwork at all. Every project is meant to result in at least one research publication, and your place in the sequence of the authors on that paper determines how your scientific achievement is perceived. As a result, academics have an incentive to get their name onto as many papers as possible while at the same time doing as little as possible for each one of the projects they participate in—as their publication record will be the major factor that the granting agencies take into account while dividing the money for future projects. Furthermore, since academics prioritize finishing projects in which they are the leading authors, they often delay giving input to the projects in which they are supporting authors, and as a result, block them. The situation is the same unhealthy we look at the employer-employee relationship. Unlike in industry, in academia bosses and their employees often have *contradictory* goals. Namely, your boss often wants you to exploit their own research ideas which they developed many years ago. Now, they work on building their name even further rather than working out your future line of research. It wasn't the case in my PhD, but I have seen this situation many times around me, and it's extremely frustrating. Additionally, in many countries (such as the Netherlands), your salary is paid straight from your lab's budget and not from the department's budget. In a way, this means that you belong to your boss, and if you want to change your boss, you need to find a new job elsewhere. The situation is different in some countries such as the US where graduate schools offer fellowships. Theoretically, you can change your lab affiliation within the same graduate school during graduate studies, but it makes your life harder and it's often perceived as a failure.

➤Games all around. You can expect that once in a while, there will extra author(s) on your paper even though they did nothing for the project. It happens because some professor owes something to another professor, because the project is produced within a consortium, or for any other unrelated reasons. Once in a while, your paper will be rejected only because a reviewer doesn't like some of the researchers on the authors' list, makes it personal, and anonymously bombs your work. Recruitment is not fair in academia neither; from time to time, you may lose a position to another candidate, even though they had a much shorter academic CV than you, just because they had better contacts than you. It's hard to get any jobs more senior than a PhD contract if you don't know anyone in the lab you are applying to. There are lots of games you will have to tolerate to survive in academia—the more competitive field, the more gamified research becomes.

➤Rare gratification. In private companies, employees usually need to accomplish several small tasks during the week and typically, they get small personal gratification for each one of them—it might be as little as a thumb up from the boss, yet still, it's a sign of appreciation. On the contrary, academics need to develop sacred patience as the days of triumph are very scarce. Once or twice a year you will score some publication and celebrate, once or twice a year you will present at a conference. Other than that, research is a peaceful grind away from the world. So, you need to motivate yourself daily and find a peer group to support each other, or otherwise, your life will get very hard.

➤Poor correlation between income and quality of work. Especially at the early stages of an academic career, your salary depends on the number of years of professional experience rather than on your skills and ability to conduct research. If you publish ten papers during your contract and your peer will publish just one while spending half of the working time on drinking coffee at the canteen, you'll be still rewarded the same. No bonuses, no special allowances. Sometimes, it can even work the other way around: the time spent on drinking coffee with colleagues can often result in getting more job opportunities than the time spent in solitude on the actual work.

➤Luck factor. There is a strong luck factor associated with an academic career. If you don't secure a publishable PhD project, and if you don't find several good mentors to support you at the early stages of the academic career, you'll have a hard time receiving your first personal grants, and staying on the academic career track for longer—no matter how talented you are. Unfortunately, many talents have been wasted because of the PhD project planned out poorly.

➤Lack of stability. Even if you are a strong researcher, you'll get unemployed as soon as your contract ends. Also, the research scene changes constantly, and the state-of-the-art solutions in science rotate as well. You might come up with something clever in your PhD, and your solution becomes obsolete ten years later just because there are other, new solutions using new equipment developed in the meantime. Even as a PI, you are not entirely safe: the research landscape can change a lot from the day you get your tenure contract until the day you get retired.

➤Quantity rather than quality. The times when you could have spent a few years developing some concept alone in your cozy office are a long time gone. If you want to stay in science for longer, you need to play a game and care about the number and impact of your research papers.

➤High frustration levels. Currently, a lot of attention is dedicated to mental health problems in academia (Woolston, 2019). Even if you manage to find an enjoyable academic job, you'll still need to work with people who are not happy about their current situation. If you are a type of person who can easily empathize with others, and usually share the emotions of people around you, this might be draining in the long-term.

➤Pulp fiction. Many people in academia put on a happy face—they only tweet about their recent papers, contracts they have just signed, some other professional achievements, and happy events such as exotic vacations. They try to create the impression that life is easy for them. It is easy to get depressed when looking at these "perfect" figures. These people play it cool while they usually work overnights and wipe everything they didn't succeed in under the carpet. Also, some people treat doing science like a game: they strategically choose projects only because the topic has the potential for a high impact publication. If you prefer saying things straight and picturing things as they are, these games might be very frustrating to you.

➤False impact. In academia, everyone dreams about major discoveries that will lead to a *Nature* paper or even to a Nobel prize. Yet, not everyone can succeed at this—these achievements are prestigious also because of their scarcity. However, everyone can launch a *Twitter* account and start collecting followers. Unfortunately, many academics wrongly take building social media presence as a sign of impact. And, they compensate for their frustration coming from a lack of academic success by collecting likes, retweets, and follows. This chase after popularity is often associated with a lot of hypocrisy. For instance, when some topic becomes popular on social media, everyone gets involved overnight, and *Twitter* becomes a machine of activism. So, if you produce viable solutions to real-world problems, prepare for a healthy dose of frustration as it will take ages before anyone will find out about your work and notice the value that you produce among the sea of memes and slogans.

➤ Safety net. You need to develop networking skills in a slightly different way than in other working environments. While in other tribes, the impact of your network grows linearly (or even quadratically!) with the number of people you know, in academia it doesn't. Here, it's much more important to create a *safety net*—find several strong researchers within your field who are willing to collaborate with you in writing grants and conducting research projects. Some professors publish in these little cliques for their whole careers. Remember that those who cite your papers often don't know you as a person—they cite you because they find your paper to be informative on the subject that they research. Thus, it's not compulsory to reach out to thousands of people, shake hands, and make a personal connection with each one of them. This is a mistake people often do in academia: they make a lot of casual friends with other researchers at conferences and on *Twitter*, and think that they now have a network. And then, when it comes to the end of their contract, they are surprised to find out that this whole "network" turns out to be useless when it comes to looking for another job or building a new research project.

➤ Modern slavery. Even though we have been living in the twenty-first century for two decades now, there are still reminders of slavery from the Middle Ages in the academic system. For instance, in the Middle Ages, recommendation letters were used to pass staff between different members of the elite—the opinion of the previous owner was the only source of information about the competencies of the low-born peasants. Today, in times of the Internet, all the information about your competencies and professional experience is available 24/7—yet still, your new owner (to read: your next PI) wants to know what your previous owner thought of you. Although the vast majority of PIs aim to be fair towards their employees and help them career-wise, there are many cases where negative recommendation letters blocked careers of talented early career researchers.

BEST ACCESS ROUTES FOR PHDS

➤ Well, it is quite natural: you need to apply for your next academic job :) Needless to say, networking works best, followed by *Academic Transfer*.

OFTEN-ENCOUNTERED TRIBAL BEHAVIORS YOU SHOULD KNOW ABOUT

➤ Networking at conferences. To stay in a loop, you need to showcase your work at major conferences in the field at least once per year. You are also expected to go to the dance floor, and dance with everyone, just as if you were attending a wedding.

➤ Twitting. Today's scientific discussion moved to *Twitter*, and this is where many researchers distribute their work and make their impact. If you want to stay up to date with the recent progress and opportunities on your field, you better join!

7 Freelancing

Freelancing means being self-employed (usually as a sole proprietorship, or otherwise, as a subcontractor to another business) and offering your professional services to individuals, businesses, and public institutions in the open market.

THE GENERAL STRUCTURE OF THE WORKING ENVIRONMENT

➤ You work on your own unless you find subcontractors for the given project. Some freelancers also combine forces for big projects, but this is not a common practice.

In general, other freelancers in your space are your competition rather than your team—although you can help each other by creating affiliate programs and referring clients to each other, of course.

WHAT DAILY LIFE IS LIKE

➤It's exactly as you choose it to be—which can be either good news or bad news, depending on your self-discipline. The necessity to keep a steady working pace is one of the most common inconveniences reported by freelancers. In most of the large cities, there are either formal or informal places where freelancers gather to work and network together—open workspaces, bars, libraries. So, if you suffer from a feeling of solitude, you might consider joining one of these communities, or otherwise, renting a desk at the nearest startup accelerator.

YOUR OPPORTUNITIES

➤A high degree of personal freedom: you don't depend on anyone, and no one depends on you. You can choose optimal working hours as well as the most comfortable working location. It can be anywhere, even at the nearest bar! The client will only care about the final product and not about how and where you worked on it.

➤When you are experienced and acknowledged enough to secure many returning clients who are willing to queue for your services, the feeling of safety and stability at work will increase and be almost as high as the sense of safety perceived by employees. Furthermore, this is one of the very few career tracks that might free you from the necessity to network at some point. Of course, you will need to network for the first few years. However, if you become recognized for your work, build a brand, and a strong image online, at some point, new clients will start finding you by themselves.

➤Freelancing professionals who manage to develop a personal brand in their area, can charge very high fees for their services and live on a very high standard. For instance, high-class software developers and business advisors can ask for $100-300 per hour. Funny enough, despite the stereotypes about the lavish life of entrepreneurs, on average, freelancers tend to be the highest-paid professional group. For instance, in the Netherlands, the median income among freelancers in 2019 was ~€49,700 net, as opposed to ~€44,100 net among entrepreneurs, and ~€43,600 among employees (Ruts, 2019). It is a consequence of two factors. Firstly, freelancers have almost no steady costs as they don't need to employ anyone in their business. They don't need to go through the process of bankruptcy to pivot their business either. They can just change the scope of their business operations in the Chamber of Commerce's records (usually possible to do online and for free), and start new business activities straight away. Secondly, entrepreneurs often get modest salaries and a pool of shares as an additional motivation-in case the company hits bankruptcy, the value of these shares goes to zero.

➤In many areas of the market, you can also build a passive income as a freelancer. For instance, if you are an author, you can create ebooks and place them on

Amazon[23]. In this way, you will receive some nice royalties from every sold piece for as long as the copyrights hold (which is 70 years after your death). If you are a coach or a teacher in a given area, you can develop and post an online course. If you are a software developer, you can spend a portion of your time programming software for some business in exchange for a pool of shares in the company—then, you'll get dividends for as long as you hold these shares. There are multiple ways in which you can secure yourself a stable passive income as a freelancer!

➤If you live in a low-income country, you can achieve additional leverage by finding clients online and earning according to the local standards in the client's area of residency while you live in a place where life is cheap. Many freelancers also travel for this reason: they choose clients in developed countries while enjoying sunshine and palm trees in developing countries.

➤You can refuse in creative ways. If a given project is not interesting for you to pursue, you can increase the hourly rates to ridiculous numbers. Then, whether you hear "Yes" or "No," it is a win-win!

➤Last but not least, unlike in corporations and other working environments where the tribal life is closely monitored, you can do well in freelancing as a night owl. Research has shown that night owls pressed to conform to this lifestyle function below their natural capabilities (Facer-Childs et al., 2019). So, if you are a night owl, freelancing might be your chance to spread your wings.

WHAT YOU WILL NEED TO ACCEPT IN THIS WORKING ENVIRONMENT

➤A sense of solitude. A freelancer is a lonely wolf, and you need to have a specific personality to enjoy this type of work. As a freelancer, it is also important to make an active effort to keep in touch with friends and meet new people. Humans are sociable by nature, therefore, after a few years of a lonely odyssey, many freelancers voluntarily come back to working on full-time contracts, even if that means that their earnings and the amount of personal freedom will drop.

➤Price tags. You need to learn to *price your work*. In academia, we only negotiate the salary once every few years while signing a new contract. In freelancing, on the other hand, you need to make sure that your remuneration will be decent while signing up for every single project that you participate in—this can mean multiple projects every month. Many budding freelancers tend to put *too low* prices on their work at the beginnings of their freelance careers. This is often true about PhDs leaving academia: in freelancing, especially among highly qualified professionals, payment per hour is much higher than payment per hour on typical PhD contracts, and many PhDs experience a mental barrier related to that. For instance, in the Netherlands, PhD contracts are worth €15-20 per hour gross while freelance consultancy services are worth at least €50-100 per hour. Many former researchers ask themselves, "How can I now put five times higher price tag on my work than I used to do in my last job? Insane!" Many budding freelancers agree to deliver their services at a little to no price for the sake of building their *portfolio* in the early stages of their business. In some areas of the market, this might be actually necessary as you'll strongly depend on testimonials from your clients. This is often

---

[23] www.kdp.amazon.com

the case if you are thinking of services heavily based on the human factor, as they are subject to the client's personal opinion and valuation, e.g., coaching, teaching, photography, graphic design, or writing (as opposed to services that have more objective market value, e.g., data science, web design, or accountancy). If you are thinking of going in this direction, remember that you need to start pricing your services as soon as you possibly can—way before you reach the limbo in which your clients get used to the fact that you work (almost) for free, and are no longer willing to pay. Also, mind that clients who pay, are more committed—and also, paradoxically, they often value your work higher than those who got it for free.

➤No leverage. As a freelancer, you might experience stress related to the fact that you have no leverage. As a freelancer, you have no passive income (initially, at least). You have no paid vacations, and you have no one who could take over your responsibilities while you are away (well, unless you hire some subcontractors to work for you). It means that in case you happen to experience some more difficult periods in which you are unable to work, you have no income at all. Also, since you lead a sole proprietorship, there is no one around you who knows how hard you work and who could take care of your well-being when things go sideways—either with your business or with your health. For this reason, many freelancers end up as workaholics who feel guilty for every hour not spent on working. To become a happy freelancer, you need to develop some level of self-awareness and mental hygiene to say, "Stop!" and take free time when necessary.

➤Competition. You can experience a lot of rejection and competition—especially at the beginning of your freelance career before you fully develop your brand. Also, you need to watch the market closely as changing trends might require you to change your offer or marketing behind it once every few years, or even once every few months. In the worst case, it might happen that your current services won't be even necessary on the market in a few years—in that case, you need to think about learning new skills and changing the scope of your activities. *Web design* could be a good example here: 10-15 years ago, creating commercial websites was a good source of income for freelancers. Today, there are so many hosting platforms that offer very cheap and convenient tools to build your own professional website that the space for freelancers in this area has shrunk; many developers who used to build websites had to change their offer and start a new business.

➤"Shall we cut the deal, Sir?" You need to learn about salesmanship—to an even higher extent than in consultancy jobs. Even if you are not a natural salesperson, in freelancing, no one can take care of salesmanship but you. You will need to learn the basics of building an image online: Search Engine Optimization (SEO), and perhaps also *Google-, Facebook-,* and *LinkedIn* ads, etc. It will also be beneficial to build a following on *Twitter, LinkedIn*, and other social media. There is one exception from the necessity to be a salesperson as a freelancer. It's the situation when you become a subcontractor to a company or an organization. In some countries, such as in Poland, the tax system favors self-employed professionals over employees. In such conditions, many professionals exchange an employment contract for an opportunity to become a subcontractor as it's financially beneficial for them. At the same time, this system also benefits employers as their workforce becomes more disposable. It means that you work as a freelancer, but you have one main client for whom you work full time, and you work together with employees. However, in some countries, freelancing in this way is not possible (e.g., in the Netherlands, as a freelancer, you are not allowed to be a subcontractor to a single client).

➤Taxes. You also need to learn about tax regulations and accountancy. In most countries, you'll need to pay income tax and sales tax (VAT) separately. The income tax is typically paid once per year, while the sales tax is typically paid on a quarterly basis. Most budding freelancers initially handle the taxes by themselves as professional accountancy services are expensive. While doing this, you need to be timely and precise, as delays and mistakes can result in painful fines.

➤Responsibility. You have to take full responsibility for your projects. You and your company are one organism—if the given client is not happy about the service, you'll need to take it on your chest and kindly apologize; there are no other people or external circumstances that you could blame the situation for. And once in a while, you *will* encounter an unhappy client even if you are best at what you do—at least 1% of the population are haters and that's a constant of the universe.

BEST ACCESS ROUTES FOR PHDS

➤The formal requirements are the same as for everyone else: you need to register your own business in the local Chamber of Commerce. In some countries, you also need to set a website for your business before you start. But, as a rule of thumb, it's always good to keep a personal website next to that—especially in market sectors where much depends on the brand (see chapter 5: *How to Land My Dream Job?*). In freelancing, PhD title can work on your behalf as it's a natural quality stamp that can testify that you can execute complex projects. So, you can proudly put it on the website next to your name.

OFTEN-ENCOUNTERED TRIBAL BEHAVIORS YOU SHOULD KNOW ABOUT

➤Freelancers who choose to work and travel at a time, form communities, and travel together. It's so much funnier to live a nomadic lifestyle in a group!

➤It is also good to keep in touch with other freelancers in your area through dedicated *Slack*/*Discord*/other groups. You never know where and when you'll be able to get another contract just because someone else in your network is too bombed with their work and needs to delegate some project to someone else. And vice versa: maybe it is you who is going to be too overloaded at some point and will delegate your client to someone else as an exchange for some nice kickback fee. Sharing is caring!

8 Entrepreneurship

Entrepreneurship means that you have set your own startup, and you are planning to grow your business around it: hire employees and gradually increase the revenue so that the market share and the value of the company grows too. In the landscape, I placed entrepreneurship further to the right than freelancing. It is because, as an entrepreneur, you have even more personal freedom to put your ideas to life than as a freelancer: you have employees, thus more pairs of hands to work on your projects. However, at the same time, you are also less secure because there are more modes of failure for your business. Statistically, most startups fail, and most entrepreneurs are "serial entrepreneurs" which means that they failed a few times before they made their business work. However, even though entrepreneurship can be a path through pain, tears, and blood, most entrepreneurs feel completely revived while getting the first invoice from the client—and this feeling is ecstatic and addictive. Entrepreneurs are also often featured in Hollywood and not always in a positive way—just to recall movies such as *The Social Network* (2010), or *Steve Jobs* (2015) and documentaries such as *The Inventor: Out for Blood in Silicon Valley* (2019).

Actually, many researchers are hidden gems in entrepreneurship, as these two tribes share a lot in terms of the philosophy and working style.

THE GENERAL STRUCTURE OF THE WORKING ENVIRONMENT

➤You have set a company to be free, but in fact, all you do is serving three gods: your investors, your clients, and your employees. So, you have to make many people happy. You also need to watch the competition.

WHAT DAILY LIFE IS LIKE

➤The daily life resembles academia is many ways. You are expected to organize your day and troubleshoot problems on the fly. You can expect a lot of meetings, and all the associated people will knock at your door when things go wrong and not when things go right. Every day is different, and you never feel that your work is done. Plus, you are the face of the project, so you need to pay attention to networking and Public Relations.

➤One difference between entrepreneurship and academic work is that, while as an entrepreneur you have a limited number of resources, as an entrepreneur you can use *any* possible resources to push the project forward—as fast as possible, as well as possible, and as cheap as possible. Let me explain. To conduct a research project, you make use of several research tools the you have at disposal. Plus, you know many people in your field with whom you could potentially collaborate. Most likely, you won't buy a part of the solution from a colleague, or copyrights to their work to accelerate your work. You won't jump on a last-minute plane to Japan just because you heard a rumor that someone in Tokyo can accelerate the progress on your project. You won't spontaneously come up with a solution for how to improve your research project just because you just had a late-night chat by beers with someone who is in the target audience for your work—and after hearing about their motivations and attitude to life, you decided to change the project to better fit the expectations of your audience. In entrepreneurship, such solutions can come up at any moment and from every side: they come up when chatting to a stranger on the bus, at a reunion party from high school, while shopping for groceries. The more mindful you are, the better for you.

YOUR OPPORTUNITIES

➤You typically start a company composed of just yourself and your co-founder(s). Before you get the cashflow in your company, you can also motivate other people to take part in your project by offering them pools of the company shares. Then, once you secure an investment or you sell enough of your products and services so that you can bootstrap, you can also hire a very small core team. If the company develops, the number of people involved grows too. So, in a few years, you might find yourself to be a leader of a large company, with hundreds, or even thousands of people working for you. Optimistic scenario for sure, but this happens.

➤ You have a rare opportunity to only work with people with whom you truly *enjoy* to work with. Since you are the employer now, you can choose people who think alike, who have a similar sense of humor, and who can teach you something useful. You can actively avoid toxic people as you are in command of your own close environment.

➤ While the company grows, the revenue and the market value of the company grow too—the sky is the limit! At some point, the income from your salary and dividends can far exceed what you would otherwise earn at corporate positions, and what is within reach to any employees in the whole job market. Getting 10x or even 50x of the average salary is a viable possibility if you are a talented entrepreneur and if you find and take over your market niche. Also, today's market undergoes fast globalization: giant corporations acquire a sea of promising businesses to secure their position on the market. Therefore, it's possible that one day, your startup will draw the attention of a big player in the market, and after signing a lucrative deal, you'll wake up as a self-made millionaire.

➤ If one of the things that bother you in academic life, is that you often lose a lot of time by concentrating on unimportant details (e.g., your boss asks you to change colors on the figure to match his/her taste), the good news is that here, this won't be the case. Quite the opposite: you'll need to fully focus on the core problems, set the perfectionism aside, and find the quickest possible way to release a beta version of the product to the market. You'll improve and upgrade the product multiple times in the process—there is even a special term for such a development strategy: a *lean* startup (Ries, 2011).

➤ Your financial rewards are not binary and don't depend on the subjective opinion of one person. Unlike in academia where you write grants and receive binary yes-no decisions, in entrepreneurship you are dependent on other people's opinions in a different way. If you present your product to 1,000 potential clients, it might happen that 950 of them choose the product and make a purchase, or it might happen that only 30 of them choose your product. It's very unlikely that none of them will buy the product—unless it's a really, really bad quality product. In general, your income should be *proportional* to the quality of your product and to your outreach (i.e., the traffic on your website), rather than being a binary outcome of the decision taken by some anonymous "expert" whom you have never met.

WHAT YOU WILL NEED TO ACCEPT IN THIS WORKING ENVIRONMENT

➤ Star qualities. The meaning of the *star quality* in entrepreneurship is quite different than in academic and corporate environments. Namely, in entrepreneurship, you need to be *authentic*. What does that actually mean? It's quite hard to define this quality but the meaning is roughly that it transpires through your words and behavior that you have a real purpose and drive, and that you inspire and infect other people with your true passion and enthusiasm. You also need to be a little bit of a *visionary*: be able to take a helicopter view at problems and predict future trends in your field. Next, you need to appear intelligent, for instance by presenting a good sense of humor and connecting with respected people. Lastly, you need to have perseverance; you will balance on the edge for a long time, even if you have a good product and business acumen.

➤ Lack of work-life balance. Most entrepreneurs work 24/7—especially in the early phase of the business, before securing a seed investment or developing a stable revenue stream. You need to be available for your team and answer questions from all the engaged parties. Plus, you need to be there for your team every single day to build the team spirit. For this reason, many budding entrepreneurs refer to themselves as "married to the company." Your work-life balance as an entrepreneur can get better later on when your company grows. At that point, you can delegate a large portion of your work to managers of the lower level. However, for the first few years, you won't be able to go on vacation without checking your phone every five minutes. You might also get surprised by how quickly you become company-centric in the process: after a few months, you start evaluating every task before you get down to it. You ask yourself, "Does this activity serve the company?" You also start cherry-picking people and leaning towards those who are on a similar development stage with their own companies—or, those who are more advanced than you. Is this calculated behavior? I would say that perhaps to some extent it is, but this is also a natural behavior when you are on the survival mode. So, it's understandable.

➤ Understanding of value and equity. Even if you know your craft and work 24/7, it doesn't mean that you will be successful. Namely, successful entrepreneurs are those who get a good grasp on two qualities: *value* and *equity*. Generating value is an essence of business: the amount of added value that you can provide will eventually turn into the company profits. Value is often hard to evaluate, especially when we are talking about non-material goods, i.e., services. To assess the value properly, you need to understand the market and the customer, plus you need to have a good imagination—especially when thinking about a product that doesn't exist just yet. *Equity* means your share in your projects. For instance, if your equity share in the company is 5%, it means that you will receive 5 cents per every dollar that the company makes. Full-fledged entrepreneurs are motivated by equity much more than by the salary because they understand its scaling effect. Thus, they fight for equity like lions.

➤ Constant rejections. If rejection makes you feel undervalued, prepare that you might experience even more of it from now on. As an entrepreneur, you'll spend almost all the time in the selling mode: selling the vision, products, competencies of your employees. And, you'll hear, "No, thank you!" very, very often—at least one order of magnitude more often than in academia. For instance, in most online stores, the conversion rate is lower than 1%. It means that statistically, more than 990 out of 1,000 potential clients who view the product decide *not to buy*. And you still need to attract these potential clients to your website in the first place! Even worse, when you hear "No," you often get the feeling that you are a disappointment, not only to yourself but also to your employees, investors, and other stakeholders. Thus, to become an entrepreneur, you need to develop a very thick skin against rejection and keep going.

➤ Street knowledge. Most entrepreneurs are street smart rather than book smart (although the top entrepreneurs are usually both). Therefore, they focus on the practicalities of everything they are doing—theoretical models and the associated background knowledge are not as essential to them. As an academic, you might be surprised and frustrated that people who have never finished their undergraduate studies yet developed business acumen and built a network might be valued higher as business developers than you. It is usually the case, even though you acquired unique expertise and became a world-class expert. So, please beware: if you want to get far, your strong academic background is not enough—a good understanding of the market, hands-on experience with building businesses, and a broad personal network are compulsory.

➤ Rationality. You need to become very pragmatic and put your emotions aside while making strategic decisions. For instance, green entrepreneurs often launch a company with a close friend just because they like that person and feel comfortable around them—rather than paying attention to that person's competencies, the value that they bring to the table, and common business interests. These mistakes often lead to failures in the early stage, before the company even launches their product. So, it's better to reach out to people who are either good hustlers or hackers rather than to those who might be your friends but don't represent any of these categories.

➤ Paranoia. Entrepreneurs tend to be a bit paranoid, and not without a reason—as long as your work cannot be protected by a patent or by strict copyrights, it can get scooped at any time. It is because in entrepreneurship, there is a common belief that ideas are worth nothing without good execution, and there is no "code of honor." If you dislike the academic community for the fact that some people scoop others, I need to tell you: entrepreneurship is much worse than that. If you share your business ideas without rushing to put them to life as soon as possible, you are almost guaranteed to get scooped. For this reason, you also need to build a *network of trust* —a circle of people whom you support, and who support you. Trust and lifelong friendships are priceless in business!

➤ IP violations. Related to the point above: once you enter the entrepreneurship space, you need to beware of the looser understanding of agreements and IP. Many people in this space (and especially, the beginners on the survival mode) often overpromise —and this might be shocking to many researchers at first. In research, people are generally decent. OK, some of them might have a difficult personality, be a little explosive, or highly introverted and hard to communicate with. But after all, whenever they don't deliver what they promised, it's usually either because in the process, the research project turned out to be impossible to execute, they got overwhelmed and burned out, or their contract has expired and they needed to rescue their well-being by starting a new project somewhere else. It's a very rare situation in academia that people working with you *intentionally* overpromise. In business on the contrary, you will meet lots of hustlers who lure you into their project with their vibrant personality and ask you to do something for them as an exchange for some elusive shares in a non-existent company. And then, they will disappear with your work. You can also expect that the copyrights will be respected to a lesser extent, and it's much more probable that your work will be stolen than it would be in research. For this reason, it's also a good idea to get some legal protection for your company, i.e., the liability insurance (in case an individual or another company makes claims that your company caused physical damage to their property) and the legal insurance (in case you need to open a dispute against an individual or a company with whom you have a disagreement on the business ground, e.g., your copyrights were broken). You should also get familiar with the concept of a Non-Disclosure Agreement (a.k.a., NDA), which is a form of a confidentiality agreement that should be signed before sharing any confidential information essential to your company with external parties.

➤Luck factor. Similarly, as in an academic career, there is a luck factor associated with building businesses. You might have a great product in your hand, but if you don't time the market well, you'll still fail. You might get a competitor that has a worse product than you but a broader network, influential partners, and more funds for marketing. And, they'll eventually win the market. It might happen that a new technological solution released on the market suddenly makes your product obsolete. Many budding entrepreneurs need to try a few times before they succeed in launching a startup.

➤Rocky start. It's not easy to start in this area. One of the multiple reasons is that, as a fresh entrepreneur, you don't have your safety net just yet. Namely, without knowing the key figures in your field, you will need to rely on other fresh entrepreneurs who are the same green as you are—and you can experience incompetence and disloyalty in the process. The successful, multimillionaire entrepreneurs, who have already developed five or ten successful companies in their professional lives, will prefer to reach out to entrepreneurs with a similarly high status while creating new ventures rather than take a green person onboard. Thus, it will take you many years to gradually leverage your skills, contacts, and status in the field to the point at which you can acquire powerful, accomplished business partners.

➤Salesmanship. If you chat with a stranger at a party and after less than ten seconds, the person starts persuading you to buy into some product or service, they might be an entrepreneur. Without salesmanship, it is hard to make any business flourish. Some people are born to sell, while others need to learn this skill in the process. If you like the feeling of *persuading* someone else to try something, you might also have a hidden talent for salesmanship! To become an entrepreneur, you also need to understand *money*: how it flows in the society, how it motivates people, and what has enough *value* for people to spend their own money on it. Salesmanship requires empathy.

➤Mindfulness. As an entrepreneur, you do not have a guardian angel. In academia, career tracks have clear stages associated with some entitlement, namely, PhD candidate, Postdoc, Assistant Professor, Associate Professor, etc. You can climb up the ladder in a finite number of ways, e.g., by winning one of the local grant competitions for young researchers or landing a position of an Assistant Professor with a tenure track. Moreover, the *rules of the game* are more or less clear: publications, citations, and grants are the currency whenever we like it or not. And, almost no-one becomes the next big name overnight. In business, on the contrary, there is no script: the progress can be much more nonlinear, and it is far less obvious what the next step is. And sometimes, you can hit a jackpot and teleport straight to stardom. You need to rely on your instinct, read people, foresee the bottlenecks, track the progress in your field, be a bit of a visionary, and adapt to the situation very quickly. You need to be present and mindful. It is hard to achieve this state of mind as, at the same time, you are under constant pressure from many directions. Furthermore, since you are the head of the project, you are in the spotlight, and you cannot reveal your stress and negative emotions to "your" people. Therefore, you will need to learn how to keep your mental health under control and how to find your internal peace—as was very well explained by Mark Leruste in his TEDx talk[24]. Many people depend on you and your peace of mind! For this reason, many entrepreneurs develop a morning routine: they read, meditate, or practice yoga and other sports to increase their resistance to stress.

➤ Control freaks won't survive. As an entrepreneur, you need to delegate tasks. It can be challenging for fresh PhDs who were the main executors of all their projects. Now, you need to find the right people and to explain the tasks to them—and then monitor the progress and make sure that they have enough skills and motivation to do the job. In the early stages, you can supervise the process, but while the company grows, then sooner or later, you'll find yourself in a situation in which you need to trust your people to do the job without your involvement.

➤ There is no free lunch. Whoever offers you a favor as an entrepreneur has some reason behind this—either directly or indirectly. To researchers who are rather empathic and altruistic by nature and who are often willing to sacrifice more time and effort to projects than they need to, this can be a major mental switch. You'll also need to negotiate every payment for every service you ever deliver—you can take nothing for granted. For researchers who don't have any experience with negotiating deals, this is usually one of the major bottlenecks.

➤ Taxes. As an entrepreneur, you need to become more conscious about the law—and in particular, about the tax law. These regulations can be very complicated. E.g., in the European Union, you need to charge your customer the sales tax according to the local tariff in your country or in the customer's country of residence, dependent on what type of product or service you sell. The tax law can also change often—and it can be very costly for you once you make a mistake. In most countries, *all companies are equal* to law enforcement. It means that penalties for breaking the tax law are the same regardless if you are a multi-billion dollar corporation, a non-profit, or a modest sole-proprietorship that barely meets ends. For this reason, you should hire a tax advisor as soon as you can afford it. Still, it's a good practice to keep track of the local taxation rules as tax advisors can also make mistakes.

➤ Pulp fiction. The public perception of entrepreneurs and entrepreneurship is very different from reality. Your distant family and friends will probably believe that you sleep on money—while, in fact, at least for the first few years, you need to worry about your empty fridge. They will think that you have an easy life simply because you do not have a boss. While in fact, you run between your employees, investors,

---

[24] www.youtube.com/watch?v=f6nxcfbDfZo

and clients for the whole day, trying to make everyone happy. For worse, despite the misleading public image, being a visionary is *not enough* to become a successful entrepreneur. People such as Elon Musk not only have big dreams but are also very down-to-earth. They have a perfect understanding of how to develop their product from scratch—they just choose to delegate the work so that the company can grow faster than it would grow otherwise. Moreover, you should *appear* successful—usually, more successful than you are. The crowd loves success stories and the tales of hardship, internal battles, and ultimate wins—but only in the *past tense*. Successful entrepreneurs tell the public about their shaky beginnings to get some public trust, but they never mention about their current problems. If you openly announce that you are depressed and your initiatives don't work, no one will be willing to work with you, invest in you, or buy your products. It's the hypocrisy, of course, but these are the rules of the game.

➤ Even more pulp fiction. Related to the point raised above, entrepreneurs often exaggerate to appear more successful than they are. You need to take this into account while interacting with people in this space. For instance, when you hear, "We work with subcontractors," it often means, "We order stuff on *Fiverr.*" When you hear, "We are already profitable," it often translates to, "We just managed to land our first client yesterday." When you hear, "We have a vision," it often just means, "We don't really know what we're doing but we'll find out later." If you hear, "I'm a serial entrepreneur," this might be a euphemism for, "I'm trying again and again, and I go bust every time. No idea why."

➤ "Could you help me?" You'll often need to ask for help. Growing a business on your own is almost impossible. You will need to get over pride and ask family and friends to help you, especially in the beginnings. It can involve asking for advice, contacts, recommendations, feedback, financial help, or just mental support. And sometimes, even asking for food when the situation requires.

BEST ACCESS ROUTES FOR PHDS

➤ Startup accelerators at universities. At university accelerators, you can get help with drafting your business plan, and contacts to some private investors. Most startup accelerators also run competitions on behalf of innovation in which you can win some small vouchers for your business.

➤ Contacting angel investors through your network, dedicated platforms, or agencies. In every country, there are dozens of consultancy companies that help budding startups in finding investors. There are also many online platforms dedicated to this purpose—you can create an account for your startup on one of such platforms and expose yourself to investors.

➤ Participating in global competitions announced by startup accelerators. Many private startup accelerators offer investment in exchange for equity. They usually accept applicants from all around the world. Examples of such accelerators are *Y Combinator*[25] (mostly interested in new online platforms and new technologies),

---

[25] www.ycombinator.com

Tech Stars[26] (mostly interested in innovation in IT), or *Shuttleworth Foundation*[27] (mostly interested in projects that evoke a social change).

➣ Participating in competitions organized by the government. In many countries, governments also launch public competitions in which you can pitch and compete for some prize ($50,000 or more). These competitions are particularly attractive as they are usually equity-free. As a downside, usually, hundreds of startups compete with you.

OFTEN-ENCOUNTERED TRIBAL BEHAVIORS YOU SHOULD KNOW ABOUT

➣ Against the common stereotype, most entrepreneurs are not motivated by making money, but rather by the possibility to gain a high level of *personal freedom*. Getting wealthy is only a means to achieve this ultimate goal. As Kevin O'Leary famously said, "Salary is a drug they give you when they want you to forget about your dreams." Entrepreneurs highly value personal freedom and mobility, yet, the majority of them don't drive Rolls-Royce cars nor live in mansions with swimming pools. Most entrepreneurs are modest, down to earth, and far from showing off their wealth.

➣ Business is based on trust—if you establish your company with the wrong person, it is instant death to the business. Acquiring business partners also requires trust. Therefore, entrepreneurs exhibit a range of tribal behaviors that help them build trust in the team and celebrate every little success. Storytelling is cultivated—if you are a good story-teller and can tell good, ice-breaking jokes, it will help you in making business deals. If you are a morning lark who avoids social gatherings, you can miss out on a lot of opportunities. For the same reasons, *loyalty* is crucial. It is often the case that people who are not necessarily the brightest and the most hard-working, but who stick to the right people and are loyal to them, get rich and wealthy.

➣ An ability to play a long-term game and to avoid conflicts is essential. Everyone knows everyone in your field. Thus, if you have any personal disagreement, it is better to prevent bloodshed and walk away. Sooner or later, you'll always bump into the same people again, and they can make or break your future business deals. Therefore, diplomacy is an essential skill in business.

➣ Since in business the sky is the limit, it naturally attracts many con artists: people who don't produce any real value, but rather, they would sell just anything, even thin air, with the sole purpose to get rich as soon as possible and run. For this reason, the ability to read people is one of the core competencies of an entrepreneur. If you are not good at reading people's real motivations, you might fall into trouble as an entrepreneur.

You can also find more considerations about tribal behaviors of entrepreneurs in one of my blog posts[28].

---

[26] www.techstars.com

[27] www.shuttleworthfoundation.org

[28] www.nataliabielczyk.com/blog/2019/7/7/what-i-learned-past-few-months

Are these all my options?

The list of the working environments provided above is not full. For instance, I listed three types of private companies: startups, consultancy companies, and corporations. Small companies (employing less than 50 employees) and middle-sized companies (up to 250 employees), a.k.a. SMEs, were not covered here. The difference between a small company and a startup is the *roadmap*. A startup aims to grow and scale in the future. For instance, a new social platform aims to become a global brand, and an alternative to *Facebook* in the future is a scalable project. A small company is typically based on a non-scalable business model and aims to keep the status quo or to increase the team only if necessary. For instance, if the company involves ten grant writers taking orders for writing public grants, the income of the company is not scalable: it's directly proportional to the number of man-hours spent on the projects. Of course, the company can grow a bit, e.g., by extending the number of team members if the number of orders from clients exceeds the maximal capacity of the current team. However, the company will never have the potential to become a worldwide corporation.

Life in SMEs is a bit of a mixture of life in corporations and in startups. On the one hand, SMEs share some features with corporations: the working conditions are usually good, the working environment is safe and stable, there is a clear hierarchy within the company, and there are some procedures to follow. On the other hand, SMEs share some features with startups: you can be highly dependent on your closest coworkers and you might experience the ceiling effect. In SMEs, you typically have less flexibility in daily life than in startups, but at the same time, the working pace is also slower and work is not as physically and emotionally draining as it can be in the startup culture.

There are also some other working environments not mentioned in Fig. 3. I skipped those environments because they are not often represented by former academics. For instance, the army and clergy fall into this category.

So, how do I know whether I'm a member of the right tribe?

It is hard to give an algorithm for answering this question. However, I believe that there are some signs. The following factors can serve as indicators:

➤ The sense of internal peace. When you find yourself in the right environment, you will get some sense of peace. All these disturbing, recurring questions of "Is this is the right place for me?" will go away. It is like finding the right people in general: around certain people, you naturally feel comfortable. So, in the right tribe, you feel safe—and even if you experience transient problems and some obstacles at work, you feel that the stress stays somewhere on the surface, and it cannot get to your core and shake this internal feeling that you are on to something.

➤ You share the sense of humor with people around you. Even if you stay in professional relations, you feel accepted as a person. The most obvious sign of this acceptance is when people around you laugh at your jokes, and you laugh back at their jokes—and it is all genuine. And, whenever you think about your coworkers, you smile.

➤ You feel strong support. You do not experience any toxicity from people around you. Your coworkers have goals compatible with yours and always leave you with new energy and inspiration to work. You wish each other the best. There are no unspoken adversities and conflicting interests—such as a hidden feeling of unfairness, conflicts wiped under the carpet, jealousy, or regrets. If you had a choice to do the same job in another team and be paid 20% more, you would still choose to stay on the team you are now. You just cannot imagine working with any other people.

More than one tribe?

The landscape of post-PhD career tracks presented above might appear highly compartmentalized. You might be asking yourself now, "These are eight boxes, which one do I fall into?" The good news is: according to my observations, most people have a personality profile that allows them to adapt to a few different environments, not just one (there are exceptions, of course, especially if you are on one of the extreme sides of the spectrum).

It's also quite common that professionals develop compensatory mechanisms by balancing activities from the two sides of the "safety-freedom" spectrum and by consciously influencing the level of risk in their professional lives. For instance, budding entrepreneurs often hold part-time jobs on the side to be able to pay their bills while they attempt to make their companies profitable. In those safe jobs, they not only earn for a living but also rest from their hectic entrepreneurial life. Freelancers often aim to secure passive income for themselves to increase their sense of safety, e.g., via developing online courses, buying rental properties, or investing in bonds. On the contrary, corporate people with steady careers often invest in the stock exchange after working hours as they enjoy the thrill and adrenaline that risk-taking gives.

These are just examples showing that you don't need to lock yourself in one box, but you can also balance between two or more of them and actively manipulate the sense of risk in your life.

Whichever tribes you decide to go for...

...I'd like to share a few pieces of advice that will help you in building your career in *any* working environment.

➤ Get yourself a mentor—or preferably, many mentors at a time.

Every mentor will give you advice based on their personal experience. What worked for them does not necessarily need to work for you. Thus, as a rule of thumb, it is better to have more than one authority to follow. It can take you years to fully accommodate to a new working environment—and those who have mentors always have an advantage over those who do not. Regardless of whether you are going to work in a corporation, in a startup, or launch your own company, it is always good to reach out to those who are more experienced than you and seek their advice. It will save you years of walking in the dark! Plus, people tend to talk about their working experience and share advice with pleasure. If you reach out to more senior people around you and ask some informal questions, they will likely take this as a sign of genuine interest and be happy to chat with you. You might even find new friends this way!

➤ Stay kind and diplomatic.

Wherever you go, it's good to remember that *kindness* and the ability to avoid open conflicts will save you from a lot of trouble. Just keep in mind that once you finish your PhD, you still have 30-40 years of professional career ahead. Whenever you cross someone, you will likely bump into this person again sooner or later. Building your career is a long-term investment. Thus, it's worth making compromises once in a while. Sometimes, it's better to agree on a business model that is suboptimal for you, step back from a project, accept a lower payment than expected, or change the team for the sake of keeping good karma around you. If someone is acting in a non-professional way towards you, make sure that you'll never need to work with them again—but it's important to get over pride and separate from this person on a positive note. People who navigate themselves in the job market well, usually have this ability to separate from former coworkers smoothly, politely, and without unnecessary drama. Some of these people are so kind that crossing them makes you feel guilty—so you won't.

Also, remember that while you might be a perfectionist—just as most researchers are—most people out there are not. When you enter industry, you might be shocked by the amount of incompetence, mediocrity, and resistance to learning. One needs to be patient and treat this new situation as an opportunity rather than a problem. In academia, we also have this culture of *helping each other to grow by giving each other constructive criticism*. It's a monastery mentality of sorts, and in many working environments, this behavior is highly unwelcome. In most large institutions and large companies, open criticism is reprehensible. In those environments, you can only criticize the performance of other employees indirectly—by *not praising them* instead of pointing out their mistakes. Typically, those who are kind and diplomatic, are promoted much faster than those who are competent and honest. Not mentioning that in academia, we often anonymously criticize researchers who live away and whom we might never meet, while in a company, you'll criticize a colleague sitting next to you —and that person will certainly remember you this!

➤ If you meet the ceiling, change!

Last but not the least, in industry, you won't always have growth opportunities. As a rule of thumb, you will have more personal space—more options for horizontal and vertical transfers between teams and for launching new projects—than you would have in academic jobs. However, there are many exceptions.

To the outside world, every company pictures themselves as *modern* and *focused on growth*: a leader of innovation in their field, and welcoming to enthusiastic, creative, and ambitious professionals. And usually, at least in the early stages of the company's life, this is true. After all, every company is born in the same way: a small team of enthusiastic and ambitious people wants to pursue their vision—so they come together and create a company. Some companies manage to keep this initial spirit of enthusiasm and innovation while the company grows and maturates. However, in some companies, something goes wrong in the process: after a few years of growth, the ego game, the internal fight for positions and influence, and the chase after profits take over. In such a setting, the managing team is no longer faithful to their original values—it concentrates on keeping the status quo rather than caring about innovation and progress.

The reality in the company is often hard to figure this out from the outside. After a few months spent in the new place, you might start feeling frustrated about the fact that despite the great premise from the job interview, your wings are cut every day. You might feel like mentally suffocating. In that case, don't hesitate to look for another opportunity elsewhere! Unlike in academia, in industry no one will ask you about the reason why you are looking for a new job. Typically, no one will ask you for recommendation letters neither. As long as you don't break any Non-Disclosure Agreements or other special confidentiality clauses contained in your contract, you are free to go anywhere, anytime. So, don't be afraid to change and don't feel guilty for it. Many people need to try once or twice (or even many more times!) before they eventually find the right tribe after leaving academia.

➤ Be careful with changing jobs too often.

It's good to stand your ground and change jobs if your boss gaslights you and cuts your wings. However, you need to be strategic with building your career. If something goes wrong in your current job, it is good to take time off to think about what went wrong and why—and plan your next career steps carefully. Try to think of employers that might potentially be better suited for you, and do your field research before you apply. The reason is that, recruiters don't appreciate to see that in the last few years, you were changing jobs every few months. It's not a good sign for them— after all, it might mean that you are disloyal and opportunistic.

The take-home message

1. Before applying for jobs, it's good to ask yourself about how you usually relate to other people and what role do you prefer to play in a team.

2. People still live in tribes and have their tribal customs. There are at least eight environments that attract PhDs:

working for a public sector and NGOs | academic jobs without an academic career track | corporate jobs | startup jobs | consulting | academic career | freelancing | entrepreneurship

In these environments, you'll experience different habits as well as different trade-offs between the amount of personal freedom and stability at work. Remember that you can develop a career in each one of these environments!

---

3. If you feel peaceful, supported, and share a sense of humor with people around you, you are probably in the right tribe.

4. Whichever direction you decide to go for, look for (multiple) mentors in your working environment, and remember to be kind no matter what.

5. If you feel that you don't have further opportunities for growth in your current place, look for other options. However, be strategic about changing contracts: changing positions too often can scare the recruiters.

CHAPTER 5

HOW TO LAND MY DREAM JOB?

Stereotypes against researchers

Even though—as discussed in previous chapters—PhDs offer a high value to their employers, landing a dream job as a PhD might be difficult for several reasons. In this chapter, I'd like to talk about the three most common stereotypes and some heuristics that can help you counteract when you encounter these stereotypes.

➤ Stereotype 1: PhDs have very high expectations regarding working conditions.

When reading a job application from a PhD, many recruiters ask themselves the question, "Do we even need a PhD graduate for this position?" The reason is that in many countries higher education is associated with a higher starting salary. In some countries, this is regulated by law while in some other countries, this works more like a rule of thumb. Nevertheless, hiring a PhD often feels like an additional expenditure to the recruiter. Recruiters can also assume that, since PhDs went through a long education process than most other candidates, they also have more options in the job market in general. And, they fear that as an employee with a PhD, you won't be loyal to the company, but rather, you will change your job as soon as you have a better offer on the table.

To address this stereotype during a job interview, you'll need to emphasize that you are a loyal person focused on finding a good working environment where you can grow and that you care about the non-material aspects of the job even more than about the material aspects. It's also good to underscore why you are willing to work for this particular employer and give them a strong impression that they were your first line of choice when looking for jobs.

➤ Stereotype 2: PhDs are nerdy.

To many recruiters, "a scientist" and "a specialist" are almost synonyms. We might have a ton of experience with public presentations, leading discussion panels, organizing conferences, managing research projects, and mentoring students, but they still don't trust in our managing skills enough to offer us executive positions. For this reason, typically, it is difficult for PhDs to get executive positions right after leaving academia.

To address this stereotype during a job interview, highlight your communication skills in your interactions with the recruiter. Bring a positive mindset to the job interview—if they experience you as a relatable, authentic, articulate person, you will have a chance to counterbalance this prejudice. Remember that the recruiter does not know you. Thus, they take you at face value-if you claim that you are good with people, you need to behave accordingly at the interview.

➤ Stereotype 3: PhDs are unable to work under time pressure.

In industry, the project dynamics typically differs from the projects as we know them. Projects are closer managed, more structured, better timed, and contain more checkpoints and deliverables. In IT specifically, a popular working scheme is *scrum*, which involves 2-4 week-long sprints. During such a sprint, the team intensively works on a group project, and every working day starts from daily standup progress meetings. In practice, this means that you'll need to present your progress to your group members every single day. Another example could be journalism: the news is hot for a few days, or sometimes for just a few hours. Therefore, if you are planning to maneuver towards science communication, you can expect that your working schedule will change to a large extent.

Moreover, in industry, life pivots around deadlines. Every client expects the timely delivery of the service. For this reason, in many companies, there is constant time pressure—the closer your contact with the client is, the more you will feel this pressure on your shoulders.

PhD students rarely need to present their progress daily. Therefore, this can be a dramatic change to their working style. In academia, the problem is often the opposite: we need to knock at the supervisors' doors and wait in line to present our progress, rather than having supervisors checking on us regularly. Also, research life often involves only a few fixed deadlines throughout the year, with other delivery dates negotiable. If you submit your abstract to a major conference, you'll need to meet this deadline—and then, of course, have your poster/presentation finished before the event; these dates are not negotiable. But if you have a research paper under review, editors are typically liberal and understanding towards postponing deadlines for revision and resubmission. Not mentioning that typically, most of your projects are individual, and if you don't meet the deadline—either for a grant call or for a conference submission —it's just your loss, while in industry you typically work in a team and the peer pressure to succeed as a group is much higher. No one wants to be this black sheep who stayed behind and made the whole team fail. Thus, even though research life can be stressful, deadlines are less of an issue compared to industry.

Many PhDs who switched careers to industry and are now working in IT, describe themselves as happy to work from 9 am to 5 pm—but at the same time, they are surprised at how *tired* they are every day after eight hours of intensive work. They feel the same (or more!) physically tired as in times when they were sitting in their cubicles for twelve hours a day as researchers.

Therefore, to some extent, this fear from the recruiters' side is understandable. If you consider moving towards one of these dynamic fields where you can expect deadlines every day, you should think about your own resilience to stress and your ability to adapt your working style to the group.

Nevertheless, most PhDs quickly adapt to their new working environments (see: testimonials in the *Appendices*). Therefore, even you apply to a top-notch, competitive high-tech company, you shouldn't feel intimidated! When it comes to job interviews, it's good to highlight projects in your research career in which you worked closely in a group and under time-pressure (such as, for instance, hackathon projects). It is also good to demonstrate that you understand the importance of timely responses by simply answering the recruiters' emails quickly.

Common mistakes PhDs make when looking for jobs

Not only the recruiter's stereotypes work against PhDs in the job market. PhDs also often lower their own chances by developing the wrong attitude towards jobs and the job search. In this section, I review the most common mistakes and make suggestions on how you can avoid these mental traps.

➤ Mental trap 1: "I want a job anywhere but in academia!"

The first common mistake PhDs make is the "escape" mindset. Burnout and depression rates in academia are, unfortunately, high (Shanafelt et al., 2009, Sarner, 2018). I'd like to avoid a detailed discussion on the reasons for this phenomenon, as this could fill a whole new book. However, I feel that in many hierarchical systems other in academia—in which there are only a few individuals on the top, such as sports or politics—there is a better understanding of the *odds* of getting to the top. In these areas, professionals have a *stop loss*. If an athlete wins no medals in their twenties, they quit or downgrade sports to a hobby. If politicians run for parliament three times and don't get elected, they quit or start treating politics as a side-hustle next to their daily job. While in academia, many people pressure themselves to remain for way too long, even though the chances of getting a permanent contract are, objectively, becoming very slim for them.

Anyway, when you push, and push, and push, and you constantly encounter a force that pulls you backward—either constant rejections from academic journals, a toxic environment, or both—at some point, you can simply reach your dead end. There are no official statistics on the percentage of PhDs who decide to switch careers to industry for exactly this reason, but from experience, I can tell that this percentage is high.

First, there is *nothing wrong* with lucky escapes. If you are unhappy about your working conditions, and if it affects your quality of life, it is likely in your best interests to change the situation for the better—which might involve changing professions. If people around you do not appreciate your hard work and dedication, then find people who do. It is an improvement and progress, rather than a failure of any kind. The only problem with this is that when you are in a bad state of mind and

97

think about switching careers, you might be prone to making bad decisions. Let me explain.

I still remember one question from the final exam in social psychology during my undergrad studies: "Who is the biggest opponent of the Labour Party? a) proponent of the Green Party? b) proponent of the Democratic Party? c) proponent of the Conservative party? d) former proponent of Labour Party?"—you get the idea. A lot of people escaping from academia are on a *rebound*. They would rather choose to go to the beach and sell ice cream for a living than take any job that has any resemblance to what they were previously doing.

I still remember a Christmas dinner that I had three years ago at my friend's home. She has been a great friend of mine since high school, and she was always obsessed with physics, astronomy, and the universe. And, she was damn good at this. She graduated from Theoretical Physics and went abroad for a prestigious PhD program. At the age of 26, she became the youngest PhD graduate at her faculty. Then, she continued and went through two good Postdoc contracts. She was only about 30, and she was slowly becoming a big name in her field. Nothing seemed to ever go wrong. And then, on one winter day, I had dinner with her and her parents, and I witnessed a conversation that I had never expected to hear. Firstly, she did not resemble herself: she always takes care of herself but on that day, she looked really messy. She also did not behave as she normally does: she is always peaceful and polite, while back then, she was clearly irritated, and her mood swung between despair and anger. She yelled, "F*k it! I will go to Africa to build schools! F*k everything! I hate academia!" Her parents were very concerned but tried to rationalize the situation. They were politely explaining that they just want the best for her and that they'll love her no matter what—but going to Africa to do volunteer construction work is not what they believed would be good for her. But that did not calm her down at all. This discussion was going on and on, and I stayed quiet not to make it any worse. What eventually happened after this quarrel, was that she took a few months off to travel and find her new self. Now, she is a happy Machine Learning Engineer in a corporation.

The message is: if you have a strong desire to escape academia, it is often better to take some time for yourself first and rest before you make any big career moves— as otherwise, you might end up with a random job which doesn't suit you on many levels. Also, beware of this psychological effect of looking for something *completely different* from your previous job. Better to specify some elements that you did not enjoy in your last research job and try to avoid those elements in your next job rather than disregard all jobs which might have any commonalities with academia at all.

Besides, the human brain cannot visualize the word "no" properly: if you keep on thinking about all the things you don't want, you'll most likely attract them in some way. It is much better to go through the self-discovery phase as quickly as possible, redefine what you want, and focus on thinking about these new goals.

➤ Mental trap 2: "I have a good education, and I will always be fine."

In his famous autobiography, Arnold Schwarzenegger mentioned that living without a plan B largely contributed to his professional success (Schwarzenegger, 2013). Well, what worked for Arnie, doesn't necessarily need to work for you and me.

Postponing the job searching until the end of the contract is a common mistake among PhDs. In a way, research life encourages you to focus on your current projects rather than to look around, especially if you are still in the PhD phase: the more unfinished manuscripts on your desk, the harder it will be to combine finishing the PhD with your new job, and the longer it will take you to eventually graduate.

As a PhD, you have a lot of skill and value, but the process of searching for the right place in the job market can still take a long time, be tedious and frustrating. Besides, there is a big difference between *finding a job* and *finding a good job*. Yes, eventually you'll be fine, but the key is to make sure that you have a smooth transition to your next job—and make sure it's a job that suits you.

Of course, the time course of looking for a job very much depends on the country of affiliation, and the local job market. Currently, if you have a good technical education and the ability to program (especially in Python), and you are willing to find a data science job, in most countries you'll be able to find it within a week as the demand for Data Scientists is so high compared to the supply in the market. However, this is not always the case. There are a few rules of thumb here:

➤ The more differences between your current job and your dream job, the more time, effort, and sometimes also serendipity, you will need to find the next position. For instance, if you are finishing a PhD, it will generally be easier for you to get a job as a specialist rather than as a manager. The time necessary to make the transition doesn't need to reflect proximity in the personal freedom/personal safety space (Fig. 3): if you are a researcher right now, you might grow into a corporate or NGO employee faster that into a freelancer or entrepreneur.
➤ The more protective the labor agreement is, the more time it takes to find a job. In countries like the US where it is common to lay off an employee without a notice period, it is also common to accept an employee for a job at the first interview and allow them to start the job almost immediately. In countries that are protective of the employees, such as the Netherlands, it is common that you'll be invited to multiple interviews and it will take you weeks or even months before the contract is signed.
➤ The smaller the company, the slower the application process. The reason is that smaller companies, such as little startups, have fewer opportunities to shift an employee around in case this employee doesn't fit the team (I'll review this topic more in detail further in this chapter). Among entrepreneurs, there is even a saying, "Hire slow, fire fast." This saying means that as a startup owner, you need to first know the person well before hiring them because signing a new contract is associated with high costs and risk. And if the employee makes mistakes crucial to the well-being of the company, you should not hesitate to lay them off regardless of how hard it might be on a personal level—the well-being of the company and the job security of other employees are more important. For this reason, you should not be surprised if a startup you applied to, will prefer to first accept you for an internship before they can offer you a full contract.

Many researchers believe that the higher their university degree, and the longer their academic CV, the easier and faster it will be to find a job. Unfortunately, it often works the other way around: the less you have done, the lower the expectations and demands you have, the faster you will get recruited. For instance, if you are a high school graduate who is looking for a part-time job as a waiter/waitress, you are likely to be recruited at this first bar that accepts part-time student assistants. But, let's assume that you are a world-class expert in the physics of nanomaterials who additionally has experience running hackathons and working as an editor for an academic journal. Then, finding that one position in industry where you can best use *all* your skills, do *all* the things you enjoy doing, plus get rewarded accordingly, will be much harder. These positions *are* out there waiting for you but it might take you much more time and effort to find them.

For this reason, it is good to start looking for jobs early on, and possibly, play "the long-term game": keep in touch with the recruiters whom you encountered on the way (Pickle, 2019). If you are now going through a PhD program, and you consider finding a job in industry after your PhD, then as a rule of thumb, it is good to start looking around *a year before* your contract expires. It is good to be systematic about it, for instance by reserving one evening per month or one evening per week for browsing for jobs online and going through informational interviews. Or—if you are thinking of starting your own business—for learning about freelancing/ entrepreneurship, e.g., about the current demand in your market sector, the local tax regulations, online marketing strategies, etc. It is also good to refresh your contacts from undergraduate studies: you can dedicate part of these "job searching evenings" to chatting to these people about their experience in the job market, either face to face or online.

Remember that both Millennials and the following Generation Z have a low level of *loyalty* towards their employers. They easily swap jobs, which makes it hard for the recruiters to find a good employee and make a long-lasting bond with them. For this reason, most employers will agree to wait for a few months for your research contract to end if they find you a great job candidate. Therefore, if you happen to find a new job earlier than expected, you most likely will not need to choose. And, you can peacefully finish your research contract with peace of mind knowing that you already have plans for the future.

Furthermore, in recruitment, *hustling* works just the same way as in any other area of life: the more options you already have, the more new options you will get. Good job opportunities tend to come to those who already have a good job or got attractive job offers and don't even need them anymore. It is a psychological effect: when you have options, you are more relaxed at job interviews and sell yourself better.

Lastly, *never* put your job search process on hold—especially in hard times! For instance, the lockdown related to the corona crisis caused major turbulence in the job market: some companies have put their growth and expansion plans on hold and postponed or called off the recruitment process for many months. Many PhDs also postponed their job search then. They were thinking, "I need to wait with applying and focus on my projects right now." Wrong! Even though some companies decreased the number of open positions, plenty of vacancies were still open—for a few major reasons. Firstly, if an employee decides to leave the company or retires, the company still needs to find a replacement as soon as possible, even if they give up on their development plans. Secondly, large organizations and companies always have some *inertia*: many of them received grants and subsidies with the purpose of hiring new employees before the crisis, and they still need to spend this money before the deadlines specified in the grant proposals even though they have limited opportunities to invite candidates for face-to-face interviews. There are two groups of employees who typically apply for these positions: those who need a new job (e.g., because their contract expired) and those who don't technically need a new job, but for some reason, they are not satisfied with their current job or want to build their resumes by occasionally swapping positions. This latter group is inactive in the crisis—these people tend to postpone their plans and wait with the job applications until the end of the crisis. As a result, counterintuitively, while applying for jobs in the crisis you sometimes have a *higher* chance of getting accepted than before the crisis. For this reason, people who were active and doubled their efforts to apply rather than waiting for whatever happens next gained the most on the crisis—and, some of them got jobs they would otherwise have no chance of getting. This happens in almost every crisis on the market.

➢ Mental trap 3: "I have a PhD and I deserve this!"

Lastly, a common mistake made by PhDs is overestimating the *value of your education* to the employer. Many PhDs applying for jobs have the general attitude that being the best-educated candidate automatically makes them the best candidate. They often go to job interviews with the assumption that they are on the top of the leaderboard, and can dictate conditions. For instance, at their initial job interview, they may flood the recruiter with questions about how flexible is the working style at the company, and if they can walk out of the office at any time as this is their preferred working style. If you do interviews in this diva style, you are almost guaranteed to be rejected.

Let's look at this from the perspective of the employer. Most employers represent for-profit institutions and companies—and even if they happen to represent non-profit, they still have a limited budget at disposal. For them, the goal is to employ someone who will give them the best *value for money*. They hire a new employee because they need an additional pair of hands in the company which will help them to either increase the profits or to lower the costs—there is no other reason. Some employees in the company produce money in more indirect ways than others. For instance, an employee who takes care of the security of the servers in a video game production company doesn't generate profits in a direct way as an employee who programs the newest video game. Yet still, the final outcome is the same: while one person counteracts hackers' attacks and prevents the associated costs, the other person creates the product.

So, to maximize the gains, employers are looking for employees who are good workers, but also *cheap* workers. A cheap employee doesn't necessarily have to do with a *low salary*. Let me explain. Let's assume that you come straight from academia and that you have never worked in a corporation before. At the same time, another candidate at the same job interview is of the same age as you and spent the same amount of time working in another corporation as the time that you spent on your PhD. The recruiter will know straight away that you have no idea about corporate procedures, and that for the first few months you'll be like a bull in a china shop. They'll probably need to assign someone else around you who will need to show you around, and teach you how the company works—and they need to pay for this person's time. Plus, there is no guarantee that after these few months you won't come to the conclusions that you don't enjoy corporate life and quit anyway—which would be extremely expensive to the company. The other candidate, on the other hand, is a much safer bet to the recruiter: they have former experience with a corporation so they know what they are going for, and they'll adapt to the company culture much quicker. In the recruiter's books, it makes them cheaper even if they are offered the same salary as you.

This example is just to give you an idea of why better-educated candidates are not always the first line of choice for the recruiters. If you go for free-market jobs, then, in fact, you start from a *worse* position than other candidates rather than from a *better* position: you'll need to convince the recruiter that you are so much better than the competition that it is worth giving you a shot even taking into account the additional costs and extra risk.

It's also good to remember that while we were writing research publications, Master's graduates who never went for a PhD were not sleeping. They have their own dreams and ambitions, plus much more industry experience than us. And if they go for a job interview, they are the same determined to get the job.

Of course, as from every rule, there are exceptions from this one as well. Some companies, in particular, the top brand corporations such as *Google*, *La Roche*, *Philips*, *ASML*, are already familiar with the PhD culture and have a strong representation of PhDs in their R&D departments. If such companies invite you for an interview, it usually means that they already made that risk-reward estimation, and they see the added value of PhDs for their teams. In such cases, you are not at a disadvantage as a candidate with a PhD.

General advice in your job application process

This is probably the most controversial part of this book, because recruitment is not rocket science, and there is no consensus about the *efficiency* of many of the classic techniques for job search and approaching the job interviews. In this chapter, I summarize the most important points related to the job search and approaching job interviews—yet, as explained later in the text, the recruitment process is *probabilistic*. It means that these techniques will *increase* your chances of landing a job but will never give you a 100% guarantee.

➢ The recruiter will attempt to find "the right" person, not necessarily "the best" one.

The classic question that academics looking for jobs in industry often ask is, "How shall I compose my resume to maximize my chances to land the job?" It's good to know that this question is *ill-posed*. The main difficulty in the application process is *not* how to frame and present your resume; 80-90% of all the effort is to learn and vocalize who you are, where you would fit, and decide how you want to pitch yourself as a professional, while only the remaining 10-20% is putting this information into a visually appealing format. The recruiters are not looking for the most beautiful resume —they are looking for someone who fits the company, who is adaptive, and who will do the job.

If you have ever applied for jobs in the past, you might have encountered the following feedback: "Unfortunately, there were candidates who better fit the position," or "Unfortunately, there were candidates who better fit the company profile." This is common feedback from recruiters. For many applicants, this sentence sounds like a euphemism, namely, it sounds like the recruiter dodges admitting that there were better candidates in the process. So, you hear this sort of feedback and you think to yourself, "Damn, I am not even invited to the interview... There were so many better candidates than me!" In fact, this feedback is most often true: to the recruiter, someone else seemed more *tailor-made* for the position than you.

Therefore, there is no such thing as *the perfect resume*. You might be the best or the worst candidate for different positions with exactly the same set of application documents. It is just a matter of whom the recruiters are looking for at the moment. That's why it is often a good idea to *shorten* your resume before you apply for the job and adjust it to the requirements for the position you are applying for. I recommend keeping a *master file* containing your full resume listing all your achievements, from which you remove the least relevant 25-75% for a given application. It's never easy to kill the babies but it is necessary to increase your chances in the recruitment process.

One tricky situation is when you have a resume that both suggests that on the one hand, you are a specialist, but on the other hand, you are a type of a leader. For instance, imagine that you have a strong publication record in your discipline, but next to that, an equally long record of organizing and leading events, supervising students, etc. As mentioned in chapter 4: *What is My Perfect Working Environment?*, in industry, managers and specialists are often enrolled onto separate career tracks. If you are then applying to a specialist position, the recruiter might look at your documents, and think, "Will this person be able to follow the instructions, or is this someone who will start their own initiatives and come into conflict with their team leader every day?" On the other hand, if you apply for a strictly managerial position, the recruiter might think, "This person has the leadership skills. But I can also see that they also have a strong nerdy part to them, and just love digging into one problem for a long time. Is this person able to let go of that technical part of their career, and focus on managing people only?" This is why it is good to make sure that if you apply for a specialist position, at least 80% of your resume should be focused on your technical skills and your prior work and achievements, while if you apply for a managing position, at least 80% of your resume is focused on the managing/logistic experience, and soft skills. This will make it clearer to the recruiter what kind of professional you identify yourself with.

➤ Take the employer's point of view.

It's always good to take the employer's point of view—it is an important point often overlooked while looking for jobs. Employers are also humans—people who sacrificed their youth working around the clock for a vision they had. Most of them had to face years of insecurity and fail many times before they ever got to the level of comfort that you have as an employee from day one. And, leading a company will never get any easier—there is always new competition in the market, the demand in the market changes, there are new taxes and other obstacles. Therefore, employers want to hire people who are not only good at what they are doing but also easy-going, team-oriented, naturally interested in contributing to the projects, and loyal.

Let's do a little mental exercise here. Imagine that *you* are the person who spent the last ten years working 70-100 hours per week to build your business. You still remember these sleepless nights and an empty fridge, the debt in the bank, and your family and friends telling you to "get yourself a real job." Yet, you persevered and you made it: now, you are a leader of a successful company hiring over 100 people, and you win awards for the innovative services that your company offers. You meet a candidate who just finished graduate school and who is willing to work for your company. What questions would you ask this person at the interview?

➤ The recruiter will check whether you fit into their culture.

You have probably heard the term "the company's DNA." As we discussed, people still live in distinct cultural circles. Fitting into the culture is the key to getting hired. Therefore, as mentioned before in this chapter, recruiters not only look for the candidate that has skills and expertise necessary for the position, but who also best *fits their company's culture* and the team. Someone who will likely stay within the company for a long time.

I would like to make one thing clear here: *fitting into the company's culture* has nothing to do with your gender, ethnicity, or religious beliefs. In fact, it is known that diverse teams are, in general, more productive than uniform teams (Hunt, Layton & Prince, 2015), so none of these aspects should have a negative influence on your chances to get the job (in fact, the recruitment process is still often biased with respect to minorities but this is yet another problem).

What I mean here by "cultural fit", is fit in the *working style* and in attitude to work in general. For instance, if the team you are supposed to work in, practices scrum and meets for daily briefings at 8 am every day while you are a night owl and you cannot imagine yourself waking up at 6 am, it will be very hard for you to fit this working schedule. If the company works in a scheme that requires them to schedule last-minute business trips (for instance, because there is a sudden problem in another plant which only you can solve), and you are not willing to take up a midnight call and jump on the plane a few hours later, the company will be in trouble. If you prefer to get close instructions in your projects while your employer has this policy that the manager is just the facilitator and the team effectively needs to self-manage, you will probably feel lost and unhappy. If your last salary was twice as high as the salary which the company can offer you, you'll most likely feel undervalued and look for something else. If you are allergic to fern, and the whole company office is filled with fern, you'll suffer. If you would prefer to work from home 50% of the time while it is essential to the company that clients can walk into the office and always find you there during the working hours, it will be a problem. You get the idea.

This possible cultural clash is the reason why the employer needs to check how much your working style and expectations fit the company expectations for this particular position. For this reason, it's good to do some research about the company before you go to the interview.

In particular, you can check the following:

a) The company website,

b) General information about the company (via googling),

c) Crunchbase[29] profile to check essential numbers such as the year of incorporation or the number of employees,

d) Glassdoor[30] information to find out about the salary range they can offer, and the experiences of former employees,

e) Your *LinkedIn* contacts to check if you know anyone how works or worked for them.

If the company is large enough, you might even be able to find videos with instructions on how to best approach the qualification procedure or the job interview at that place.

As preparation, you can ask yourself the following questions:

a) What is the motto of the company?

b) When was this company created, and by whom?

c) How many employees do they have? Do they have international offices?

d) Who is the current CEO?

e) What is the main product that this company produces? What is the main revenue stream? Is this a Business-to-Customer (B2C), a Business-to-Business (B2B), a Business-to-Government (B2G), a non-profit, a government-funded agency? Try to understand what their business model is,

f) How do you imagine a working day at this company or institution? During the interview, you can even ask the recruiter how the reality differs from your preconceived views! It will be seen positively—as a sign of involvement and genuine care about meeting each other's expectations.

Related to the last point, it's also good to verify your *beliefs* before applying. What do you really think about the employer you are applying to work for? If you are planning to move towards the private sector, you need to warm up your heart to the private sector in the first place. Many researchers look down at private companies, and especially at the owners of these companies. They have a general opinion that entrepreneurs are vicious bloodsuckers with cash machines in place of hearts. It's hard to develop a thriving career with such an assumption, or even to get accepted for the job in the first place.

Money is a measure of value, and there is always another person at the end of the food chain. Private companies can only survive on the market when they produce products that either customers or other companies (that sell to their own customers) are willing to buy. The public sector, including academia, is very different: it works by *forcing* hard-working people, including nurses, schoolteachers, or street cleaners, to

---

[29] www.crunchbase.com

[30] www.glassdoor.com

pay a hefty income tax. Then, the government redistributes this money, e.g., to universities, *hoping* that the researchers will produce results useful to society one day. This often doesn't happen though, due to the publication game. It's easy to look down at the private sector but as a matter of fact, private companies often have a more direct positive influence on society than many academic research teams will ever have. And, they only cash in their money *after* they produce the value instead of getting their salaries on credit and based on (usually, far-fetched) promises, as it happens in the public sector. It's good to give it a thought before applying for jobs and develop some genuine appreciation for what private companies do. Recruiters will also instantly notice your positive attitude!

➢ The recruiter wants to see your engagement.

Today's employers not only pay salaries but also invest in their employees: send them on business trips and to professional workshops, take care of their general development, and aim to build a relationship that lasts for many years. This is why the recruiter will enjoy any signs of your engagement and genuine interest in the company. As mentioned above, it's good to prepare for the interview by learning the basics about the history, vision, and business model of the company. However, it's also good to prepare a few questions related to the company and their culture which you might ask the recruiter during the interview. It's also good to indicate that you are interested in contributing to life within the company. Some ideas below:

> "I'm curious about what the daily workflow is within this particular team. Can you tell me how a typical Monday looks like? How can I make sure that my work is the most synergistic with my colleagues' work?"

> "Currently, we have a deep crisis in the market. I'm curious about how the company is doing at the moment, what the plans for development are in these hard times, and how I can contribute."

> "Can you tell me a little bit more about the working culture in the company? Do the teams meet with each other regularly? Do you cast some regular extracurricular activities together that I could help with? Is there a company blog or newsletter that I could contribute to?"

> "How can I additionally prepare for this position before I start? Are there any books or documents I should read?"

Furthermore, if the job is a full-time position, yet you would prefer to work part-time, I would *not* mention this during the interview. It is because some recruiters treat this preference as a sign of *low engagement*. Namely, they assume that you are asking for a part-time arrangement because you might have some other professional activity going on in your life, such as a side business. And perhaps that other activity is more important to you. Therefore, in such a case, as a rule of thumb, it's better to get to work full-time for a few months, demonstrate your expertise and engagement, and then politely ask your employer to reduce the number of working hours per week, e.g., to 32 or 24. If the employer values your work, they will most likely agree to this arrangement as they will prefer to keep a good employee around. And if they say, "No," you still have a job, and you can think of alternatives.

Of course, it is also essential to show your engagement by simply answering any post-interview questions the recruiter might send you by email in a diligent and timely manner. Don't wait for a week to answer an email from the recruiter—for the industry standards, that's way too late!

➤ Check your visibility online.

It might sound trivial, yet still, many job seekers forget about this one. It is good to check back on your social media accounts and examine what *Google* will return when you google your own name. Remember to google from a different browser than the browser you use daily as otherwise, you'll get biased results—preferably, from a browser with no cookies. If you notice materials that you would prefer to erase from the internet, you might have no control over those materials—for instance because these are photos posted from your friend's social media account. Thus, you'll need time to contact the person who manages this resource and ask them to remove the content. It can take weeks, and this is why it is good to start the job searching from this step.

Also, take care of your image on social network websites such as *LinkedIn*: make sure that you picture yourself as a young professional rather than as a student. The same holds for other social media. For example, *Facebook* is more of a social platform than *LinkedIn,* but it does not mean that a respected company would be eager to hire a candidate who presents themselves in a bathing suit on the profile photo for an executive position.

Lastly, you need to be careful when building your image on social media because industry standards for networking online are different from academic standards. In fact, *every* working environment has its own online culture—their own memes, insider's jokes, and standards for what behaviors and opinions are or aren't professional. For instance, academic *Twitter* is welcoming to sharing any job-related frustrations publicly, including burnout, depression, and failure of all kinds. In many areas of industry, this is not acceptable though—as soon as you employer learns that you shared anything that puts the company in a bad light on *Twitter*, you are out with no questions asked. Recruiters will also likely screen your online activity, especially if you apply for any representative functions where you are supposed to network and contact clients. Thus, once you are in the job application process, I would generally advise to keep conversations about your daily struggles at your current job private, and concentrate on sharing knowledge and neutral advice once you are active in public.

➤ To attract the recruiters, you need to build your online image.

Building a personal website is also a standard. However, many industry professionals rely on their *LinkedIn* profile, and they successfully build their careers without developing a custom personal website. Thus, an up-to-date *LinkedIn* profile is probably even more important to start.

While polishing your *LinkedIn* profile, think about what you want to achieve. What works well with recruiters on *LinkedIn* is presenting yourself as more of a professional with a research background than a researcher. It's good to underscore your interest in the branch of industry that you aim for and list all the projects that (even remotely) relate to projects in this industry. A trick that often works for PhDs is to introduce yourself as someone who *already represents* a profession that you are planning to eventually occupy. For instance, if you aim to make a switch from PhD to data science, building your profile as a Data Scientist with a research background, will likely help. This approach works only if you are planning to find a job that is very close in nature to your PhD—a far stretch from your PhD might be disappointing to recruiters who decide to contact you.

Also, once you figure out what your core competencies are, they should be mentioned in your *LinkedIn* profile description. It will make it so much easier for the right people to find you! Furthermore, mentioning those of your transferable skills that recruiters often search for—such as orientation on teamwork or the ability to finish projects on time (of course, as long as it is true!)—will help. Some job seekers wonder whether they should openly indicate on *LinkedIn* that they are actively looking for jobs —especially when they are still employed. Fortunately, *LinkedIn* offers an option to make your job search status visible to recruiters only[31].

➤ You need to learn how to convert your academic CV into a resume.

There is a difference between a *CV* and a *resume*. In academia, we prefer to use a CV. CV showcases our *credentials* and *technical aptitude*: our education history, certificates, publications, grants, other achievements, professional affiliations. However, the format preferred in industry is a resume. A resume is a *brief form* (1-2 pages) focused on our *competencies,* work experience, and notable achievements. In most cases, the full list of publications is not necessary as it won't be of interest to the recruiter (a hyperlink to the full list of publications is enough). The good news is that converting your CV to a resume is not hard, and you can find plenty of good tutorials on how to do this online.

➤ The details of the application matter.

Firstly, remember *not to write in code* in your motivational letter. You don't know who will read your letter and what background that person has. And as a matter of fact, most recruiters don't have a technical background that would allow them to interpret some of your achievements. For instance, if you say, "I organized a hackathon," it might not tell the recruiter too much about your logistic skills. In this case, it would work better to say, "I organized a hackathon, a 3-day event hosting 120 participants in which 12 teams competed in a challenge to design a solution for the problem of air pollution in our city. I came up with the concept of the event, and I was responsible for registering participants and building the infrastructure on the site, including the equipment ad setup for broadcasting the event online."

---

[31] www.linkedin.com/help/linkedin/answer/67405/let-recruiters-know-you-re-open-to-work

Next, when you are putting together your resume and motivational letter, check for typos, and especially, whether the name of the company/recruiter is spelled correctly. Nothing makes a worse impression than sending out a letter full of typos in which you picture yourself as a diligent person. It is good to write the documents and then check them once again the next morning when you relaxed. You can also use apps or browser plugins such as *Grammarly[32]* or *Hemingway[33]*.

Of course, not every recruiter is as harsh as others when it comes to reacting to typos. It is a very personal thing. Some recruiters give a chance to good candidates even if the writing is not perfect, while others do not. It is a bit like with journal editors. Some editors believe that the quality of your English neither proves nor disproves the quality of your research findings. Others will immediately reject your paper if it is written in poor English. According to *LiveCareer*, 59% of recruiters reject candidates due to grammatical errors or typos (Bruzzese, 2018). Since you do not know who is sitting on the other side and reading your letter, it is always safer to assume that this person is scrupulous and non-forgiving.

The same holds for the sense of humor. Certain areas of the market, such as marketing, are based on creativity and out-of-the-box ideas. In those areas, it is well received if you do something funny with your job application—for instance, if you print your resume on a cover of a chocolate bar and send it to the company by post. Or, if you send them one shoe and add a note that now that you have already got one foot in the door, you would appreciate it if you can show up at their office and step in with both your feet. In many other areas of the market, such creativity would not meet with understanding though. It all depends on who is sitting on the other side. One recruiter would find it funny and invite you, while another recruiter would think, "We don't need such a quirky person here," or "Gosh! This shoe stinks!" So, this is a risky strategy. I would summarize it this way: if the recruiter likes your joke, your chances to get the job increase (but not to 100%). However, if the recruiter doesn't like your joke, your odds of getting the job drop to zero. In my eyes, this game is not worth the risk—but if you are a gambler, please go ahead!

One quite controversial subject when talking about job applications is *keywords*. Big companies (in particular, companies with a good brand) often get hundreds of applications per position, and they need to prescreen them before they even let their recruiters read the content to cut on the costs of the recruitment process. According to *LiveCareer*, 64% of the recruitment companies screen incoming resumes (Bruzzese, 2018). Well, it is hard to answer the question of how to best approach this problem. There is more than one method to prescreen the applicants' documents: there are multiple software packages with different standards, and you don't know which one the given recruiter will be using.

Therefore, as a rule of thumb, it is good to read through the job offer once again and spot expressions that describe the job and the preferred qualifications. Then, use the same or very similar phrases to describe yourself in your own letter (of course, as long as this is true). For instance, if you read that the dream candidate should have "a

---

[32] www.grammarly.com

[33] www.hemingwayapp.com

continuous drive to keep learning," then it is good to reflect that in your letter describing yourself as a person with "a drive" who "never stops learning," or "enjoys learning new skills." If they expect you to be "analytical," it's good to rephrase this and mention that you have "an analytic mind," rather than looking for synonyms such as "systematic approach to solving problems." It is because you do not know how intelligent the screening algorithm will be and whether it will understand that you are talking about the same quality. As mentioned before, it is also a good idea to cut some unnecessary content from your resume to better adjust it to the position. The software not only picks up on keywords, but also calculates the *concentration* of the keywords in the whole text. Thus, the more off-topic text, the lower your odds of getting through.

Network, network, network!

I cannot stress the value of networking enough. Networking shouldn't be just something you do at times when you happen to be looking for a new job. Instead, it should be your modus operandi throughout the whole professional career. There are at least four solid reasons for making professional networking your regular activity.

Firstly, some jobs are *impossible to get* without networking. Namely, some jobs —especially in startups—are never announced publicly. For those positions, the candidates are scouted by the employer through professional circles. Sometimes, the founders create a new position only after they meet a professional whom they would like to see in their team. Some other jobs—especially in the public sector—are announced publicly to make a show while the preferred candidate is already waiting for their contract. In such cases, the only way to get the job is to be personally connected with the employer or to find yourself at the right time in the right place.

Secondly, networking has a much higher *conversion rate* than sending out job applications for publicly announced positions. When you network and actively ask for opportunities, you might have little to no competition, while any good job that appears online attracts hundreds of candidates at a time. Moreover, while networking, you can present yourself as a professional and make a personal connection with the recruiter-instead of becoming yet another candidate behind the resume. Networking is a bit like leapfrogging the whole crowd of applicants and proceeding straight to the interview! As a result, in terms of the probability of getting hired, one hour of networking will give you a much higher return than one hour of browsing through online job boards.

Thirdly, it's much easier to learn about yourself and figure out which tribe you should join if you encounter people representing various environments. It's not about comparing with others; it's about noticing the similarities and differences in habits and in the way of thinking. Don't guess—get the data!

Lastly, networking is a form of a *long-term investment*: the profits from networking grow over time like compound interest. While networking, you shake hands with lots of people—who then migrate, change jobs, bump into each other, figure out than they know you, mention about you to other people… And the network grows. Therefore, for the sake of general career development, it's good to regularly reach out to people regardless if they are in the same sector of the market as you:

shake hands, introduce yourself, invite to contacts on *LinkedIn*. Also, you never know who will come back to your life, and when—sometimes, your contacts from undergraduate studies becomes relevant only after fifteen years or more. Or, while chatting with some peers from high school, you can suddenly realize that now, you have much more in common than you used to. And sometimes, your friend from the school desk can even become your employer! Thus, it's good to reach out to your friends from school and studies once in a while—send a friendly email for Christmas or poke on social media. Since networking *is* investing, it's good to treat it as such and *diversify:* reach out both to the people whom you don't know yet, and those whom you've already met in the past.

Especially if you have a PhD title in humanities, networking is the key to land jobs. As a humanist, you might lack specialistic technical expertise or programming/laboratory/engineering skills that are now highly valued in the job market, thus, finding yourself in the right place at the right time is even more important than more PhDs in STEM.

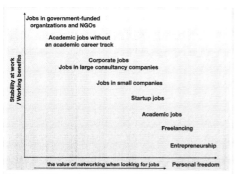

Figure 4 The value of networking when looking for jobs, depending on the tribe. Networking is always an important aspect of a job search, but the more to the right on this landscape, the more it influences your chances of landing the actual contract.

Networking will greatly help you, particularly with getting jobs in companies and labs that are so small that the employers have limited ability to shift employees around in case something goes wrong (Fig. 4). Let me explain. Let us assume that you get employed in a company with 10 departments and a total of 1,000 employees. After six months, it becomes clear that you and your direct superior are not a match as you have a very different vision of how to manage projects. This situation starts affecting your job satisfaction and mental health. You knock at the door of the HR department and explain that you have had enough. What would they do? They might tell you that if you do not communicate with your superior, they will need to let you go. But this would mean that they need to give up on all the cost of acquiring you as an employee and training you for at least half a year. Most likely, they will propose you another position in another department instead—and then, you will need to start over in another team. As they have 1,000 employees, they have *room* to do this. And what will happen if you are in a lab which has 15 employees, and you have frictions with your daily supervisor in this lab? The chances of finding another project and other supervisors for you in the same lab are much slimmer. The same holds for a small startup company. In business, it is even worse: if you set your own company with a co-founder with whom you happen to have a different vision of the business, it is instant death to the company.

For this reason, small companies, research labs, and entrepreneurs are usually not eager to make any deals with anyone they *have just met* for the first time. If you are thinking of setting up a company with someone, it's usually with a person you have known for years and whom you trust more than you trust yourself. If a postdoctoral researcher is accepted for a position in a given lab, it is usually someone who has already met the PI on multiple occasions before. For instance, someone who met the PI at conferences, who was collaborating with the PI on research projects, or previously joined the lab as a visiting researcher. If a new employee is accepted at a small startup, they are usually first asked to go through a trial period, or a paid internship, for a period of a month to three months. As mentioned before, there is even a saying in business, "Hire slow, fire quickly." The reason is exactly this effect: in a small company, there is no space to shift an employee around if something goes wrong. And if the company is still in the startup phase, one miscast, unproductive, or misbehaving employee can take down the whole company. This is also why one shouldn't blame small employers who only hire those whom they've previously met: after all, they care about the ultimate success of their team, and they simply lack the resources to risk accepting strangers.

Anyway, it is good to be aware of this effect as it influences your chances of getting into a given environment if you are "from the outside": if you don't know anyone in industry, it will be much easier for you to get into a corporation, or a large, government-funded institution, than into a startup.

Research has demonstrated that networking has a real influence on everyday life, including a *sense of luck*. Richard Wiseman is a Professor at Hertfordshire University who spent years investigating the nature of luck (Wiseman, 2004). In one of his experiments, he put two individuals, Brenda (who identified herself as a very unlucky person) and Martin (who identified himself as a lucky guy) in the same situation: they had to get to a cafe designated by the experimenter and wait inside. Dr. Wiseman had put a 5-pound bill on the pavement in front of the café. He had also placed four of his accomplices at four separate tables in the cafe. One assistant dressed like a successful businessman, while the other three assistants dressed simply. Martin got to the café as first. He picked up the bill from the pavement, and without hesitation, he joined the business guy's table. He then offered the businessman a coffee and started chatting. After five minutes, they were talking like best friends. Brenda also got to the cafe, but she didn't notice the bill. She also joined the businessman's table, but she didn't say a word and waited for the experimenter in silence. From this anecdotal study, Prof. Wiseman concluded that the common feature of all the lucky people is that they build a network of connections and never miss an occasion to grow this network. So, networking should be one of the focal points of your career development in general, regardless of your plans!

As a matter of fact, your circle of influence grows proportionally to the size of your network. Therefore, building new connections should become your *habit*—one of the things that you do daily, just as brushing your teeth or exercising. Here, I would like to share several pieces of advice on how to make your networking more efficient.

➤ Prepare for networking events.

Firstly, it's good to take some time to prepare for every networking event that you are about to join. These events usually host a few hundred to a few thousand people squeezed in a small area for a few hours. Thus, it's going to be hard to find the right people in time without a prior preparation. Take some time to screen through the website of the event, create a must-see list, and schedule meetings in advance if that's possible. Self-discipline is crucial at these events—otherwise, you'll do a random walk, and spend the whole day bumping into people whom you know and chitchatting. And then, you'll get back home with a feeling that you didn't benefit from the event at all. People who are good at networking, are not just lucky: they usually enter the room with a plan on their mind.

➤ Polish your skills in networking through *LinkedIn*.

LinkedIn is still the online avenue where recruiters meet job seekers. It gives so many options! For instance, you can browse for professionals working in companies that are of interest to you and politely ask them for informational interviews. You can then briefly introduce yourself, explain that you are interested in applying, politely ask them how it feels to work in this place, and whether any vacancies are coming up. You will get some percentage of positive responses (hard to give hard numbers on the range), which will then allow you to collect very valuable information about the company from first hand and get an advantage over other candidates.

LinkedIn is also a great platform to reach out to recruiters. First of all, you need to know that there are *various types* of recruiters. Namely, some recruiters are employed in companies while others are independent (the difference is easy to notice by checking the *LinkedIn* profile) or work for agencies specialized in hiring professionals in certain sector. As the rule of thumb, the company recruiters are the most valuable for you as a potential job seeker, as they know the most about the plans of the company, and about the specific needs of the employer. Of course, independent recruiters can help you as well!

You can filter recruiters who are of interest to you by typing appropriate search phrases in the *LinkedIn* browser, e.g.:

"recruiter" + "*[insert the name of the company]*"
"recruiter" + "*[insert the name of the industry]*" + "*[insert the geographical area]*"

If you have a free *LinkedIn* subscription, you can only contact users who are your second-hand contacts—for most people, it still gives plenty of opportunities. For the job search period, you should also consider trying the premium subscription to increase the number of possibilities. While contacting recruiters, make sure that the title of your message is informative (e.g., "Inquiry from a Data Scientist searching for new career opportunities") and customized for every company. Going with a mass mailing and sending generic messages to companies just won't work. Industry recruiters are bombed by private messages every day. Therefore, make sure that you are brief and concrete. As a rule of thumb, an efficient InMail message consists of three components:

Part #1: Greetings at the beginning of the message (it's good to greet the recruiter by name), and a blitz pitch explaining who you are as a professional in one sentence.

Part #2: Reference to the company in a positive context, e.g., "I learned about *company name* from…", "I admire the *company name* brand for…", "I have been tracking the development of *[insert the name of the company]* in the market since…"

Part #3: Expressing a wish to introduce yourself further, e.g., by saying something along the lines, "I'd be delighted at the chance to present myself to you and talk further about how I can contribute to your team."

Greeting at the end of the message, e.g., "Thank you for your time and consideration. Yours sincerely, *[insert your name + your academic title]"*

The hardest part of writing such InMail messages to recruiters is to find a way to customize them and express your interest in the company so that it sounds genuine. To do this properly, you'll need to get familiar with some basic facts about the company and/or with their website and think of any memories/facts/people you might mention that link you to the company. Please find some examples below:

"My name is Ana Brown, and I'm currently looking for new career opportunities in the video gaming industry as a software developer. I've been using your game apps for years. I've had a great user experience with your products and I enjoy the exceptional design of your games. Thus, I cannot imagine a better team to join this market. I would be grateful for information if you are planning to grow your team soon."

"Congratulations on the recent *The Coolest Product of The Year* award! I've been following the development of your company, and I'm impressed with how much growth you've achieved within the last three years. I'm currently looking for opportunities in this field, and I would be delighted if I can present myself to you in person."

"My name is Ana Brown, I'm a young professional with a PhD in computational neuroscience, and I'm passionate about new developments in Brain-Computer Interface technology. I have been reading your company blog for the past few months, and I always feel inspired by how your team leads the innovation in your field. Thus, I would love to contribute to this project. Thus, I would be grateful if I could receive any information about upcoming vacancies in your team."

"I recently attended the annual Innovation for Health conference, and I had a great pleasure to listen to the talk of the CEO of your company, John Smith. His vision for innovation in the field was truly inspiring, and I would love to be a part of this venture. I would be grateful if you could share information about the upcoming vacancies in your team with me."

Such a customized message demonstrates that you are familiar with what they do and that you have a genuine interest in working there. Recruiters working in reputable companies get tons of private messages on *LinkedIn* daily; if you start the message in a customized and engaging way, they won't classify you as a spammer.

How to approach job searching in different working environments (a.k.a. tribes)

Apart from networking, there are a few different channels that can allow you to find your dream job—the choice of the optimal channel depends on the tribe you are willing to join. Below, I am listing information on the most popular ways to search for jobs, and I summarize this information in Table 3.

➤ Finding job offers online.

Googling feels like the most natural and intuitive way to search for almost anything these days. To a large extent, this is also true about searching for jobs. You can find jobs in most sectors online. There are a few major categories of online services where you can search for jobs:

a) Job boards where you can post your resume or browse through posted job offers using search keywords. Some of these job boards are assisted by machine learning algorithms that scrape information from your resume to present it to the right employers. Job boards were the most efficient mean of recruitment for a long time (31.7% of all recruited employees, Zappe, 2015) but recently started losing the competition with social networks for professionals and businesses (McLeod, 2014). However, using job boards can still be recommended, as it costs relatively low effort: you need to either fill in a questionnaire or load a resume in a single file—then, you don't need to do anything anymore, just wait. Also, one additional benefit of using job boards as a PhD, is that employers who have a preference for hiring PhDs, will easily find you (by simply using "PhD" as a keyword). On the other hand, public institutions don't post their jobs on job boards all that often. In particular, academic employers usually don't put their offers on job boards, unless these are dedicated websites such as *Academic Transfer* or *Nature Jobs*[34]. The

[34] www.nature.com/naturejobs/science/register

most popular job boards are: *Indeed*[35], *Monster*[36], *CareerBuilder*[37], *Ziprecruiter*[38], *Jobs2Careers*[39], *Experteer & The Ladders*[40] (specialized in executive employees), *Dice*[41] (specialized in tech), and *Nofluffjobs*[42] (specialized in IT). To sum up, using job boards works best if you aim to get a corporate job or employment as a consultant. It can also work when looking for academic jobs (with or without an academic career track), but for that purpose, you need to access dedicated job boards.

b) Online social networks for professionals and businesses. Social networks merge the concept of building your own network with building your professional career. By using these social networks, you can keep in touch with professionals in your circles, but, at the same time, you can make yourself visible to employers worldwide and inform them about your availability in the job market. The employers not only see your resume loaded onto your profile but can also observe your activity in the community. If you post interesting posts and articles or share content from other users—which indicates that you are passionate and knowledgeable about what you are doing in your professional life—it will help you in making a great first impression. You also have the option of actively searching through the database of offered jobs, and you can use multiple filters (for salary, location, etc.). The most popular social networks at the moment are *LinkedIn*, *Viadeo*[43], and *XING*[44]. Using these channels works best if you aim to work for the public sector if you are looking for an academic job (with or without an academic career path), or a corporate/consultancy jobs.

c) Dedicated services such as *Honeypot*[45] (specialized in software dev and data science). If you subscribe to such a service, you'll be contacted in person and go through an online interview, which aims to help you fill in your online profile in an optimal way. Then, your resume will get posted online so that employers can approach you.

---

[35] www.indeed.com

[36] www.monster.com

[37] www.careerbuilder.com

[38] www.ziprecruiter.com

[39] www.jobs2careers.com

[40] www.eu.experteer.com

[41] www.dice.com

[42] www.nofluffjobs.com

[43] www.fr.viadeo.com

[44] www.xing.com

[45] www.honeypot.io

➤ Googling for research conducted in industry.

Let's now assume that you would like to move towards industry but at the same time, still keep doing research. This is quite an often-encountered situation as lots of academics came to academia for the sake of the research but leave because of the dysfunctional system. If you are looking for a research position in industry, you might first get a proxy of where most research in your neighborhood is done. You can search for the following information online:

a) The list of companies with the most populated R&D departments. In many countries, e.g., in the Netherlands, such lists are publicly available[46]. R&D departments are usually the most PhD-friendly departments,

b) *Scopus* database[47] where you can search for names of companies that are of interest to you; if the given company published any research papers, you should be able to view this information.

This approach should work best if you are looking for research jobs in the public sector or corporations.

➤ Tracking the leaders in the field.

If you were looking for yet another research contract, would you type a few keywords related to your research subject in *Google* and just go with the top records? Or rather, would you first think about the leading labs in your field, about their way of doing research and the lab culture that they have developed? And then deliberate whether you fit there, start tracking the positions coming up in your dream labs, and personally ask about the upcoming vacancies? Well, it's good to use the same strategy while looking for jobs in industry.

You can start by creating a list of companies that are of general interest to you, e.g. because they are the market leaders in the sector that you target, they have a good opinion as employers, etc. Once you have that list, it's good to track these companies, namely, to follow them on *LinkedIn*, and regularly visit their website and their company blog (if they have any).

Checking the vacancies on the websites of these companies will allow you to leapfrog and skip one step of the recruitment procedure. It's because the offers posted on job boards and *LinkedIn* are often released by external, private recruiters. If you apply through such an external recruiter, you need to go through two steps of recruitment: first, you need to be qualified but the external recruiter and passed towards the internal recruiter in the company, and second, the internal recruiter also needs to accept you. If you, instead, apply directly through the company website, the internal recruiter within the company will receive and read your application without the middlemen involved. That gives you much better chances of success. Also, mind that in many countries, there are *no quality standards* for external recruitment agencies, and many of these private recruiters have a very superficial knowledge about the market sector which makes their decisions quite random.

---

[46] www.technolution.eu/uploads/2019/06/rd-top-30-2019.pdf

[47] www.scopus.com

Furthermore, many large companies such as *Google* developed their own online career centers where you can subscribe for personalized newsletters—so that you'll get notified whenever new, interesting positions are announced in your area. No need to mention that it's worth to subscribe!

➤ Contacting agencies specialized in hiring PhDs.

If you are not convinced about which direction to go, you might consider professional recruitment agencies—e.g., agencies specialized in hiring PhDs (but not only). The modus operandi of such agencies is that they offer you the contract (it is often a contract for a fixed period, e.g., for three years), and you effectively become their employee. Then, the agency puts you on projects in private companies. They make income from the difference between what the company pays the agency for your work and the salary that the agency pays you. The benefit for the private companies to work with such agencies is that this model allows them to have a *disposable workforce*. Namely, they can dispose of you at any time (without the severance pay), and the agency is then obliged to find you another project in another company. In countries that are protective of the employees (e.g., in most countries of Western Europe), it is hard for an employer to lay off an employee. If they decide to terminate the contract, they usually need to give a few-months-long notice and bear huge financial costs—even if the employee is highly inefficient at what they are doing. For this reason, many employers prefer this umbrella model of hiring. They agree to pay more per month than they would otherwise pay for the employee's salary (as the agency needs to earn on top of the salary) but, on the other hand, they have more freedom to shift people around and resign from the employee's service at any time.

If you decide to go with such an agency, you will need to accept that you might lack a sense of belonging. You will work at companies, but at the same time, you will be an employee of someone else, and your working conditions depend on another employer. On the other hand, you have guaranteed employment, at least for a few years—and if one project, or one company, does not work for you, they will move you elsewhere.

One note to make here is that for these agencies, *you are the product* they sell. With professional recruiters, it is a bit like with real estate agents: they want to sell as much as possible in as little time as possible, rather than looking for hidden gems on the market, and spending weeks or even months on finding the most appropriate client and negotiating the highest possible price. For this reason, they are usually interested in *easy cases*: people who have a very clear career path, and a very well-defined set of competencies that are currently valued in the job market. For instance, if you did a PhD in the physics of nanomaterials, have always been passionate about doing research rather than managing people, and are looking for a job in industry as a specialist in the physics of nanomaterials, you are probably an *easy case*: there is a high demand for experts like you, and it will be easy to demonstrate your competencies to clients in the recruitment process. If you, however, have a very unique set of skills, e.g., you were doing a PhD in nanomaterials while at the same time intensively blogging and organizing hackathons and conferences on a regular basis, and you are passionate about managing people and projects, it might be much more confusing for recruiters. Most managers employed in corporations come from the corporate world rather than from academia, thus, they won't know where to place you given such a background. Thus, I would say that agencies hiring PhDs are a good solution if you are a highly qualified specialist, rather than a natural leader, a community builder, or a free spirit. They work well if you are searching for jobs in the public sector, corporations, startups, or consultancy companies.

Today, there are also new, interesting solutions dedicated to PhDs (check: *Appendix 1*). On these online platforms, you can apply for a mentor from industry who will advise you career-wise. The online dialogue with your mentor can also potentially result in getting employed by the company that your mentor represents.

➤ Hackathons, conferences, seminars, and meetups.

In some environments—such as startups, freelancing, and academia—it is even more essential to make personal contact and build bonds than in others. As mentioned above, these are the environments where the ability to shift labor around is the lowest.

Many startups recruit new employees at hackathons, where they can test the candidates' skills in action. Thus, meetups (e.g., events listed at the *Meetup*[48] platform) and little evening conferences are a good occasion to make personal contact and introduce yourself to the right people. The dynamics at such events is usually higher than at scientific meetings: conversations are short and to the point; if the other party concludes that business-wise, you have nothing in common, they will shift their attention to another person. For this reason, it's good to be brief in introducing yourself, and have a 90-second elevator pitch at hand. Such a pitch shouldn't go to deep into the nitty-gritty details of your craft, but rather, briefly summarize the topic you are working on, your role in your projects, and some of your core competencies. A good phrase to start such a pitch, is:

> "I help *[insert a group of people, e.g., "research groups in my institute" or "patients with ADHD"]* with *[insert the purpose of your work, e.g., "better storing and documenting their codes and datasets" or "better controlling their emotions"].*"

Rather than naming a list of things you are good at, a neat way to end such a pitch is just saying,

> "If you need any help with *[insert a skill]*, just let me know."

It is a good ending because it gives the other person a choice of whether to ask more questions now or end the conversation on a good note by saying, "Thank you, we are in touch." Plus, it places you in the position of an expert.

Furthermore, even though we live in times of smartphones and *LinkedIn*, it's also good to bring old-school, paperback business cards with you. You would be surprised how many people in business still collect them. Plus, it's good to finish the

---

48 www.meetup.com

pitch (in particular, when it is phrased as suggested above) by handing in your business card.

Fresh freelancers also need to polish their networking skills, as this can make or break their business. The usual way of starting as a freelancing business is to develop a product or a skill set, and then use your network to collect recommendations, and find your first clients. Personal networks can also be built through meetups, little conferences, and hackathons. Moreover, in most large cities, there are bars or open workspaces where—in either a formal, or an informal way—freelancers can meet regularly, and work or chill together.

In academia, building personal contacts through face-to-face meetings is also priceless. It's often the case that researchers find new jobs for themselves at conferences or hackathons. It is a recommended approach, especially if you feel that you are not supported in your own research environment and, for some reason, you cannot count on recommendation letters from your superiors. An opportunity to present yourself in person can help you to get around these issues. A good approach to building your personal contacts, which can turn into a new job, is also to approach labs you're interested in, in a vanilla way—without even mentioning that you are looking for a job. For instance, you might kindly ask the PI of a lab whether you could join their weekly seminar—as you are interested in their research line. In most cases, you'll hear an enthusiastic, "Yes, of course!" And then, you can get to their seminar, get familiar with some faces, impress them with some smart questions, and usually also join them for lunch—all without putting pressure on them by introducing yourself as an official job seeker. This is usually a good starting point for collaborations or signing job contracts in academia.

Lastly, if you are thinking of starting a startup, visiting meetings is almost a must. You'll need to build your core team, and the more trusted people you can find, the better for you. Some people are lucky to fill in all the important vacancies (CEO, CTO, CFO, CMO, and others) at the very start of their adventure, in the conceptual phase of the project. However, for most budding entrepreneurs building the team is a long process that often starts at meetups, hackathons, conferences, and after-parties in bars.

To sum up, going to meetings works well if you are thinking about a startup job, freelancing, academic job, or setting your own startup.

➤ Self-promotion.

Lastly, in many areas, a little bit of self-promotion is essential to building a brand and going forward. It is also the case in academia in which setting up a personal website, and networking on *Twitter* (Cheplygina et al., 2020) has slowly become the standard.

Self-promotion is especially important if, instead of looking for your next boss, you are searching for your next client: if you are thinking of becoming a freelancer or an entrepreneur. In both these cases, a personal website or website of your project is highly recommended from the early start. It's also recommended to set up a whitelist where people interested in your services, or in your future services/products, can leave their contact email, and further receive updates from you.

If you are a freelancer, you might also consider creating a profile on one of the dedicated platforms such as *Upwork*[49]. You can actively search for good projects and apply for them by submitting your offer. You can also decide to use these platforms passively: create an account and wait for the offers. The quality of the offers sent to you will most likely be lower than it would be if you actively searched for good deals, but on the other hand, it costs you a minimal amount of energy. Also, platforms such as *Fiverr*[50] are no longer only meant for little, casual 5-buck jobs. These days, lots of professionals announce their services on *Fiverr*, and the price tags for these services can amount to thousands of dollars.

If you are a freelancing consultant, you might also consider offering your services at one of the platforms dedicated to professional online consultancy services such as *Clarity*[51]. At *Clarity*, you can put a price tag on your consultancy services and set your rate per minute—and these services are usually rewarded well (the pricing plan starts from $1 per minute).

Channel \ Tribe	Working for the public sector	Academic jobs without an academic career path	Corporate jobs	Startup jobs	Consulting	Academic jobs	Freelancing	Entrepreneurship
Networking	✓	✓	✓	✓	✓	✓	✓	✓
Job boards		✓*	✓	✓		✓*		
Online social networks for professionals and businesses	✓	✓	✓		✓	✓		
Browsing for research jobs in industry	✓		✓					
Tracking the leaders in the field			✓	✓	✓			
Agencies hiring PhDs	✓		✓	✓	✓			
Hackathons/meetups/ startup accelerators				✓		✓	✓	✓
Self-promotion						✓**	✓**	✓

Table 3 How to approach job searching concerning different working environments. *) You need to use specialized job boards here. **) A personal website especially matters here.

Lastly, if you are starting your own business, you might also think about using paid ads on social media such as *Facebook*, *LinkedIn,* or *Instagram*. The choice of the right medium will depend on the scope of your business of course. The ability to set up these ads properly, and achieve the maximum ROI (Return on Investment), is more of a streetwise rather than book-wise knowledge. Usually, you need to approach this

[49] www.upwork.com

[50] www.fiverr.com

[51] www.clarity.fm

like a research project: conducts trials using many versions of the ads, compare the results, and choose the best strategy based on this comparison.

To sum up, self-promotion works best in entrepreneurship, freelancing, and to some extent, also in academia.

Is the recruitment process always fair?

What about the underrepresented groups—women, ethical minorities, people who visually stand out? It is a controversial subject, but I will dare to say: *it obviously should be*, and let's hope that one day it will be. But in practice, it's still not always the case, unfortunately. And in some tribes—it is not true at all (Fig. 5).

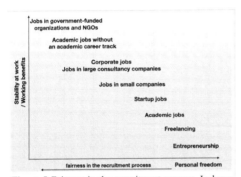

Figure 5 Fairness in the recruitment process. In large government-funded institutions and large companies, you can typically expect fair, centrally regulated salaries and working benefits regardless of the minority you represent. Unfortunately, small private companies can still be more of a jungle, and it might require good negotiation skills from you to secure the working conditions comparable with those of employees coming from privileged groups.

In large, government-funded institutions, it is usually illegal to offer varying salaries to employees occupying the same positions, regardless of their gender or any other external factors. It is also why I marked an academic career as an exception in this picture: since these positions are usually directly or indirectly funded by the government, the national labor agreement protects the employees against unfair salary schemes. So, if you are going for an academic career, you can feel safe that your salary should not significantly depend on the minority that you represent. In the corporate environment, there is also pressure on remunerating employees' work equally.

Unfortunately, this fairness is much less pronounced in small companies and freelancing. Budding entrepreneurs are usually in survival mode and try to cut costs in every possible way. Usually, startups don't offer a fixed salary associated with a given position—they'll pay you as much as you can negotiate. As women tend to use their elbows when negotiating a salary to a lesser extent than men, and they are more compromising, they often end up with a worse offer than male employees who accepted the same position. They also often suffer from prejudgment, and as freelancers, they get worse bids from potential clients. In some countries such as Iceland (Wills, 2018), there are attempts to improve this situation by regulating salaries and delegalizing wage differences between genders in any professional setting. However, we are still far from complete fairness, and solving this problem will take a long time.

What about my language?

Many researchers decide to transfer to industry once they work abroad. Many of them would prefer to settle in their current location, yet they don't speak the local language. This is understandable; in academia, we live in a bubble in which we speak English 24/7. Plus, we often have so little free time left that we prefer to choose some more relaxing activities than just spending this time on loading our brains with a new language.

But then, the question arises: what about my language skills? How does this influence my career opportunities? Where can I go without knowing the local language? Well, it would be negligence to say that with a limited aptitude to speak the local language, you'll have the same career opportunities as native speakers. You won't. Especially for the roles that require close contact with clients, such as a Medical Science Liaison, a perfect command of the local language is required. However, for the roles within the company, especially in the departments such as R&D, it's often the case that English *is* the working language. It's also true that even when the command of the local language is expected, it might be acceptable for the employer if you speak the language on the *communicative level* at first and express your strong motivation to improve. Locals are typically very patient with foreigners who make their best efforts to speak their language, yet make mistakes here and there. As an example, most American companies are densely populated by ex-pats hired because of their competencies and working experience, and not because of their proficient English. And how do the American companies function in the market? Very well. American employers also recognize the need to make their crew more multiligual as the shortage of foreign language skills is negatively impacting their revenues (Franks, 2019).

Therefore, please don't be afraid to apply for local jobs. If your language is not proficient, it's good to indicate this in your letter and refer to your language level (e.g., as Intermediate), but also express a strong will to settle and polish your language skills. It also might be a good idea to pick up some courses while you are looking for jobs. Firstly, your language will improve, and secondly, you will be able to demonstrate to the recruiters that you, indeed, make your best efforts to adapt.

Other tips for your job application process

Lastly, I would like to bring together some other tips concerning job hunting that should work for most researchers regardless of the discipline.

➤ Learn about the local standards for resumes.

There are differences between standards for resumes in various countries. One example is the dilemma of whether or not you should put your photograph on the resume. In North America, this is not welcome as the hiring procedure should be as

123

unbiased as possible concerning demographics such as age, sex, or ethnicity, as well as potentially distracting factors such as facial features. In Europe on the contrary, e.g., in Germany, putting a headshot on your resume is still expected. Probably the fastest way of figuring out what the local standards are at the moment is to ask a few friends in your area to share the resumes which they have recently applied with for publicly announced jobs—and got successful. After viewing 3-5 of them, you will get the picture.

➤ Make your resume letter transparent.

As mentioned before, the content of your resume is more important than the format. However, neatly formatting your resume will help in job applications. As the famous eye-tracking study by *TheLadders* has demonstrated, the average time spent on evaluating one application by a recruiter can be as low as 7.4 seconds[52]. It is why creating a good first impression is so important. There are dozens of free guidebooks on how to format your resume available online—for this reason, I won't focus on this topic here. One comment I'd like to make here is that, if you are familiar with *LaTeX* syntax, you might also consider putting your resume together in *LaTeX* using one of the beautiful templates available on *Overleaf*[53].

The opinions about the format in which you should send resumes are mixed. According to some sources, sending a resume in a .doc format is a must as recruiters might need to copy some information to special forms before passing your information to recruiters of higher rank within the company. It is often the case in large companies that need to do pre-screening of applications because they receive hundreds of resumes per position. Your resume in editable format can look very different when opened from another system though. Therefore, if there is an option, I would submit *both* the editable version and the rendered .pdf.

➤ "Shall I mention about my *Coursera* courses in the resume?"

Many PhDs take the initiative and acquire new competencies by taking online courses on *Coursera*[54], *Udemy*[55], *Khan Academy*[56], and other websites to better prepare for jobs in hot sectors such as (currently!) data science. Then, the question arises: shall I mention my online courses in my resume? Will this be treated as a legitimate achievement? Or rather, will this be seen as desperation?

Well, there are courses and courses—some are more prestigious than others. A course released by a respected institution such as Stanford University that ends with an online exam might be more credible than some other, more anonymous courses in which the course certificate is easy to get. But the truth is, you will get the best results if the courses you take include some deliverables that you might link to your

---

[52] Note however that the methodology used in this study received some criticism (Slack, 2019).

[53] www.overleaf.com/gallery/tagged/cv

[54] www.coursera.org

[55] www.udemy.com

[56] www.khanacademy.org

application, e.g., a *GitHub* repository that contains your codes from the course assignments. Then, the recruiter will be able to view your work and assess your practical skills.

To sum up, as a rule of thumb, it's good to mention online courses thematically related to the position you are applying for—it can only help you, and in the worst case, it won't make a difference. If you took a lot of courses, you might consider cherry-picking the most prestigious ones. Don't forget to link the outcome of your online projects!

➤ Brace yourself and prepare for interviews the best you can—not only in terms of what company you apply for but also in terms of general negotiation strategies.

One useful skill that we don't acquire in graduate school is *negotiating*. In most countries, PhD salaries are fixed, and we never need to negotiate the salary. This drawback will certainly come out in the interview at some point. In my experience, this lack of negotiation skills and focus on the content of the projects rather than on financial conditions not only hamper your chances for a good remuneration as an employee but can also negatively impact your working conditions as an entrepreneur. Namely, when the new startup is being established, the initial division of shares between founders has the major influence on all your future motivation and personal benefits from the company. If you cannot negotiate a decent, fair portion of the cake then, you'll always have a feeling of being undervalued, and your motivation to work will soon evaporate.

First of all, why is the question about the salary expectations so hard for job candidates? Well, it's hard for a few independent reasons. Salary talk is nothing else than negotiations—and in any negotiations, the side that has more information is in a privileged position by default. The recruiter knows precisely (1) what they are prepared to offer to the employee on this position, (2) what the salary expectations of other top candidates for this position are, (3) how well you rank in their books compared to other candidates in the competition. You don't know any of this!

Furthermore, you are usually in a weaker position than the recruiter; unless you have some scarce competencies that they badly need, you need them more than they need you. Namely, if you don't accept the contract, most likely some other competent candidate will—so in the worst case, they might lose these 2-3 hours spent on reading through your documents and interviewing you, and the man-hours of the recruiting team respectively. On the contrary, you can potentially lose weeks or even months of employment and a chance to develop your professional career in the direction you wish. The side that has more to lose, is usually in a weaker position to start with.

Lastly, the recruiter is a professional who went through the process of recruiting people hundreds (or even thousands) of times. Thus, they will know much better how to maneuver in negotiations than you. So, if you feel insecure before negotiating the salary, you have good reasons. It *is* stressful—to everyone. If you feel stressed in this situation, it is actually a *good* sign: it means that you are not insane and that you have a healthy degree of self-preservation instinct.

So, how to best approach this question? Well, most textbooks and professional recruiters will tell you, "Do your research through *Glassdoor* and find out what the range on this particular positioning in this particular company is." Yet, it is not as easy as it seems! The point is, the bigger the company, the more information you can get online. *But* at the same time, the bigger the company, the less flexibility the recruiter has when it comes to proposing a salary. A corporation is like an army, and the rules for salaries are very strict and depend on the position title, and the professional experience of the candidate—otherwise, the corporation would encounter issues with integrity because some employees might feel undervalued or mistreated. So, you might read on *Glassdoor* than in the company that interests you, the spread of salaries on the position of Senior Data Scientist is 50k-70k and you might think to yourself, "Great, it seems that I can earn up to 70k!"—only to learn at the interview that it is only so in theory. And that to the professional with your experience in this field (or lack thereof), the recruiter can only propose a number between 52k and 56k and not a penny more.

And how about small companies? Well, in startups and small companies, people who are in power to employ you, are usually engaged in the recruitment process from the start. They often have more power to adjust the salary to the candidate because they co-own the company and dictate the rules. They are often also able to better recognize your individuality and appreciate your unique skills than the corporate recruiters. However, small companies are much harder to research online—they have low numbers of employees and the number of information scales accordingly. Plus, employees working in small companies don't share information all that eagerly because they don't feel anonymous.

Altogether, your research will give you a vague picture of what you can ask for. The first question to answer to yourself would be: is this range motivating to you? Would you feel appreciated by this remuneration for your hard work? If the answer is "no," perhaps it is better to look for another option; taking a job with a plan to look for something else straight away usually backfires. If the answer is "yes," think of two numbers: the amount that would make you feel highly valued and shake hands right at the spot, versus your "minimum": the minimal amount that you would agree to work for. You need to have both these numbers on your mind before going to the interview.

And now comes the interview. Firstly, I would like to say that there is no consensus in the recruitment industry upon the *optimal* strategy for negotiating salaries. I will mention some popular approaches here and mention which strategy is the most efficient in my opinion.

➤ Approach #1: You should always give a range of salaries during the interview.

Well, if you say, "50k-70k," the recruiter hears "50k." They are paid for getting someone to do the job for as cheap as possible, so why would they agree to pay you more if you already revealed that you would be willing to accept 50k? It won't happen.

Plus, there are just two scenarios possible. Firstly, let's assume that your range and your employer's range overlap: your minimum is lower than the maximum they are prepared to pay you. Well, in that case, by explicitly revealing your range you lose a chance to be offered the maximum of what they were prepared for. In other words, you lose the opportunity. The second scenario is even worse. What if you overdo and your range is above the employer's range, i.e., your minimum is higher than the maximum they are prepared to pay you? Well, in this case, the negotiations will be broken as the recruiter gets a clear message that you will not agree to work for the remuneration they were planning to offer. In either case, it is just a suboptimal strategy.

➤ Approach #2: You should just browse through *Glassdoor*, find the salary range for this position at this company, and set the range that starts in half the range and ends at the top of the range.

It is also a suboptimal strategy. Firstly, it requires proposing a salary range. Secondly, as mentioned before, *Glassdoor* information can be misleading and lead to unrealistic expectations. Beware that at this stage, the employer usually already has some ranking of preferred candidates, often graded. Even if you are the top candidate in the employer's books, claiming an unreasonably high salary will not serve you well and might cause the employer to go with the runner up instead. Therefore, if you give the recruiter at a large company a number that falls way beyond their range, they might resign from offering you a contract.

➤ Approach #3: You should wait for the recruiter's number and negotiate up from this point.

Firstly, a professional recruiter most likely won't reveal what they are prepared to pay you, and they will do everything they can to let you give your numbers first. There are exceptions, of course, e.g., traineeship positions are often associated with fixed salaries which the recruiter is prepared to openly inform you about. However, for most positions, the salary can be negotiated, and in all these cases it's in the recruiter's best business to learn about your expectations first. And, they usually have years or even decades of experience!

Refusing to respond to this question is not a good idea as it might lead to the premature end of negotiations—the recruiter might simply interpret your lack of cooperation as stubbornness and lack of team spirit. You just have to say *something*.

➤ Approach #4: Give your numbers in a way that is not confrontational but rather, encourages the recruiter to negotiate with you.

You can, for instance, say, "If I was offered 65k today, I would feel highly valued and shake hands right now at the spot. Is this possible?" If this number falls out of the range that the recruiter is prepared to offer, they will simply say, "Not really, but for the start, we can offer you…"—and then, the recruiter will make a counteroffer. As long as your proposal is not outrageous, they will most likely be willing to negotiate.

In my opinion, this is the best strategy: it doesn't indicate to the recruiter where your minimum is and at the same time, they will need to reveal the amount they are prepared to pay you in their counteroffer—and that gives you plenty of information about the range for further negotiations.

Additionally, please find some general advice on salary negotiation strategies below:
a) Regardless of which strategy you choose, you should come up with two numbers before the interview, i.e., the minimum amount you require to accept the contract

and the desired amount that will make you feel highly valued and shake hands straight away.

b) *Wait* with negotiating the salary for the moment when the recruiter asks about it. Most employers won't ask you about your salary expectations early in the recruitment process, but rather, they will wait until your second or further interview (there are exceptions, of course). It is *not* a good idea to raise this topic by yourself during the interview; it's much better to wait until the employer starts the conversation. It will also work on your behalf if you first had a chance to enchant the employer with your competencies and personality and let them desire to work with you and talk about the money later on. Thus, patience pays off here. If the recruiter happens to ask you about the salary very early in the conversation, try to postpone the negotiations for as long as possible. You can always say that you first need to get more information about the responsibilities, the team, and the working conditions before you will be able to come up with your final number. If you say this politely and with a smile, the recruiter will go along with it as it doesn't sound like "no."

c) On the other hand, when it comes to this moment, don't be afraid to negotiate. If you receive a draft of a contract, it means that the recruiters want to see you in the company and that they are willing to negotiate with you! The salary talk is a clear sign from the employer that you are a serious contender for the job—usually, recruiters only schedule such conversations with the top 2-3 candidates for the position. Thus, if you politely explain your expectations, smile, and justify all your questions/requests, the worst that can happen is a polite, "Unfortunately, this is beyond our current capabilities"—and further negotiations.

d) As mentioned before, it is often the case that the recruiter needs to stick to a particular salary range—for instance because it's a corporation and there are fixed salary levels within the company. Remember that it doesn't matter how much cash you get per month—it matters how much stays in your wallet after you pay all your bills. In that case, you might try to negotiate other benefits that can reduce your fixed monthly costs: a company car, a reimbursement of the commuting costs, covering health insurance costs for your family members, covering the kindergarten costs, covering relocation costs, etc. Sometimes, it is enough to smile and ask. Remember that if, say, $100 more stays in your wallet every year, then over the next 30 years, this difference will accumulate to over $30,000 (and much more if you invest this amount every month; if you can gain 4-5% interest per year, this amount will grow to $100,000 and more). Therefore, celebrate any little success in negotiations! Even if it seems to be peanuts at first glance.

➣ Apply to companies that already hire other PhDs.

…and, for positions where you expect other PhDs to apply. If your education level is much higher than the education level of all the rest of the applicants, it is a bit like entering a shady club as an uptown girl. Most guys will be too scared to approach you as they assume that you are used to a different standard of life than they could offer you, or they assume that you are always surrounded by guys, and you might get bored with them quickly. And, those guys who nevertheless decide to approach you, might do it for all the wrong reasons: because it is prestigious to show up with an uptown girl next to you, or because they know they can profit from dating a rich girl.

And now, imagine that you are the only applicant among 100 applicants that holds a PhD title. Many recruiters might think, "Well, if we don't reaaaally need a person with a PhD for this position, and if we propose them a contract that we use to offer to people with the Master's title, they'll likely be unhappy about the financial conditions." Or, "This person has such a good education and might go work everywhere, so why did they choose us? They are probably in a bad financial situation so this is an emergency for them; as soon as they'll find something better, they'll switch jobs in a split second." Or, they might think, "We don't have any PhDs in the company yet, but it might be good for marketing purposes. Perhaps, it's better to accept this person and put their name on the company website." Or, "PhDs are hard workers, so if I hire this person, they'll probably be willing to work double hard, and produce more than others for the same salary." None of these options sounds very good.

Of course, it is often hard to check if other PhDs already work in the company that interests you. You can search for this type of information through their website, *Glassdoor*, and *LinkedIn*. You might also find a friend of a friend who works there. As a rule of thumb, large companies with R&D departments should have some population of PhDs working for them.

And to be honest, this rule is just a heuristic that works well for most people. In fact, you have two choices worth considering: you either should look for a place where PhDs are common or exactly *the other way around*: a place where PhDs are so scarce that the doctoral title next to your name gives you some edge in the market and additional credibility. For instance, a PhD title can slightly increase your chances of landing an investment for your startup as it gives some evidence that you are capable of successfully bringing large and complex projects to the end. This second path is much more difficult than the first one though. Namely, this approach is burdened with a huge risk that, as the only PhD around, you will end up in an environment that you won't mentally fit. It also requires much more patience and adaptation/self-navigation skills before it ever pays off.

➤ Don't sabotage your own job search.

The common mistake that many people make when looking for jobs is that they spend 5-10% of the time looking for job offers online, they find a bunch of offers that are merely OK-ish, and then spend the rest of the time writing motivational letters and applying. To my mind, this is not the optimal approach. It is well worth to spend much more time looking for job offers that sound great to you and that you feel excited about—so excited that you feel your heartbeat while reading—even if this means much fewer job offers in the pipeline. There are two main reasons for this.

The first reason is that, if you respond to offers which you are *just OK* with, there is a high chance that the recruiter on the other side will have a similarly (non)-enthusiastic reaction to your application - since this job doesn't fit your expectations and/or experience in 100%, your resume also won't fit the expectations in 100%. The second and even more important reason is that, in case you apply for jobs for which are far from your dream job, you might sabotage yourself. What I mean is: if deep inside, you believe that you don't want to end up in *this* job, you might subconsciously write an application in a dry, uninteresting way and give the recruiter no reason to think of you as the right candidate for the job.

➤ Track your job applications process.

It's good to document all the vacancies you've applied to so far. While applying to a particular company, you don't send letters for various positions that are very different from each other. It is perfectly fine to identify a few different types of positions that you are interested in—many people do that with great success. For instance, let's say that you would enjoy working as a Data Scientist, but you are also interested in science communication and science education positions. You need to make sure that you don't apply for these different types of jobs to the same company —this might lower your credibility to the recruiter. You will need to tailor your resume and rewrite your motivational letter for every application—so, if the same recruiter happens to read all these letters, they will be confused about who you are and to what extent any of these documents represents the core of your expertise and job preferences. On the other hand, if you apply to two or more positions that are close in the scope of responsibilities, e.g., a Junior Data Scientist and a Senior Data Scientist, the recruiter will accept this approach. It is also good to be transparent and mention in the letter that you already applied for another position within the company.

➤ Take the aptitude tests seriously.

Many companies conduct batteries of tests before admitting you to the final round of job interviews. Some companies do this at the very early stage, even before the first interview, while other companies do this at the late stage—there is no rule here. Although many commercial aptitude tests and personality tests out there rely on a weak methodology, companies still rely on them as some proxy for the quality and fit of the candidates. It usually happens when the employer gets so many candidates per position that they need to make a strict selection of candidates. Therefore, the results might influence your chances of getting invited to the interview.

Generally, there are three main types of tests:

a) Classic IQ tests. The Raven's Progressive Matrices Test (Raven, 1936) is the most classic IQ test to date. The test is based on the concept of *fluid intelligence* associated with a pure processing speed—as opposed to the *crystallized intelligence* that depends on the semantic knowledge you have acquired over a lifetime). The idea behind the test is that fluid intelligence is something we are born with, and it should not depend on our language or culture. For this reason, this test does not include any tasks that require linguistic skills or semantic knowledge. Instead, all the tasks involve looking for patterns in a set of pictograms. This test is widely used while making admissions to the MENSA association and in many other applications. Because of its popularity, it's not used by companies as often anymore—it's just too easy to find examples online and prepare for it. However, companies often look for similar, culturally neutral IQ tests based on the concept of fluid intelligence and order these tests from companies specialized in testing cognitive skills of all kinds. Even though there's a low probability that you will get Raven's test, I would still recommend going through this test online to practice solving this type of task—you might be challenged with something similar. Also, remember that many companies might ask you to first go through the full version of the tests online but then rerun a shortened form of the tests during the interview at the company's headquarters to validate that you were honest in the process. Thus, if you decide to cheat and solve the test together with friends, this might backfire later. I would advise you to be honest here and to solve the test all by yourself.

b) Motivational questionnaires/tests. Although the recruiter will assess your motivation during the interview, some companies also attempt to put a number on your motivation level. In the associated tests and questionnaires, you will get multiple questions about the situations in which you feel (de)motivated, e.g., "If you are participating in a project as a leader and you are held accountable, does this increase/decrease your motivation to pursue the project?" To be honest, most questions in such tests are burdened with *social approval*, and I don't think this assessment can ever become a reliable tool to assess motivation. Social approval means that you know straight away which answer is expected of you so that you can bias your answer to adhere to these expectations. It's sad to say, but most people choose to bleach themselves to appear super-motivated. Thus, it's not necessarily a good idea to be fully honest in these tests and mention about your moments of weakness (which we all have!)—you might easily land in the left tail of the Gaussian then. In this case, I would advise you to go for the answer that would sound better to the employer every single time when you hesitate between two options—sounds ugly, but it increases your chances to end up with a good score. And if you happen to be an employer who is reading this book: stop using this type of test! :) They are extremely biased by design.

c) Personality tests. It's also a common practice to conduct personality tests, e.g., OCEAN, or CANOE based on the concept of a five-dimensional personality model (Goldberg, 1993), or DISC based on a four-dimensional personality model (Marston, 1928). I would say that there is no one preferred profile that you should aim for here; the preferred personality of a candidate is highly dependent on the position, the team, and the company's vision. As a rule of thumb, all companies look for team players who are punctual, reliable, and with no neurotic traits. Other than that, preferences can vary. Thus, the best advice here would be: take the test seriously. Be honest, give it time, don't rush with the answers, and make sure that you fill the test in a relaxed state of mind and without any additional stimulation such as strong coffee—as this can make you more impulsive and substantially influence your results. Plus, be attentive to questions that relate to the level of your neuroticism and make sure that you don't come out as a complainer—no one wants to see a complainer in their office!

➤ Prepare for some magic questions that might come up during the job interview.

There are some questions that you might expect in the interview, and that always surprise unprepared candidates. One classic example is, "How do you see yourself in a perspective of five to ten years?" A different form of this question—asked with the same purpose—is, "How do you define success?" Almost everyone struggles with these types of questions!

First of all, no one expects you to have a clear vision of where you will be in five years' time. The whole point of the question is to figure out whether this job fits into your long-term career plans. Again, it all boils down to looking for an ambitious but *loyal* candidate. The recruiter wants to see that you are truly excited about the job and that this job fits into your career plans rather than being a mere plan B, or a "solution for now." Thus, if the recruiter hears an answer that is in any way contradictory with that the company offers, it will be a red flag to them.

So, how can one approach this question? It is good to make your answer truthful but rather general. You don't know the structure and policies within the company/organization in as much detail as the recruiter. Thus, if you are too specific, you might say something that is not possible to achieve, and the recruiter will know that. It's also good to reassure the recruiter about your interest in building your career with them. Of course, you cannot see the future, and many scenarios might play out, but the recruiter expects you to show your enthusiasm and a strong motivation to stay around.

➢ Don't speak about past negative experiences during your job interview.

Some PhDs choose industry as a new path of personal development even if they had a very positive experience in their academic job while for others, it is a lucky escape. If you had any negative experiences in your previous workplace, remember that if you mention any of this experience during the job interview, it will be seen negatively. For instance, if you make critical comments about your previous boss, the recruiter will think, "This person talks badly about their past employers. I don't want to be the next one in this chain!"

It's also better to avoid talking about difficult times at work, e.g., a sick leave. The sick leave is a construct that exists in some of the developed countries. Going on a sick leave means that your mental health does not allow you to continue working for some time (which, unfortunately, often happens to young academics). Usually, the employer is still obliged to pay the employee a salary during this period. Regardless of the reasons behind your past sick leave(s), it will not look great to the employer. They will think, "This person is weak on their mind and cannot handle stress. If I sign the contract, I might need to pay for yet another sick leave in the future—and God knows for how long." As a result, most likely, you will get rejected then, and you'll get some arbitrary explanation for this decision.

So, it is good to prepare for the question: "Why are you searching for a job outside academia?" before you go to the interview. You can treat this as an exercise in diplomacy! It is good to go for either neutral or positive answers such as "I was always interested in this market sector, and I see my future in this area," or "I would like to see more practical, real-world applications of my work than I experienced while doing fundamental academic research."

➢ It's a good practice to send an email to the recruiter after the interview.

There are cultural differences between countries in terms of whether or not you should email the recruiter after the job interview to thank them for the opportunity and express your further interest in the job. For instance, in Northern America, this is a common practice, while in Europe, this is rare. I believe that kindness always pays off in one way or another—and if you are the only candidate who emails the recruiter after the interview, that's even better for you. Thus, I would recommend to send such a polite note within 24 hours after your job interview.

➤ Learn to get over rejections.

As a researcher, you are probably thinking right now, "Rejection? Tell me about it." But wait a second. Rejection when applying for jobs is not the same *type* of rejection as getting rejected while publishing papers. Namely, when your manuscript is getting rejected, it is a piece of your work that represents some concept. On the other hand, if you are rejected as a job candidate, it is YOU as a person who gets rejected—not your project, your idea, or your product. It is the reason why when you are applying for jobs, you need to prepare for a whole new level of rejection.

Furthermore—bringing back the analogy between recruiters and editors of the academic journals—you will rarely hear the truth about *why* you didn't get the job. Most of the time, you will get "feedback" that "other candidates better fit the position" even if the reality is different. You might get rejected because the recruiter found one worrying sentence, either in your motivational letter or during the job interview. For instance, in your letter, you included the information that you hold a sole-proprietorship as a side-hustle—which might suggest to the recruiter that all you want from the job is a paycheck. Or, during the interview, you asked if it is possible to work three days per week, which might suggest to the recruiter that you cannot commit enough. Or, perhaps, the position was promised to someone else. Or, the recruiter has a subjective feeling that they don't want to work with you, and they cannot even explain why. As a consequence, you will never know the truth unless you have insider information. It also means that dwelling too much about the rejections is a loss of your time.

It is good to keep in mind that recruiters need to be discrete about the employer's hiring policies and it is often treated as part of the company's IP. They are also a bit like fashion designers who need to pick a model to take part in their fashion show. They have their own private taste, plus the show is usually arranged in a very specific style in which all models need to represent the same face and body type. As a result, not necessarily the most beautiful models get chosen for the catwalk, but rather, the ones that happen to find themselves at the right time and place, and meet the expectations for the given show—even if they have the oddest face. Homework for you: watch one season of *America's Next Top Model* and you'll instantly get better at handling rejections in the job application process.

➤ If you take a major career turn, you need to accept that your earnings might drop for the time being.

The stereotypical view of industry is that the private sector is associated with better working benefits—but this is not always the case. If your first job in industry is very close to your PhD research line, you might enjoy a senior contract and most probably, also an increase in your salary. However, if you are taking a major career turn and getting into a new field in which you'll need to learn the know-how from

133

scratch, you might need to accept that your position will be more junior or even have a traineeship status. It might also imply a temporary drop in your salary.

Some PhDs are disappointed to find out that their first industry jobs are not as much of an Eldorado as expected. It is, however, not strictly associated with career turns from academia to industry, but rather, with *every* career switch—it is often the price to pay for changing a profession and trying something new. Nevertheless, it is most often the right decision to take this financial hit as an investment in yourself that will further help you increase the number of long-term career opportunities. Plus, the drop in salary is only temporary.

For the first few years after leaving academia, you might experience some disadvantages of your PhD compared to those who spent all this time in industry. You will have all the technical knowledge, but you will miss the insights about the industry, the right contacts, and some soft skills that allow professionals to maneuver between others and get promoted. But at some point, you will learn all you need to succeed. And then, once you integrate what you now know about industry with your strong self-management and analytic skills developed in your academic career, you will outrace other professionals in your field and become unstoppable! You just need to be patient and treat your new job as an investment.

➤ An unfinished PhD makes things even more complicated to recruiters.

If you are still going through your PhD, and especially if your contract has already expired, many recruiters—both in academia and industry—can ask about your PhD title, or at least, about the scheduled date of the PhD defense during the recruitment procedure. There is also some probability that you won't even get invited to the interview if you don't have the PhD title next to your name yet. The primary reason is that the recruiters don't know the details of your PhD program, and cannot predict how much longer the completion of your PhD might potentially take. Some PhD candidates take years to finish their thesis after their contracts expire. While working for their next employer, they still spend some part of their mental power on finishing the thesis after working hours. Your employer not only pays for 40 hours of your time per week but also for the fact that you come to work rested and energetic every day—therefore, they can see the necessity for you to finish your thesis on the side as an argument against employing you.

Therefore, if you are still in the pre-defense phase, it's good to proceed towards submitting the thesis to the committee as soon as you can. You'll get many more job opportunities if you can inform the recruiter by when you'll receive your PhD title—and ideally, defend and get the title.

➤ Remember that the recruitment is about the odds.

Once the human factor is in the game, there is always an element of a lottery in it. Even if you are the most appropriate candidate for the position, you are never guaranteed to get recruited. It is a bit similar to taking an exam: sometimes you study hard, and you feel confident that you learned everything, but the teacher will come up with surprising questions about details which you overlooked, and you will get a worse score than you should, or that you feel you deserve. The whole recruitment process aims at spotting the right person for the position, but it is always only based on a certain probability. Therefore, you can use some of the techniques mentioned above to increase your chances, but these will not guarantee success. If you get rejected, do not get discouraged, and don't let this influence your self-perception!

The take-home message

1. Researchers often need to face recruiters' stereotypes, and make a few common mistakes in job interviews. Learning about these mental traps before you apply for jobs, will also help you in presenting yourself well to the recruiter.

2. Recruiters aim to make a safe choice: find an employee who has enough competencies necessary to do the job—preferably demonstrated in practice— and mentally fits the tribe. It doesn't always mean that the candidate with the strongest resume will get the job!

3. Start the job search early on, and dedicate some time to find job offers for the jobs which you *really* want to get. Write high-quality applications, both content-wise, and layout-wise. Do your research about the companies you are applying to.

4. Verify your beliefs about the private sector. You need to develop trust in the societal impact of the projects you are applying for.

5. Network as much as you can, and take care of your online visibility and image. You are your own PR agent from now on!

6. The optimal choice of the job search strategy depends on the type of working environment you are going for.

7. Learn some basic negotiation strategies before going to job interviews. Wait for the recruiter to start talking about the salary!

8. Track the companies that are of interest to you.

9. Take the aptitude tests seriously.

10. If you represent a minority, in some environments in the private sector, you might experience less fair working conditions than in the public sector. In those tribes, you will need to be assertive to get a good offer—it's possible though!

CHAPTER 6

SELF-DISCIPLINE

Self-discipline is key

Unfortunately, it is sometimes the case that broad research experience does not result in instant opportunities in industry. Somewhat paradoxically, the more talent and skill you have, and the more advanced you are in your academic career, the more time it might take you to find a job suited to those skills and talents. Therefore, it is good to prepare yourself mentally for a potentially protracted process and to maintain mental hygiene throughout.

Once your contract expires, you will need laser focus to transition to your new profession smoothly. It entails a commitment to go for some activities (such as polishing your resume, networking, etc.) but also *avoid* tempting but detrimental actions and behaviors. For instance, after the academic contract expires, many PhDs lose their sleeping rhythm, start binge-watching *Netflix*, neglect meetings face-to-face, and spend excessive amounts of time on social media. It is unhealthy, and in the long run, it will decrease your chances of landing your dream job. Job interviews don't typically go well when you are tired, unfocused, and out of energy. Maintaining self-discipline and a positive attitude throughout the process is the key!

Let's say this clearly: working on your own *is* hard. Firstly, you'll miss the casual, everyday contact with people. Chatting to others—even if it is just a little small talk around coffee—gives us a sense of belonging in the long run. Without these daily little personal contacts in the workplace, from exchanging smiles in the corridor to birthday greetings and small celebrations, one can slowly descend into depression. Secondly, it's hard to work from home because you lose your reference for comparing your performance with others. *Comparing* is a very natural behavior, and we subconsciously do it all the time. For instance, would you be concerned that taking a lunch break for the whole hour is counterproductive? If all your coworkers take the same lunch break (as this is a general habit at your workplace), you probably wouldn't have these concerns. But, when you are working from home, you can't see in real-time what other people in the same situation are currently doing and whether or not you are falling behind. It can generate a sense of guilt and an impression that you never really do enough. Thirdly, working from home is hard because you face more temptations than usual. No one is looking at you from behind your shoulders to check whether you keep on working. The dopamine generators like *Facebook, Twitter, Netflix,* or *YouTube*, are all there, smiling at you from the open tabs in your browser. The fridge full of tasty food is nearby. The beam of sunlight from the window makes you think that it would be nice to do some gardening or go on a walk in the park.

It bears mentioning that keeping self-discipline is a piece of more general life advice that goes well beyond the job search. You might have heard of the famous research study on the determinants of life success that originated in Dunedin, New Zealand, in 1971. In this study, over 1,000 newborn children got enrolled since the day they were born—and the study is going to last for their whole lives. The subject of the study is "life success" in the broad sense—from health, through relationships, to financial wealth. So, what came out of this huge, (so far) 50-year research initiative? As it turned out, the best predictor of life success is *self-discipline in children* (Moffitt et al., 2011). It matters more than your IQ, the social status of the family that raised you, or even your emotional intelligence. Just food for thought!

And now, coming back to the job search:

Keep a stable daily rhythm, and organize yourself an office

One of the biggest sins you can commit after your contract expires is to lose your daily rhythm. As mentioned before, unfortunately, many people do. Sometimes, they believe that they just found themselves on unplanned and/or unwanted vacation. So, they want to take advantage of the situation by doing whatever they wish whenever they want for the time being. And sometimes, they do this involuntarily as they miss self-discipline to keep the weekly rhythm once they no longer have daily duties such as obligatory weekly seminars, lab meetings, and such. Failing to work out a new lifestyle in which you can stay healthy, productive, and keep regular face-to-face interactions with other people, can lead to a severe mental breakdown within a few months (or sometimes, even a few weeks). For this reason, caring about yourself once you are home is *as important* for your odds of landing a job as caring about how you present yourself at job interviews. After all, home is your corner: it's the place to which you return after every job interview to rest and recharge before the next one.

If you don't rest properly and lose your daily rhythm, the voice of your *intuition* might also become too weak to be heard. Intuition is your internal, subconscious navigation system that helps you in making good decisions and reaching out to the right people (I will further elaborate in chapter 8: *Self-Discovery: A Process That Lasts For a Lifetime*).

For all these reasons, if you are now in the process of looking for jobs and your contract has expired, I would strongly advise you to *approximate your former working style* while adapting to your current situation. It's good to imitate the same *weekly*

138

rhythm as before: wake up on weekday mornings and do some work until late afternoon (or whatever your preferred working pattern is)—even if this work is limited to searching for employment options and drafting motivational letters. Applying for jobs is an intellectual effort, and this mindset will help you stay focused on the task.

Figure 6 Natalia's home office.

And what about the office? If you are still allowed to work at your desk in your former institution, e.g., to finish some lagging research projects, it is, in general, a good idea to take this opportunity. Otherwise, there are also public libraries that you might be willing to access for free. If none of these options are available, you can still organize a nice, cozy office at home. You can also arrange facilities that you otherwise would not have in your office. As an example, my home office looks like this (Fig. 6). One advantage of this office is something I would never enjoy while working at a university or in a company: close proximity to a wine stand. And the fridge is only a few meters away. Just show me another office as cool as that!

When working from home, it's also important to also *save your mercy for other people*. What I often notice in people who can successfully carry on with working in isolation, is that they have *double standards for empathy*. It sounds counterintuitive, but to stay in command of your life while working from home, you need to treat yourself *worse* than you would treat other people. Namely, in situations when you would recommend someone who works for you (or your student) to rest—as they feel tired, dizzy, demotivated, or ill—you need to tell yourself to keep quiet and continue working instead. If you are not hard on yourself and let yourself rest every time it feels right, your mind will soon create more and more reasons to complain and take breaks.

Actively reach out to people

As mentioned before, another common disadvantage of ending contracts is that you might no longer have as easy access to people as before. At the office, you must chitchat with other people at least a few times throughout the day—even if this is only a few sentences exchanged at the coffee machine. It might have seemed unimportant and even distractive when you were an employee, but face-to-face contact is a basic human need, and you will soon feel the lack of it.

It's often the case that the social life of researchers pivots around work, especially if they are in graduate school. You go to lunch with colleagues on every working day, grab Friday drinks together, participate in the same *WhatsApp* groups, and other online circles... Pretty much every week, there is yet another barbecue, birthday party, graduation party, wedding, or a movie night you'll get invited to. You don't need to make much active effort to be around people in such conditions. This situation might suddenly change when your contract expires, and you disappear from your office. From experience, people in academia are so busy that some of them might start forgetting to invite you to places if they no longer see you around. And of course, all of a sudden, you start missing all those little off-topic, cheesy conversations by the coffee machine which were so annoying to you before.

It is a difficult situation because it is associated with losing a large part of your social peer support system and a feeling of isolation. What to do then? First, if you hear from your former colleagues less and less, don't panic. In 99 cases out of 100, this negligence is because people in science are overworked and do not have enough mental capacity to track all their friendships within and outside academia—and not because they actively decided to cross you off their friend list. You have to accommodate the fact that from now on, you will need to be more proactive to have a social life: call people and ask them out by yourself, schedule *Zoom* calls with friends living abroad, invite friends over to your place for dinner, or late-night drinks, etc. It takes a friend to have a friend.

But let's look at the bright sides of the situation. Namely, the good news is that, along with your newfound social distance, you will also experience more personal freedom. Now you can cherry-pick and spend time with the people whom you like the most and with those who contribute to your life in meaningful ways. As a matter of fact, in almost every competitive working environment (such as a research institute), some toxic people only take your energy. They undermine your achievements and make you feel bad about yourself, or they ignore you in obnoxious ways. Now you can have full control over who is a part of your life and who is not. And, you can focus on reaching out to the people who make you feel good and motivate you.

Facebook steals your life

We experience hundreds of distractions every day. On average, our generation absorbs five times more new information per day than the generation of our parents. Our brains have not undergone appreciable evolutionary development to accommodate this new "information economy," and so we are vulnerable to distractions.

Researchers (including the present author) often assume that—since from early childhood, they have always been the smartest person in the room—they are too reasonable, logical, or intelligent to succumb to marketing strategies used against them online. Unfortunately, this is far from the truth. Social media notifications stimulate the same reward loop in the brain as cocaine or gambling (Kuss & Griffiths, 2017). To make it worse, major social media players such as *Facebook* or *Twitter* hire teams of thousands of marketing and machine learning specialists—many of them being PhDs! The sole purpose of these teams is to work on designing algorithms to hook us in—by serving us personalized information, notifications, and clickbait content in a way that we cannot help checking out our social media and fishing for yet another dopamine shot. The recent movie *The Social Dilemma*[57] (2020) very well explains this problem. And, no one can stand this amount of persuasion—we are all equally vulnerable.

Especially after your contract expires, it is tempting to spend a lot of time on social media. You grow even more susceptible to the siren's call because your regular, daily contact with people is so limited. So, you go online, chat with friends, catch up with people you have not talked to for a long time or live abroad, you score some social points by liking other people's content and sending them birthday wishes. It feels like making progress and building *a network*. But is it real? Social media use is the same as any other potentially addictive, reward-driven behavior, so don't lie to yourself and say that you are networking when you're just procrastinating.

That said, social media isn't inherently bad, and it isn't going anywhere. Invitations to many events are sent through *Facebook*, and many papers are only becoming noticed in the scientific circles only because of *Twitter*. Of course, some hipsters disconnect from social media, but expecting this from everyone is unfair and misses the point. Social media is there for you and not the other way around.

Figure 7 Franz app. It is a free app that allows to log into all your email and social media accounts at once. In the same way, you can also disconnect from all your accounts all at once, and dive into deep work.

Therefore, it is good to limit the use of social media to some time slots during the day or the week. Also, ask yourself, "What do I expect from social media? What do I want to achieve?" You could think of reducing your number of social media accounts and focus on the ones that best suit your needs. For instance, if you are mostly interested in tracking and discussing new trends in science, or in observing and cheering research progress of your friends and colleagues living all over the globe, *Twitter* might be a good solution. *Twitter* gives you a better opportunity to select the content you prefer to see by following only individuals of your choice. This platform also contains fewer visual distractors than *Facebook* and some other social ad-heavy media (although recently, *Twitter* has also been flooded by flashy GIFs...). On the other hand, if you use social media to rest from work, and you are more interested in getting updated about what happens in your friends' lives rather than being notified about their new initiatives, *Facebook* might score higher in your ranking than *Twitter*.

Also, to be better protected from the dopamine boosts coming from social media throughout the day, you might completely disable notifications from your social

[57] www.netflix.com/title/81254224

media account on your phone, and install apps such as *Franz*[58] on your laptop. Franz is an app that allows you to log into multiple accounts at a time, from your email accounts, through your social media accounts to *Slack*[59] or *Trello*[60] groups and other popular collaboration platforms (Fig. 7). When you log into *Franz*, it will show you all the notifications received at all these accounts at once. If you log off, you are free to work in peace and you won't be bothered by anyone. As you certainly know, periods of deep work (Newport, 2016) during the day are crucial for productivity, and this tool might simply help you in getting in and out form this "deep work" mode conveniently while maintaining your fluent access to social media.

It's also important to clean your working memory from all the garbage consumed through social media—daily or weekly—by going for activities away from your laptop or a phone, e.g., sessions at the spa, gratitude walks in the park, a dinner with friends, a good movie, a dancing class, etc. You don't lose opportunities by sleeping 8 hours a day so what will happen if your phone will be off for another two hours during the day? Probably nothing.

How to keep your motivation high?

So, how to stay motivated in this period between contracts? Unfortunately, even though science has developed to an extent when we can send rockets to space, we still do not know much about human motivation. In a sense, we know that it *does not work* in the way that we wish it did. The human brain wires in a way that every activity which doesn't contribute to our most basic life functions—such as eating, sleeping, or proliferating—becomes a source of fear and can lead to procrastination.

For this reason, I believe that motivational techniques that focus on starting a task *as soon as possible* usually work better than those that involve rationalizing *why* you should perform a certain task. I highly recommend getting familiar with *the 5-second rule* by Mel Robbins (Robbins, 2017). Mel's point of view is that, given this natural tendency to fear challenging tasks, we only have about 5 seconds to start performing the task before our brains talk us out of it. This opinion is shared by a lot of successful individuals. For example, "Just do it!" is a tagline of *Nike* and a life motto of Michael Jordan. What also helps in keeping focused is writing down your goals or motivating statements (for instance, "I am now on my way towards my new dream job!," "Just reaching out for my first million!," or "Watch out b*s, here I come!") and putting them somewhere in front of your eyes: on the wall, in some little photo frame on your desk, etc.

Can working from home turn out to be good for you?

Yes! Even though for all the reasons specified above, working from home is hard for most people, it might also turn out to be your *preferred working style*. One

---

[58] www.meetfranz.com

[59] www.slack.com

[60] www.trello.com

benefit of the home office is that it gives you yet another opportunity for a little self-discovery. Namely, you might suddenly discover that you have an affinity toward working in peace and quiet, without distractions or a dress code—and that you actually enjoy working from home. You might also notice that you were simply born with self-discipline that allows you to work from home efficiently. This might also be a strong indication that you might enjoy working as a freelancer and/or entrepreneur. Also, while working from home you'll have some advantages, time-wise. The clearest advantage is the absence of the daily commute. But, please don't squander this time on unhealthy behaviors! Meditation, exercise, and healthy home cooking are all good alternatives and productive uses of your newfound time.

Actually, when the corona crisis broke out, lots of people around the world realized that working from home has its perks and that they would actually prefer to work from home in the future—so, you might come to the same conclusion! Not mentioning that given this recent moment in human history, in the near future, working from home can become the new normal.

What to do with delayed research projects?

One common problem encountered by PhDs moving to industry is delayed research projects. This is all the research that you hoped to finish and publish while your contract was still going on, but that you did not manage (most likely, for the reason that isn't under your control). These projects in limbo can cause you additional stress while you are looking for a new job. After all, they took many years of dedicated work, so you can't just abandon them without a second thought. And it is often the case that the projects are efforts shared with multiple people.

So, what to do in such a situation? In brief, you have three options:
a) First, find a new job, and then try to finish the projects after working hours,
b) First, finish the projects, and then move to search for jobs full-time,
c) Put your unfinished projects on hold, or delegate them to other researchers.

And, even if you choose to finish the projects, you still have the following choices:
a) Be selective about the projects you plan to finish: choose only projects which give the best chances to be published, and drop the rest,
b) Finish all the projects regardless of how impactful they might be.

There is no simple answer to which line of choice is the best one here. Of course, if finishing some of the projects is the prerequisite for you to graduate from your PhD, you should finish them—either now or later. Other than that, there are no clear rules—this depends on your priorities and on your resilience to stress.

As a matter of fact, from the very day your contract expires, looking for a new job should be your top priority. Many researchers keep on finishing their projects for many months after their contracts expire and postpone the job search. This is a huge mistake, and further impedes their chances to land a good position as the first job in industry. There are two main reasons for this. Firstly, because when you get used to working for free, it will make you a weaker negotiator when it comes to talking about

143

the salary at the interviews. Secondly, because you get a hole in your resume which won't look good to your potential employers.

Thus, what I would say here would be: "Be selfish!" and make a choice that will maximally increase your level of comfort. If you cannot multitask and marrying job search with finishing your projects felt hard to you, don't finish them! Don't feel guilty—at the end of the day, an unfinished project is an outcome of the negligence of many people, never just one person. After your contract expires, it is only a matter of your goodwill whether you are willing to continue working. In academia, project leaders (i.e., PIs) take too little responsibility for the projects, and they are usually not evaluated for how well their project members perform. As a result, it is often hard to finish a project in time because your own project leaders block you from doing that. So, if you feel that you did not manage to finish your projects in time for reasons independent from you, you don't have any moral obligation to finish them after your contract expires.

Personally, I chose to slowly finish off almost all my projects one by one while I was already indulging in new professional activities. However, I didn't do it for my supervisors, for my parents, or anyone else—I did it only for myself. I just like having this self-image of a person who always finishes her projects no matter how much time it takes. I think the fact that I slowly but steadily go forward in my life, is my core competency, and I like looking at such a person in the mirror. Yet still, I wouldn't do this only because my supervisor, my parents or anyone else pressed on me. *Time* is the only thing you can never claim back. So, if you are not convinced that finishing your projects is a valuable way of spending your time after your contract expires, don't do this.

One thing that you need to learn while making a career switch towards industry, is to learn to *respect your own time* better. In academia, we are often taught that our private time is worthless, that we should serve to the god of science 24/7, and live like Shaolin monks. When your academic contract expires, you are in full charge of what you do every single hour that you are not paid for. You need to learn that your time has a price tag to it, and that you should finally stop giving away your working hours for free. So, if your former employers insist for you to finish some projects, you might consider setting a simple freelance business, and start charging them per hour. They would either pay (and freelance jobs are usually paid 3-5 times more per hour than working on a contract), or immediately stop insisting on doing the work—so that's a win-win for you.

How to deal with itchy questions from family and friends

When you decide to switch careers, you should prepare for the ride. You'll encounter certain drawbacks, such as itchy questions from your family and friends, especially from friends who are still in academia. Many researchers looking for new career opportunities in industry still need to struggle with a stereotypical look at industry careers, which are still viewed as a failure in some academic circles. Especially if your parents always dreamt about a professor in the family, and you are now going to shutter their vision, you might need to go through a serious conversation with them. Friends who decided to stay in academia might also make your life harder. Phrases such as "resign from an academic career," "leave academia," or "unemployment benefits" still have negative associations, and certainly don't help you feel more confident. How should you deal with these itchy questions about your plans then?

Mind that not everyone in this world is happy with their professional life, and not everyone takes action to change this situation. If you step up for yourself and look for new solutions, you'll always be salt in the eye to those who don't have the energy or willpower to do it. As a matter of fact, happy people who never stop developing and transforming themselves are a minority. These are people who live for real, while most people just sit on the sidelines, make comments, and occasionally throw stones at them. So, just don't bother about these people.

I believe that the key is to always look forward. If you are still employed and consider finding a job in industry, it is good to look for other people around you who have similar ambitions and are willing to exchange information with you. Maybe you can organize a brainstorming session together, or even become a mastermind group? If you already finished your contract, it is good to focus on reaching out to people embedded in environments that you consider joining. For instance, if you are planning to work in the pharmaceutical industry, think about all your contacts who switched their careers to pharmaceutics. Go out with those people, spend some time with them. If you are thinking of setting your own company, try to find people who already have their own companies, and hang out with them. You get the idea.

One thing is for certain: changing a career path is an advance to your career and not a failure. If someone is trying to persuade you otherwise, it is good to educate this person—or leave them alone in their bubble.

Actively suppress black thoughts

It is natural to experience occasional black thoughts when you are looking for a new job. Especially if you had a bad personal experience in academia, it might happen a lot. For those who have experienced unfairness in the workplace, there are two major attractors. The first attractor is activism: if you are mistreated, you say "No!" aloud, and fight back. In case you say "No!" to the whole system such as academia, this can effectively mean spending the rest of your life as a person fighting for better science full-time: setting/joining foundations, running mentoring programs, educating politicians, writing books and articles on this topic, and actively working on new, more ethical research practices.

The second attractor is starting your professional life anew in industry. In that case, the faster you work through all the dark things that happened in your academic career, the faster you forget about them and start your new life with a positive attitude, the better for you.

So, in case you are gravitating towards the second attractor, it is good to keep mental hygiene and not let black thoughts occupy your head for too long. Gratitude-powered activities such as writing support/recommendation letters can give a lot of extra energy too. If you have a bad day, talking highly about other people can substantially improve your mood, even if it's just a thumb up under some *YouTube*

145

movie or a warm review on *Amazon* :) Moreover, a 10-day mental diet as proposed by Tony Robbins (Robbins, 1991) can help a lot. The only rule of this diet is that you commit not to worry for ten days straight—that's all.

Every day incremental progress is the key

What motivational speakers such as Brian Tracy (Tracy, 1993) use to say about persistence is true. Namely, small everyday steps have a large impact in the long run—most people overestimate what we can achieve in a year and underestimate what they can achieve in ten years. Also, forming good habits takes time (and I believe it takes much longer than the proverbial 21 days). So, if you are in the period between two contracts, make sure to take little steps every single day. Even if you don't have inspiration for some reason, and you don't feel productive on a particular day, make sure that at least you learn something new on that day. Every hero had their own origin story: drawbacks, failures, and periods of low productivity. But they all have their eyes set on the long-term goals.

Lastly...

Before you sign your first contract in industry...

...you should sign a contract with yourself first. What are your boundaries? Where are your buttons? What behaviors and situations would you allow for in the workplace, and what wouldn't you ever accept? At work, we often compromise way too much and agree to do things that we would advise our own friends to avoid. If you list your minimum requirements for the job, sign this list, and promise to yourself that you will change your job as soon as these terms are broken, you will instantly feel much more safe and secure.

You need to be your own advocate from now on!

The take-home message

1. If your contract expires, and you don't have a new job yet, remember to keep a steady daily rhythm while looking for jobs. Limit contact with social media.

2. Actively reach out to other people, and maintain social contacts. Search for people who are in the same situation as you and support each other!

3. Be strategic about delayed research projects. You don't need to finish them all!

4. Ignore comments from fellow researchers about "leaving academia," "ending your career" and such. You don't end; you start.

5. Work on your mental hygiene, and find relaxing activities.

6. Before going to job interviews, sign a contract with yourself first!

PART III

How to further develop your career

CHAPTER 7

WORK ON YOUR PERSONAL FREEDOM

Money is a measure of freedom

In the previous chapter, I provided some tips on how to successfully go through a period of unemployment. In this chapter, we will talk a bit more about how to increase your comfort zone, and how to become more resilient to stress related to changing jobs.

Let's take one more look at Fig. 3. When we talk about personal freedom here, we talk about freedom at work: the ability to define your personal career goals and to choose your projects and teammates. Does this mean that you can do whatever you want with your time? The professions associated with high levels of personal freedom, such as entrepreneurship, freelancing, or an academic career at the senior level, imply having no direct boss, but at the same time, they require acquiring *clients,* or *readers.* If you are a freelancer or an entrepreneur, you won't become any successful as long as you don't care about what your clients think of your products or services. Therefore, in these professions, your *client* is effectively your boss. Even as a PI, you are not entirely independent from the opinion of other people—if you didn't produce any new concepts for the last twenty years but rather, you are still cutting coupons from the work you did as a PhD candidate over twenty years ago, and press on your PhD students to propagate your concepts, you are slowly becoming a walking joke to other PIs. For the scientific community, it matters if you demonstrate creativity throughout the career—even when you are bombed with bureaucracy, and you effectively have no time for research anymore. If you are stuck for a long time, grant agencies won't be happy about your proposals and will award the money to someone else.

So, are you free as a person in these professions? Not entirely—you still need to care about what someone else thinks of you.

And now, let's think about safety at work for a while. Yes, in large governmental institutions, you are *relatively* safe. Most probably, you won't *lose a job,* and you can peacefully continue working there until you retire. However, will you

149

be safe from other potential work-related dangers such as mobbing, patronizing behaviors, or microaggressions from your boss or some competitive colleagues? Not necessarily.

The only people on planet Earth who are both free and safe and who don't need to care about what others think of them are those who have a constant inflow of money, namely, savings or a substantial passive income. In other words, wealthy people.

As Francis Bacon famously said, "Money is a great servant but a bad master." It is so true! If you need to find a job very soon just because your account is empty, you'll be stressed—no surprise here. As such, you'll always sound more needy, present yourself worse at job interviews, and possibly, also agree to accept jobs below your qualifications or jobs that you are not excited about at all. I *notoriously* hear stories of researchers who took the very first job they were offered—just to fix their finances. Therefore, it is essential to eliminate such a possibility.

Talking about money is a taboo in Western culture

On Friday drinks, what do you usually talk about with your colleagues? Some new projects? The incoming conference? What did your boss say this week? Who dates whom? Vacation plans? Plans for the weekend? A newborn from a colleague? An incoming surprise birthday party for yet another colleague? In graduate school, I noticed that there is one topic that is *always* missing from these evening chats: personal finances. How to make money? How to invest your savings? How to save more? How to gain passive income? In other words, *how to be free?*

In Western culture, money is a taboo. Just try to talk about money, and other people will immediately change the topic. In most countries, there is absolutely no training in economics and finances throughout the whole education process—quite as if the government was tactically skipping it from school education. Well... The conclusion is: it is worth learning a little about this topic on your own as no one else has an interest in helping you to acquire personal freedom but you.

The first thing to learn about money should be that, despite the negative public image, money *doesn't* make people worse than they were before acquiring it. Hollywood movies tend to picture wealthy people as snobs, sex-addicts, wreckages, blood-thirsty psychopaths and/or weirdos. Let me give just a few examples of movies such as *The Big Short, American Psycho, Hostel, The Talented Mr. Ripley, The Wolf of Wall Street, The Iron Man, The Devil Wears Prada, The Great Gatsby, Fifty Shades of Grey, Charlie and the Chocolate Factory, Harry Potter series*[61], *Superman*[62], or *Interview with The Vampire*[63]. In fact, having money will not make you any more snobbish, more self-indulged, lazier, or more abrupt towards others. It does not make you any better as a person neither. Money gives you more opportunities—if you were

---

[61] Lucius Malfoy is a billionaire in the books/movies.

[62] Lex Luthor is a billionaire in the comics/movies.

[63] Lestat de Lioncourt is a millionaire in the book/movie.

an ass before acquiring it, you will have even more chances to be an ass afterward. On the contrary, if you were a good person before, you'll get even more chances to do good once you become wealthy.

Also, there is a stereotype that wealthy people are fat cats who never got their hands dirty with real work. In reality, only 20% of all wealthy people inherited their wealth, while 80% worked hard to get where they are now. Also, their success is due to a vibrant, magnetic personality, empathy, the ability to listen to their clients and employees, and to make everyone around them happy. Of course, there are some sociopaths out there, but the vast majority of wealthy people are nowhere near that.

The second thing to learn about money is that people who tell you that money is not important are either unaware of what money is, or they don't want good for you. As, again, money is the measure of your freedom and safety.

The financial cushion

To feel relatively safe and not pressured about the next career choices, one needs to develop a financial cushion first: accessible savings that can pay the bills when necessary. How big should this cushion be? It is a bit dependent on the country. In countries where recruitment is more dynamic and where you can typically start working as soon as you get the contract (e.g., in the US), as a rule of thumb, you should have enough savings to survive for 3-6 months. However, in countries where the recruitment process is more conservative and where the recruitment process often lasts for many months (e.g., in the Netherlands), as a rule of thumb, you should have enough savings to survive for 9-12 months.

How to build a financial cushion? The most straightforward answer is: save the difference between earnings and costs. If you don't have any savings, you should do at least one of the two things: increase your monthly income, or reduce your monthly costs.

Of course, as a busy academic, it is difficult to find additional time for working on the side to increase your income. One idea might be to write a book about your research subject—yet, this will take a lot of time and effort. You might also think of building a passive income by creating an online course. If you have good teaching skills, you might consider offering consultancy services—this would allow you to possibly make an extra income without the necessity to learn new skills .There are websites such as *Kolabtree*[64] where you can make a profile and offer research consultancy services or websites such as *Clarity* where you can announce, e.g., coaching services. It is also possible to make some extra money while spending relatively little time as a private teacher in statistics, mathematics, English, etc. Sometimes, it is good to think a bit out of the box here. When you think "a private teacher," the first image that comes to your head is probably some spoiled teenager whom you need to babysit. But today, there are also lots of wealthy, educated people over 40, or even 50, who overslept the math class in high school. Now, they want to improve their analytic skills, be more up to date with science, learn about machine

---

[64] www.kolabtree.com

learning and AI, and "what all this buzz is about." People want to learn at any age—ambitious people in particular. Mind that as a teacher or as a consultant, you'll most likely need to register a sole proprietorship and take care of your taxes (more about freelancing in chapter 4: *What is My Perfect Working Environment?*). The easiest way to build a financial cushion as a researcher is still to limit the steady, monthly expenditures: it takes less amount of time and effort than acquiring an extra income and gives guaranteed results every month.

Cutting costs

Below, I list a few pieces of advice on how you can approach your monthly costs to eliminate unnecessary expenditures which pull your finances down.

➤ Learn how to tell the difference between assets and liabilities, and focus on acquiring assets.

To put it shortly, assets are goods that leave cash in your pocket, while liabilities are goods that take money out of your pocket. It sounds like a simple division, but it is not as simple as it seems. The same products can be assets or liabilities, depending on the situation. Also, some products can gain or lose your money in indirect ways. Even people experienced with finances often have a dilemma about how to classify some of their purchases!

For instance, a car can be an asset or a liability, depending on circumstances. In general, a new car leaving straight from a car showroom is a liability—it loses almost half of its value on the day of purchase. Second-hand cars are always way cheaper than the new ones, so you'll never be able to redeem a large portion of its price even if you sell it literally on the next day. Now let's imagine that you get yourself a second-hand car for $4,000, and this car saves you one hour per day on commuting time. You can spend the same one hour earning an additional $50 as a freelance writer on a side, and after one year, you'll have $12,000 extra in your pocket. You can also spend this one hour a day learning a new skill which is in high demand in the job market for one year, and then get a new job with a salary of $300 higher. Within the next five years, this difference between salaries will amount to almost $20,000 extra in your pocket.

Another example might be buying art. If you buy a designer sofa worth $10,000, then over the years, it will most likely get fatigued and lose almost all of its value. If you get yourself a *Louis Vuitton* purse for the same price and then take good care of it, after a few years, it can substantially grow in value. *Louis Vuitton* purses are considered a profitable investment, by the way (Sowray & Murray, 2019).

Lastly, let's consider the *Netflix* example: is *Netflix* subscription an asset, or a liability? This, again, depends on the situation. This case is quite complex. If you don't watch *Netflix* and keep your subscription just because everyone around you does, it is an obvious liability as a steady monthly cost that doesn't produce any value. If you, however, watch *Netflix*, and it helps you in saving money by avoiding movie theaters, and additional expenditures coming from buying access to single movies, then your savings will likely exceed the monthly subscription costs. *Netflix* could also become an asset in indirect ways. For instance, if you often socialize by watching movies by beers in a group with your coworkers, it might lead to building bonds and getting more opportunities at work—for instance, new project ideas created during such a "Netflix evening." Or, if an evening seance of a B-class horror movie on *Netflix* is some weird form of relaxing to you (and for quite some people, it is!), you might be more effective at work during the day. But again, if you spend a lot of time watching movies on *Netflix* alone, and that prevents you from effectively socializing, it can become a liability again. You get the idea.

➤ Save pound wise, not pennywise. Think long-term.

Many people who aim to improve on their savings become too strict about their rules, and start saving on the things which they should not bother about. For instance, if you spend a quarter in the grocery store comparing labels of two jars of beans and trying to figure if the cheaper one is good enough, you'll lose time worth much more than your eventual saving. It is a better choice to be pound-wise, and to focus on making a few key choices which save you the most every month: choose a place to live that has a good quality to price ratio, cut on the commuting time and costs, resign from unnecessary, expensive branded items, find a reasonably priced bar for regular Friday drinks.

It is also worth to spend one evening per year on looking through your steady costs: your energy provider, Internet provider, healthcare provider, etc. It might be the case that another provider currently has more attractive monthly rates or there are new options on the market. Also, in many countries, tax law changes from year to year. Therefore, it is worth to check once per year whether you might be eligible for some new tax benefits, or some other public allowances.

At the same time, *health* is not worth saving on; your body won't care about the labels on the clothes, but it can protest against bad food and lack of exercise in harsh ways. If you think about your well-being long-term, there should always be some room for good quality food and for sports in the equation.

➤ Evaluate the real value of the products you are buying.

Financial intelligence is yet another type of intelligence; something different from fluid intelligence, a talent for mathematics, or programming. A lot of intelligent people have issues with evaluating *the real value* of the items they are buying. So, they purchase whatever they feel like buying, and often don't even know why they make their decisions.

Every transaction is an exchange based on the *assessment of value*: if someone sells you a product at price X, it means that they believe that this product is worth *no more than X*. If you buy this product, you believe that the product is worth *not less than X*. So, if a given purchase seems to be a good deal, it means that you disagree with a professional salesman who believes otherwise. They might see aspects of the product which you don't see, or otherwise, they would price the product higher. What I mean is: most so-called *good deals* are what you were manipulated into, and not good deals. For this reason, it is good to develop your own, objective assessment of value and concentrate on buying things that have the best value to price ratio for you.

➤ Pay yourself first.

As a rule of thumb, at least 10% of the salary should be set aside each month as savings. A separate bank account serves well for this purpose, and it's good to deposit this amount on this account right after receiving the salary. Financial advisors usually refer to this habit as *paying yourself first*.

➤ Be a bit opportunistic with travels.

Travels can eat quite a lot of savings; popular vacation destinations usually aren't cheap, and they might require distant flights. As a researcher, you might be able to take time off around conferences to reduce the costs of your vacations—and many researchers do so. You might also sign up for online newsletters such as *Fly4Free*[65] which will notify you whenever there are new, attractive flight offers to exotic destinations. If you are interested in one particular destination, you might set an alert for one particular connection, e.g., at *Skyscanner*[66].

➤ Prevent inflation of lifestyle.

Inflation of lifestyle is a phenomenon that happens when along with your income, your steady costs also grow so that eventually, your amount of savings stays the same (and for many people, this amount is ground zero). This is a surprisingly often-encountered situation: PhD students getting a steady increase in their salary during their PhD contracts, yet saving nothing from their salaries at the end of their contracts. It happens because once they receive higher salaries, they move to bigger apartments, buy themselves new furniture, go out more often, go to more expensive restaurants, and eventually, still spend everything they earn.

It is good to be aware of this effect, and actively prevent it. Sometimes, the only thing you need to save a lot of money is *not to raise costs* while your salary steadily grows over the years.

➤ Change the way of thinking about saving.

Lastly, one stereotype about saving money is particularly detrimental. Namely, for many people saving is unpleasant as it makes them *feel poor*. Saving is not the domain of poor people! Wealthy people are usually even keener on saving than everyone else—saving is just a healthy habit. Warren Buffett, currently worth about 80 billion dollars, still feels excited when he finds a store offering a can of coke half a dollar cheaper than the coke on the opposite side of the street. So, saving should be treated as a habit, a game in which you cannot lose too much, and you can win a lot of personal freedom!

Take care of your personal finances in daily life

To get control over your personal finances, it's good to plan and monitor them. There are multiple strategies for how to manage your personal finances, and just like

---

[65] www.fly4free.com

[66] www.skyscanner.com

with diets, there is no "one fits all." In this chapter, I will mention a few popular strategies that you might try in daily life.

➤ Save on the fly.

This technique boils down to simply asking yourself if you need a given product or service *before every purchase*. This technique is beneficial for those who are already fluent in evaluating products, identifying liabilities, and comparing prices— otherwise, your life and the lives of people around you might become difficult as you'll hesitate while making every single purchase.

Saving on the fly saves *the most money* as you cut the costs on every possible occasion. However, it can also generate the most conflicts with your environment, e.g., if you have a partner or friends who are not big on savings—they might classify you as a short-handed and stubborn person.

➤ The bucket method.

The essence of the bucket method is financial planning. In this scheme, you share your monthly income into buckets of "personal allowance" each month. The buckets can be, in example: rent—30%, commuting costs—5%, utilities—5%, health insurance—5%, food indoors—20%, food outdoors—5%, social activities—5%, clothing—5%, travels—5%, sports—5%, savings—5%, investments—5%. It is just an example—the list of buckets should be custom.

This technique has a few advantages. For instance, it pushes you to revise what you bought throughout the month, think about it, and compare your expenditures with the previous month. It can also prevent you from obsessive saving: if you choose to save on the fly and you are very determined to pull your costs as low as possible, you might soon resign from anything that is not essential for keeping you alive—sports, social activities, travels, or dining outdoors. Throwing money into all the buckets will make your daily life more harmonious, and you won't overspend in any direction. The downside is that bucketing requires recording everything you buy and some regular effort with personal accountancy.

➤ 50/20/30 budget rule.

It is also a form of financial planning but works according to different rules. Senator Elizabeth Warren proposed this simple system in her book (Warren & Warren-Tyagi, 2005). 50/30/20 rule boils down to sharing your after-tax income between three main buckets: needs—50%, wants—30%, and savings—20%. Needs are the obligatory monthly costs: rent, health care, groceries, commuting, utilities, etc. Wants are entertainment: travels, dining outdoors, concerts, movies, sports, parties. "Savings" include both savings and investments in this technique (for beginners, savings are good enough). It is a simple and intuitive system that can be a tradeoff between the other two strategies.

➤ Regular measurement.

Some people report that they lost weight without introducing any diet plan— they just *measured* their weight every morning. Why did they lose weight though? Well, due to their competitive nature, they subconsciously adjusted their behaviors to make a step towards their dream weight every single day. These little daily morning rewards were more than enough for them to keep disciplined. Similarly, with finances, you can introduce a habit of checking your savings account balance every month or every week. If you are competitive enough, your brain will bake some strategies to make this number grow all by itself.

Get access to the right people

Building savings is like building your muscles in a gym—it is always easier and funnier when you are in a group. If you can find people interested in this topic around you, great! If not, you can easily find them online, e.g., in the world-wide *FIRE*[67] community. *FIRE* stands for "Financially Independent, Retire Early." It is the movement of people who aim to gain personal freedom by building savings and passive income. In every country, they have their online forums, *Slack* channels, and gatherings in person. You might also consider subscribing to one of multiple *YouTube* channels dedicated to savings and investments, such as the channel by Graham Stephan[68], Nate O'Brien[69], or the Financial Diet[70]. There is a high rotation of content on *YouTube,* so at the time you are reading this book, there might be dozens of new, even better channels.

Also, broke people usually have friends who are broke too. You might think of the wealthiest person you know, and interview them to find out what are their strategies for building wealth!

Lastly…

Creating savings is only a part of the game. In the long run, to build financial independence, you'll also need to *invest* at least a portion of your assets. Investing is difficult-for a few reasons.

Firstly, it is always associated with taking risks and involves some degree of stress. Secondly, since you can potentially lose money, you first need to work out a functional investment strategy, which is quite challenging-although online finance gurus will try to convince you that investing is super easy, barely an inconvenience. Thirdly, when you have to do with relatively large amounts of money, your lizard brain can take control over you. It will push you to make very irresponsible decisions, e.g., invest in highly speculative assets or trust to wrong people in the hope to maximize your gains. Lastly, with investments, it is like with diets—there is no "one fits all." Depending on your personality, some methods might work much better than others; while some people are born to invest in the long term, others prefer to trade.

For all these reasons, strategies for investing private assets are beyond the scope of this book. The only advice I can mention here is that you should invest at least 10%

[67] www.wikipedia.org/wiki/FIRE_movement

[68] www.youtube.com/channel/UCV6KDgJskWaEckne5aPA0aQ

[69] www.youtube.com/channel/UCO3tlaeZ6Z0ZN5frMZI3-uQ

[70] www.youtube.com/channel/UCSPYNpQ2fHv9HJ-q6MIMaPw

of the time you spent on earning your money on learning about investments before you decide to risk your savings.

I wish you and your family a lot of wealth!

The take-home message

1. Money is a measure of safety and freedom.

2. To feel safe while looking for jobs, you should build a financial cushion.

3. The easiest way to create a financial cushion is to control your monthly expenditures by developing a strategy for managing your personal finances.

4. Reach out to other people for financial advice. Sharing is caring!

CHAPTER 8

SELF-DISCOVERY: A PROCESS THAT LASTS FOR A LIFETIME

Career goals

Let's first think about some fundamental issues related to setting career goals in general. Goal setting is very challenging. Doing it the wrong way can lead to frustration and hamper your performance at work (Ordóñez et al., 2009). Even though there are some classic techniques for goal setting, such as S.M.A.R.T. (Raia, 1965, Grant, 2012), goal setting is still the Holy Grail in the self-development literature. Here, let's focus on goal setting in the context of professional development.

Please take a look at the following question, and then *take a break from reading for a few minutes, and deliberate on this question on your own before you come back to reading.*

> What is the main reason why setting and reaching career goals is so hard?
> a) Usually, we have too many goals at the same time while the day only has 24 hours,
> b) We often set contradictory goals, which is a form of self-sabotage,
> c) Goals can be too general (i.e., not motivating enough) or too specific (i.e., too frustrating),
> d) Goals are moving targets.

Let me discuss all the options mentioned in this question and explain which answer I would choose and why.

Firstly, we live in a crazy world, with too much stimulation and too many expectations at a time. How should we stay ahead of the competition and excel at work while at the same time working on friendships, relationships, health, hobbies, spirituality—and still finding time to document all this and put it on *Instagram*? There are just too many targets at the same time and too much peer pressure to be successful.

No wonder that in many first-world countries, burnout rates are higher than ever before even though, paradoxically, the economic situation is also better than ever before in human history (Wigert & Agrawal, 2018, Sarner, 2018, Savage, 2019).

Secondly, it is often the case that our goals are contradictory on some level. For example, I know expats who are planning to develop their careers at their current location, but at the same time, deep down, they miss their maternal country so much that they cannot imagine spending the rest of their life there. Some people do not miss their home country, yet still, they dream of finding another place they could call home. I have a friend who is an expat living in the Netherlands, just like me. The other day, we were chatting about life. At some point, she brightened up talking about how much she loves Mediterranean culture and how warm and lovely Mediterranean people are —unlike the Dutch people whose accompany she doesn't enjoy. She added that she dreams about living there, in the Mediterranean sunshine. I was a bit puzzled, so I asked, "Well, you chose the Netherlands, right?" She did not give me any answer to this; she just looked at the window deep in her thoughts. She is a very bright, energetic, and hard-working lady, and she could choose to live anywhere. Yet, she picked the culture that she doesn't identify with.

Some people set contradictory goals by building two careers at a time—and these careers are just an impossible match. For instance, some people try to develop a career in sports after working hours, and come to the office tired every day—and in the end, they neither perform at work nor at sports competitions. We often sabotage ourselves this way.

Thirdly, it is hard to hit the right level of generality when setting professional goals. Let us assume that your main goal is to *become a good person who makes an impact on society*. Well, it's great—the world will probably benefit from you achieving that goal. But, is this goal even motivating at all? It isn't easy to visualize how you are supposed to get there in practice. Will you jump out of bed every day thinking, "This is going to be a great day, as I am on my way to make an impact?" Does this goal let you imagine the steps that you need to take and let you make the right career decisions? Probably not—it is too vague. What will happen if you, on the contrary, choose a very particular and well-defined goal? You might put yourself at a high risk of frustration and burnout. Let me give an example.

I have a friend who lives in Seoul; yet another bright, energetic, and hard-working lady I am lucky to know. I have been tracking her career for the last ten years, and here is what has happened. At the end of her Master's studies, she made a strong resolution to become the CEO of *Samsung*. Initially, I thought that it was a good party joke, but I soon realized that she was dead serious about this. She applied to *Samsung* and became an employee—one of these young, career-aggressive corporate yuppies, fully delved into their culture of success. And, she started getting promotions. Up, up, up! She had to adapt to the hard, intense corporate life in Seoul. Especially as both an expat and a woman, she had to face quite a lot of challenges and work twice as hard to get any promotion. Yet, for all this time, she had her eyes set on the main prize: the seat of the CEO of *Samsung*... Just like all these career-aggressive corporate yuppies around her. How did the story end? No surprise here: with a massive, severe, a few-year-long burnout. Then, from a corporate rat, she made a 180° turn, and recently launched her own initiative in which she helps startups to take off.

The conclusion is: too well-defined goals can easily turn against us. It's good to take a general direction with your career but if you cannot be happy without getting to one particular, competitive position—well, it can become a huge problem.

Lastly, on the way towards our goals, we gain a new experience, and we change in response to this new experience. The goals also often change, which makes them a moving target. As we all know, moving targets are much harder to hit than fixed targets. And this is, in my opinion, *the hardest aspect* of defining and reaching professional goals.

Why is it so hard? It's because we need to *notice* that we changed and that our ultimate goals should change respectively. And, if we don't notice this progress, we cannot act on it. Many researchers stay in academia for far too long because of the *inertia* effect: they are offered some convenient Postdoc contracts after their PhDs, decide to stay in the same place, postpone reflecting on their lives for as long as they can, and in the end, fail to realize that they have changed in the process. And then, they wake up ten years later—frustrated, confused, and looking for their first jobs in industry. For the same reason, i.e., for the sake of the fact that our targets are moving, we are often hard on ourselves, which leads to a lot of regrets. We ask ourselves, "What if...?" way too often. For instance, one can say, "If I had known that after my PhD I would end up in data science, I would have moved towards data science straight away." I also used to torture myself with these thoughts far too often. I questioned my every decision, including my PhD itself. It's good to look back at the past sometimes and realize that everything that happened was necessary to happen.

Redefining who you are

We all change—every single day. I spent eight years doing brain research, and I must say that we still don't know that much about its functioning... At the moment, over 100,000 full-time researchers study the human brain worldwide—either directly or indirectly by building animal models of cognition and perception. However, we still don't know almost anything about how *the coming of age* happens.

Sometimes, it strikes me how different my thinking is, compared to as little as 2-3 years ago: thinking about people, work, friendships, society, money, anything important in life. How is this possible? Single days only consist of solving little issues that you have on your to-do list, from finishing little projects, planning the to-do list for the next week, through shopping, going places, watching movies, to chitchatting, chilling, discussing (and sometimes arguing) with other people. And then, in some way, your brain is taking all these little impressions together, throwing them into one pot, and slowly cooking something over time in the back of your head. Most people don't have any access to this subconscious part of their cognition (and neither do I). Yet still, even if you "just" live your life, without planning for any particular self-development, you still catch yourself becoming a new person over and over again. For this reason, coming of age will never stop.

You might also get surprised by finding new, undiscovered talents at pretty much any age. In most countries, the school system is still outdated and does not help in discovering your *real* talents. If you have a talent for math—fair enough; there is a chance that your math teacher will spot this talent, and let you and your parents know. But what about talents for dancing, mountaineering, investing, or salesmanship? These types of talents are much less likely to be discovered early in your development. Most people talented in these areas only discover these capabilities by themselves and from experience. Who knows, maybe at the age of 50, you will turn out to be a genius in some area you haven't even heard of until then. I would even say: if you keep on challenging yourself hard enough, it is even a likely scenario.

Intuition

Intuition is an often overlooked yet crucial factor for success. As Albert Einstein used to say, "The intuitive mind is a sacred gift, and the rational mind is a faithful servant. We have created a society that honors the servant and has forgotten the gift." As mentioned in chapter 5, using intuition is a clue to making good decisions—in particular, in situations in which you have *incomplete information*, i.e., you need to solve a puzzle, infer the true motivation behind actions of another person, or predict behavior of a large group of people (e.g., whether a given product will sell to a chosen target group).

Now, let's approach one question related to intuition. Please take a look at the following question, and then *take a break from reading for a few minutes, and deliberate on this question on your own before you come back to reading.*

> Which of the following statements about intuition is *false*?
> a) Intuition works best when we are relaxed,
> b) Intuition helps in making good decisions,
> c) Intuition is something we are born with,
> d) Intuition is a form of intelligence.

I will discuss all the options mentioned in this question, and in the end, I will explain what I think is the right answer.

Firstly, as mentioned in chapter 6: *Self-Discipline*, intuition works best when we are rested and relaxed. It, indeed, helps you in making better decisions. Have you ever wondered why some people always find themselves in the right place at the right time? And, they seem to be the lucky ones? Usually, these are not the most hard-working individuals in your workplace. They might not even be the smartest ones. How does this happen then? I was wondering about this for a long time. And, at some point, I noticed that the people who are best at picking up on opportunities are those who have the best work-life balance and who know how to switch off their brains when necessary. Those who *allow themselves* to have quality time and not worry too much about the future. Even if, at the moment, you are career-oriented and you don't think about having a family, this is one good reason to let go from time to time and to take care of your social life.

I will discuss all the options mentioned in this question and, in the end, I Secondly, intuition is a form of intelligence (Gigerenzer, 2008, Dohmen, 2018) rather than just a way of guessing. There is even a saying, "Intuition is the highest form of intelligence." Actually, the ability to perform well in any area *is* intelligence. If you are good at catching numbers and relations between them, you might be gifted with fluid intelligence. If you learn new sports and dances fast, it is a sign of kinetic intelligence. If you can read intentions from faces and you know how to behave in various situations, it is evidence for emotional intelligence. And, if you pick the right options in cases when you have incomplete information, it is a sign of a strongly intuitive mind—which is a form of intelligence as well.

Actually, we still don't know much about the neurobiological mechanisms underlying intuition. Some people naturally rely on intuition in decision making more than others (de Vries et al., 2008). Intuition was at the roots of many groundbreaking scientific discoveries and is often pointed to as the key factor to success, especially in professions that require extensive contact with other people. For instance, over 62% of business executives have an intuitive rather than a logical approach to decision making. Great leaders in many industries also reportedly used intuition to make seemingly irrational but, in fact, groundbreaking moves in their enterprises. Let me bring just a few examples (I deliberately chose famous stories so that some of them ring the bell):

➤ Henry Ford solved the problem of decreasing demand for his cars by *doubling* his own employees' wages. He just felt that if his workers could afford the cars they produced, they would start to buy them, and it would stimulate the sales in the whole society—and he was right.

➤ J.K. Rowling was a divorced single mother suffering from clinical depression. The other day, she was waiting for a delayed train, and all of a sudden, some seemingly crazy idea came to her mind. It was when the world of *Harry Potter* was born. Before she reached her destination, she already had the synopsis of the first book and all the main characters in mind. She was finishing the book at public cafeterias while living on social benefits amounting to 70-pound per week. In such a situation, the decision to put all the energy into writing a book about a wizard boy was counterintuitive, to say the least. The synopsis of her book got turned down by pretty much every major publishing house in the United Kingdom. However, she was persistent and tried over and over again. Many years later, she commented on this situation with words: "I had nothing to lose, and sometimes that makes you brave enough to try."

➤ Arnold Schwarzenegger is famous for a variety of reasons, but not many of his fans know that he was also a pioneer in cinematography. Namely, he was the person who injected *humor* into action movies. Today, we cannot imagine blockbusters such as the *Mission Impossible* series without humorous scenes and funny punch lines. But back then, in the times of *Conan the Barbarian,* the plot and the dialogues in action movies were always deadly serious. Adding humor to an action movie seemed the same abstract and inappropriate as adding humor to a scientific publication or a funeral speech. Arnold felt confident about his concept though. He had to fight with directors and screenwriters like a lion to persuade them to smuggle any humor into his movies. He faced a lot of resistance on the way as most movie makers were afraid that humor would make the movie look grotesque. But he eventually succeeded, and the rest is history.

➤ Carl Lewis was one of the most successful athletes of the '80s. He dominated sprinting and long jump, and by 1990 he had already won six Olympic gold medals. To the surprise and horror of his trainers and sponsors, at the age of 30, and in the middle of his professional career in sports, he went vegan[71]. Despite the objection from his environment, he persisted, and in 1991, his results were just outstanding—better than ever before. Until the end of his career in 1999, he still won three more Olympic gold medals.

➤ Elinor Ostrom, a Professor of Political Science at Indiana University Bloomington, was interested in the concept of the tragedy of the commons since the very early stages of her academic career. When she was publishing the book summarizing her finding in this field, *Governing the Commons: The Evolution of Institutions for Collective Action* (Ostrom, 1990), she couldn't predict that her work will inspire the design of new technologies for building decentralized networks such as blockchains, and to the creation of new, trustless models of governance. In the end, her work also brought her the Nobel prize in Economic Sciences in 2009.

➤ Steve Jobs put together two things which had never been viewed as compatible: computers and art. Before his ideas came to life, computers were perceived as items whose only features were their practicality and performance parameters. The idea of a *beautiful computer* seemed the same outrageous to an American consumer as, say, an artsy vacuum cleaner or a designer mop. Nevertheless, Jobs used his intuition to predict that the added value of having an artsy, aesthetic computer at home would hook the public opinion. Needless to say, he was right.

➤ Martin Garrix quit from high school to become a DJ. Why did his parents allow that? In 99 cases out of 100, quitting school at such a young age, and moving towards the world of the entertainment industry to become a professional DJ, would end up with drugs, alcoholism, burnout, depression, or even death (check: Avicii). But somehow, these two individuals trusted that their son won't end up like this and that everything will turn out for good.

And now, is intuition something we get at birth? Not really—and it is a detrimental myth. To feed your intuitive mind, you need to gain a lot of *life experience*. It is why, e.g., learning from mistakes often leads to achievements: you need to get a grasp of what works and what doesn't work in general. If you fail many times, your intuition will get stronger. For instance, if a few of your business partners turned out to be dishonest with you, you'll become much more sensitive to the little signs in other people's facial expressions, voice, and wording—which might indicate that you are dealing with a conman. If you happen to pursue a few research projects

---

[71] www.youtube.com/watch?v=zBcyUqspQjk

which turn out to be dead-end projects with no results after a few months/years of hard work, you'll learn better how to manage risk in your future projects. And, when you design your new project, you'll immediately start analyzing in what ways this project resembles your previous research projects and in what ways it is different. And if conceptually, this project has more in common with your unsuccessful projects than with the successful ones, it will be a red flag.

The message is that we shouldn't be too hard on ourselves. Everyone made some decisions in their life that they would take back if they could. Intuition for making the right decisions is developed slowly and through life experience.

To sum up, intuition is a very powerful tool. I like to think that this should actually be the *first* line of aid when making important decisions, before even reaching out to others for help. Actually, from my experience, when asked about the most helpful ways to make career decisions, 85% of people point to *internal* rather than *external* processes: learning from their own mistakes and listening to the voice of intuition. For comparison, only 15% of people declare that external points of reference, such as advice from family and friends, and following inspirational stores of successful people lead them to the best decisions.

So, if your intuition tells you that you might be on the wrong track with your career, you are probably right, and the sooner you'll commit to change this situation, the better.

Mental trips

I see this scenario very often: a PhD graduate experiences an existential crisis, so they pack their belongings and take a gap year to travel and "discover the world," or "redefine themselves." There is nothing wrong with traveling, and I know success stories from people who came back from such travels with a perfect plan on what to do next, and it all turned out well for them. But here, I would like to encourage you to practice "mental trips" rather than regular trips. Let me explain.

In the common view, networking is a great way of getting jobs. I fully agree with this opinion. But I feel that there is one more huge benefit of networking: an opportunity to enter other tribes and test whether you fit the group. The other tribes might be next door, and each one of them will have a different culture. As academics, we often close ourselves to other academics, which is a rather uniform environment and doesn't give us enough opportunity to explore other options. Below, I list some ideas of how you might sneak into other tribes to learn something about them, gain new contacts, and also learn about yourself:

➤ Browse for local meetups in your city. Perhaps, it is good to get out of your comfort zone and choose a topic that you don't know much about—anything from politics, through economics, to tinkering?
➤ Search for evening conferences in your area. In business, it is quite common to cast small meetings for 50-200 participants starting at 6-7 pm so that people can reach the place after working hours.

➤Check student clubs and associations at your university as they might have interesting profiles. Besides, undergraduate students can be very entrepreneurial, proactive, and fearless. It's often inspiring to hang out with them!

➤Ask friends who work in corporations whether they could smuggle you to an annual open day so that you can see how their company looks from the inside. On such occasions, employees are usually allowed to bring their family—a close friend should also be accepted too. Furthermore, in corporations, it's common to cultivate Friday Afternoon Drinks, and these events often happen in public bars—so that anyone can join. You can get a much better picture of what life in that company looks like if you join such an event for the whole evening. And, after a few beers, people will just tell you the truth about their daily life!

➤Ask friends who have their own companies about where and when they meet other entrepreneurs. Entrepreneurs tend to flock together and party together in informal circles. It is why it's often hard to find such information online. Ask a friend to bring you to such an informal meeting the other day.

➤If you have any friends who are freelancers, you can invite them for a walk in a park or dinner and ask them about the pros and cons of their job.

It's good to embark on these mental trips not only when you are looking for your first job outside academia but also later on. It is not necessarily the case that your first job in industry will be your ultimate destination—it is highly unlikely, given how fast the job market is currently developing! Therefore, it is better to work out a *habit of talking* to people who live and work beyond your comfort zone in your free time.

Talking to other people about their professional careers and about the reasons why they found themselves in their current position can be very refreshing. I still have a vivid memory from a neuroscientific conference in Rome over a year ago. Just as at every major scientific conference, we could enjoy a festive conference party. The party took place at a club in the suburbs. On the road to the main gate, the guests were welcomed by two dozen middle-aged men dressed as ancient Roman warriors, standing on two sides of the pavement with swords and trumpets. I walked through the gates and tried to dance and enjoy the party as planned, but I couldn't stop thinking, "Poor guys… We are partying here while they are standing outside." So, I walked back and ignited a conversation with them. "How much are you paid for this? Are you treated well?"—I asked. To my surprise, they burst into laughter. "We are not paid for this! We walk around Rome as Roman warriors at night. It is a great hobby!" It turned out that these guys are members of an association cultivating old Roman traditions and that they feel honored to have the opportunity to wear original ancient war clothes.

The other day, I went to the gathering of *Venture Cafe* in Rotterdam. *Venture Cafe* is an international organization casting open meetings where startups can hook up with investors[72]. During the meetup, I had the opportunity to approach a stand where professional tax advisors were answering questions about taxes. I chatted with two tax advisors—a young lady and a young gentleman. Since the conversation was going well, and they were eager to answer all my questions, I decided to go one step further and also ask them about their jobs. So, I asked, "Why did you decide to

---

[72] www.venturecaferotterdam.org/venture-cafe-global-network

become a tax advisor?" The lady's face lit up immediately. "This job is so creative!"—she said. I thought to myself, "Say what? I must be tripping…" In her eyes, the opportunity to restructure companies to lower the taxes was an exciting and creative activity though. I also asked the young gentleman the same question. "I love helping people!"—he said enthusiastically. I didn't want to give up too early, so I asked them more questions, trying to figure out if they were speaking the truth. But, at some point, it became clear that they were both honest with me: they just loved their job and found digging into tax regulations inspiring, regardless of how abstract this sounds to me.

To sum up, it is a good idea to challenge yourself and talk to other people about their jobs—as they can shed new light on what they do, and let you think about their jobs in ways in which you have never thought about them before.

Thus, homework is as follows:

Homework

In the next two weeks, talk to five individuals about their professional lives. These should be people with whom you *don't* normally talk about their working experience, e.g., the secretary of your department, the chef at the university canteen, your neighbor from across the street, your distant relative, a stranger met on the bus. Ask them about their "story of self": how they found themselves in the current position, whether they like their job, what are the pros and cons, and whether they have any regrets. You'll gain a broader perspective of the job market, and the struggles other people have. Do you notice any parallels between these issues and your own experience?

Job market is a fluid

As Heraclitus famously said, "The only thing that is constant is change." The same holds about the current job market. Today, we can project that an average employee will swap jobs even fifteen times during their professional career (Marker, 2015). The job market is changing faster than ever before, and it's hard to make plans for more than a few years ahead. Below, I share some of my personal forecasts for how the job market will change within the next ten years:

➤ There will be tons of new professions in the job market. Most individuals will have specific, individual functions represented by the few.

Western world economies are based on *services,* and this trend will further progress. Therefore, it is easy to predict that in ten years, there will be lots of new professions related to media, social media, communication, logistics, and all kinds of online and offline services. For instance, in recent years, it has become common for universities to hire *Twitter* representatives full time. Who could predict this ten years ago!

Furthermore, we live in times of high *specialization.* For instance, most YouTubers become famous and wealthy because they are world-class experts in some narrow discipline, such as: applying mascara, making funny movies of their cats,

167

playing GTA, or reviewing horror movies—and not because they *know a lot about life*. Similarly, my prediction is that in the future, people will solve the same, specific problems for various clients rather than solving a broad range of issues within the same company. For instance, you might be a world-class expert in solving conflicts that stem from age differences between employees and get hired by companies to walk in and solve this particular problem at their side. Or, you might be a Data Scientist specialized in analyzing trends in the fashion industry, and you are hired by different designers and clothing companies to analyze their data and recommend new sales strategies. You get the picture.

Of course, people who do well in their professional life are usually high functioning in general: well connected, sociable, likable, healthy, energetic, optimistic, creative, with common sense, and common knowledge in many different areas. It is good to represent all these qualities—and next to them, find a niche in which you can create your brand. You don't need to become a household name—it is perfectly fine if your name is only known within your narrow professional field.

➤ Empathy and creativity will be rewarded higher than now.

Many PhDs orient themselves towards data science these days. In general, the market for data science looks great and the prognoses for the future are more than positive (Columbus, 2018, Magnimind, 2019). However, I'm not as enthusiastic as some of the experts. I feel that it's hard to predict what will be the market for data science jobs from a perspective of ten or twenty years. It could go either way: it might be that one day, almost everyone with higher education works in data science. Or, it might also happen that most of the data science positions will one day become redundant because of high automation, similarly as most of the stock exchange brokers were replaced by computers. A broker used to be a very prestigious job thirty years ago!—and it's not the case anymore. If one day a deep neural network will learn how to produce new pipelines to mine new datasets, this might be the end for most people hired in this industry. If it's now possible for a machine to learn the game of Go on the master level all by itself and win against first-league players (Silver et al., 2017), then automatizing data science might also be possible one day. I wish the data science jobs all the best but this is simply unpredictable now.

What is for certain, is that jobs in which humans cannot be easily replaced by machines, are the safest bets for now. For instance, writing insightful books :) Or, any jobs that involve empathy and understanding of emotions, such as managing people, mediation, or salesmanship. Even a waiter might be much better paid one day, as *good service* is one of the crucial factors that decide whether the client returns to the restaurant. We live in times when many people can no longer verbalize their emotions, and replace all the effort with sending emoticons through text messages. Growing up in the culture of emoticons kills the ability to vocalize and express your emotions with words and gestures. My prediction is that in ten years, people who can notice, process, and understand other person's emotions and intentions, and who can respond in an adequate, and empathic way, will be one of the most valued professionals regardless of the market sector—as these abilities will be so scarce.

For the same reason, I also predict that creativity will become an even more essential factor for success than it is now. The whole world's economic condition is improving, although not everywhere at the same speed. For this reason, most people will be willing to invest more in quality products, customized items, designer items, exclusivity. Instead of listening to pop songs at the wedding, they'll invite a composer to write songs for this occasion. Instead of going to the restaurant for a romantic dinner, they'll order a chef to come to their own place and cook for them. Instead of gardening on their own, they'll find a specialized company that will design and create their garden for them. So, if you have the soul of an artist, the good times are coming!

➤ Deep work will be valued higher.

The public usage of smartphones and access to social media caused that many people experience problems with working memory, and with focusing on just anything —I would give this phenomenon a working title of "evoked ADHD." In the future, this situation might only get worse. My prediction is that in ten years from now, the ability to dive into the deep work state of mind (Newport, 2016) will be a point to mention in your resume, as it will be such a rare skill at that point. It might even happen that employees will get additionally rewarded by their employers for taking a conscious decision to deposit their phones for the whole working day. So, perhaps it's a good idea to take care of your ability to focus, and to reduce the time spent on social media, already now.

Furthermore, the ability to marry your ability to work in the "deep work mode" with public communications and networking will be highly valued. These days, most professionals develop in one of these two directions. The first group grows into top-class specialists fluent in some narrow discipline who use social media sporadically and rarely communicate in public. The other group grows into leaders and communicators who are very active online, meet and interact with lots of people, and have an overview of certain problems, yet are no longer able to perform focused work. In many professions, it is optimal to spend 50% of the working day on deep work, and the other 50% on networking and communications-yet, few people have enough self-control to stick to this scheme. So, you have enough cognitive flexibility and self-discipline to switch between the two modes, you will become valuable to employers.

➤ If you want to get far, learn how to assess added value, and execute projects.

Since Generation Z has appeared in the job market, we observe a massive shift towards projects related to sustainability, the environment, and solving big societal problems. This is a great trend, however, there is one downside to it. Namely, there are more and more "visionaries" who "want to change the world for the better" yet have no hard skills. They chose studies related to their interests, but never learned anything about statistics, programming, economy, or even proper technical writing—and prefer to communicate mostly through short messages and emoticons.

As a result, there are more and more *talking heads* who would prefer to lead projects and manage a team of individuals who will put their ideas to life, rather than make their own hands dirty. These ideas are often impossible to execute, yet, their authors live in their own world. They can't evaluate the added value of the projects, they don't know how to set realistic milestones and deliverables, and how to make the teamwork. As a PhD, you have all the skills necessary to properly assess the project value and the odds of success, to plan and execute projects. You have all the skills to break down the project into smaller pieces and write down a viable project proposal step by step. So, keep and cultivate these skills as they'll be more and more scarce in the future.

➤ Becoming non-fungible will lead to better job prospects.

Fungibility means that you are *replaceable*. For instance, one-dollar bills are fungible because it doesn't matter which one-dollar bill you choose to pay for a can of coke. In many professions, *people* are also fungible. For example, will it matter for the owner of the local grocery who is the shopping assistant at their store? Probably, as long as this is a clean and honest person who has a habit of welcoming clients with a smile, it won't matter as much what the *identity* of the shopping assistant is. Similarly, if a software developer gets hired to program a new platform, it does not matter to the employer who programmed it. It matters whether the platform faithfully reflects the solution architecture, how much the whole project costs, whether the final product is functional, and if the project is finished before the agreed deadline.

However, there are also many professions in which you *can* become irreplaceable. These are usually professions in which you can add a personal touch to what you do. For instance, if you are a teacher who has developed a unique teaching style and has a very smooth, natural contact with the students, then replacing you with another person will be hard. This is because handing the same training materials to another teacher hoping that they will get the same teaching results, is nonsense. If you are a graphic designer with their own style, many clients will be willing to pay extra for your services rather than getting cheaper artwork elsewhere. If you can write entertainingly, you might get a personal audience that is willing to come back for more content every time you release a new text, whether it's an essay, a blog post, or a book.

I believe that in the long run, non-fungible professionals always perform better in the job market than the fungible ones—even though they often have a rocky start to their careers. Therefore, it's a good mental exercise to deliberate every career path that you consider, and ask yourself, "Does this job make me irreplaceable?"

➤ Professionals who can "speak with machines" and service them will be in demand.

As mentioned before, I'm not entirely sure about the future of employment in data science, as a large part of the jobs classified as data science jobs today might potentially be automatized in the future. However, machine learning and AI are going to dominate technology and kill many professions. The rise of AI will stir and change the job market as we know it. On the one hand, robots will replace many types of blue- and white-collar jobs. On the other hand, there will be a high demand for professionals who can *communicate* with machines: engineers and programmers. So, if you like tinkering by electronic equipment, good times are coming for you. Perhaps, new professions that require speaking to machines but without the necessity to write code will be created. I mean interacting with machines e.g., by using interfaces that allow for building complex, conditional commands from simple blocks—which requires understanding logic rather than programming skills. In any way, the ability to interact with machines and service them will be highly valued in the future.

➤ Flexibility to attack one problem from various sides will be the desired competency.

Today, most professionals need to find a personal mission in their jobs to stay motivated—the paycheck and stable lifestyle are not enough. However, most professions are defined by the main *activity* or the primary *role* to play rather than by the *mission*. E.g., a manager is supposed to manage a team, a researcher primarily performs and publishes research, and a public speaker gives public presentations.

To my mind, this desire to follow the mission is so strong that the job market will adjust to it. Namely, in the future, jobs might be defined by the *problem* one is solving. For instance, when you ask someone, "What's your job?", then instead of replying, "I'm a researcher" or "I'm an activist," they will tell you, "I solve the problem of air pollution with CO2." And, this will mean that they juggle twenty different roles to approach this one problem, from researching air pollution and proposing or designing new solutions, through giving talks to students, writing press articles, to popularization through appearances on the media, and speaking with the government officials. Many people will make their mission their profession. Thus, I believe that cognitive flexibility and the ability to play various roles in pursuit of one goal will be the desired profile of the professionals of the future.

In summary, it always pays off to observe the global trends in the job market. If you are a good observer, you'll be able to foresee demand faster than most people. And, you might even be able to *create* a position for yourself. For instance, as mentioned in the previous chapters, many research institutes are now interested in hiring social media representatives. If you knock at the door of the nearest institute and introduce yourself as a researcher who has a strong social media presence and is interested in becoming a *Twitter* representative for them, they might come to the conclusion that they actually need one, and create a vacancy for you.

Also, observing the job market gives you the first-mover advantage: being one of the first individuals who spot a new opportunity always gives an edge. For instance, some of the YouTubers who came to the platform in the early days, around 2010, now enjoy a large base of followers and high earnings even though their content is not unique. They spotted their chance early on, committed themselves to the *YouTube* career, learned the rules of the game, and were persistent. Similarly, there are multiple budding industries in which you can build your brand early on, and profit from it. For instance, if you can code in *Python* or *JavaScript,* you'll easily learn programming languages dedicated to blockchains such as *Solidity*. Nowadays, there is a shortage of *Solidity* developers and you can earn as much as $100,000-$200,000 per year in this area. There are good online courses where you can learn coding in *Solidity* and other languages from home such as *Ivan on Tech Academy*[73]. It's a friendly and supportive community, and definitely a good platform to take your first steps as a blockchain developer.

---

[73] www.academy.ivanontech.com

A note on being plain

Lastly, I sometimes wonder: if you are a highly educated and intelligent person, is it *easier* or rather, is it *harder* for you to get a satisfactory job? Those who invested their whole youth in professional development—by extensive studying, internships, building their resume, reading books, and practicing self-development—now have very high expectations towards their jobs. If you have a perfectionistic attitude to yourself, most likely you'll also have a perfectionistic attitude to your jobs—and you'll always have some sense of void: the desire to improve, transcend yourself, do something extra, try something else.

I feel that we have an exaggerated view of what professional success means. It is often due to poor advice from parents and peers and the public image of success gained through (social) media. According to this image, you should be unique, express yourself, have a following, develop an impact in some field to become a successful professional. Isn't being a "plain," who is not famous, not a boss, not a millionaire, yet likes their job and people involved, good enough anymore?

In a way, this problem is related to yet another atavistic fear of not being important enough. In the old times, occupying the bottom of the social hierarchy could result in a deficiency of food, physical pain, or even premature death. Today, in the developed countries, pretty much every white-collar employee can live peacefully and without falling into the danger of getting ill or getting killed. It is no longer necessary to climb up the ladder to be safe and sound. Today, success is not necessarily to be the boss—success is to wake up with a smile in the morning and go to the office with that smile on your face. And, this is the kind of job I wish you the most!

The take-home message

1. Goals change over time—professional goals included. Thus, monitor your goals and don't blame yourself for changing your plans.

2. Use intuition while making career choices.

3. Reach out to other communities beyond your comfort zone.

4. Track the progress in the job market as it is rapidly changing.

5. You don't need to be famous or get to the top of the food chain to be happy and fulfilled at work.

CHAPTER 9

ALWAYS GO FORWARD

Set your eyes on the right prize

Many researchers are depressed, chronically stressed, or even traumatized. Yet, they often suffer from learned helplessness and stick to academic positions at all costs —even though they might find alternative jobs outside academia or better academic jobs elsewhere.

One reason for this phenomenon is that many early-career researchers believe that to develop a *fulfilling life* in the academic system, they first need to *survive* the early phases of an academic career: draft and defend the PhD thesis, and go through a few Postdocs. And that eventually, at the end of this long journey, once they land a tenured position, they'll get rewarded with a truly fulfilling professional life. To many people, the word "professor" is a synonym of the word "freedom." Well, this is *not* the case. When you don't feel free in academia, getting promoted further and further won't make your life any better. The further you get, the more you'll be tangled in the webs of mutual dependencies. You will encounter more and more people who only take care of their own business, and the percentage of time spent on doing research (which attracted you to academia in the first place) will shrink. You will also get more responsibility for others, more representative duties, more unwanted bureaucracy, etc. And, the world is *not* just: you won't be rewarded for your current efforts and the associated pain in any way. As elaborated in chapter 8: *Self-Discovery: A Process That Lasts For a Lifetime*, setting professional goals properly is key to develop a fulfilling professional life. Therefore, it's good to sometimes ask yourself if you keep your eyes set on the right prize.

Let's spend more time to deliberate. This time, please take a look at the following question, and then *take a break from reading for a few minutes, and deliberate on this question on your own before you come back to reading.*

> Who has *the most freedom* as a person?
> a) Master's student,
> b) PhD student,
> c) Postdoc,
> d) PI.

The answer that intuitively comes to mind when reading this question is probably the PI. Is "free" really free in this case, though? Well, let's imagine one day from the life of a typical PI. You just came back from an international conference at 2 am again. So, you are trying to put your face together in the morning. You fill your stomach with *Paracetamol*, praying that you get over the jet lag and the hangover before you reach the building of the institute. You cannot just call off the lab meeting because of the hangover, right?

So, you crawl to your office. Checking email first. Over 120 new messages since yesterday—mostly spam: publishers, vendors, institutions, and companies who want to sell you something, plus people from all around the world who read your articles and have questions, editors asking for reviews, invitations to join PhD defense committees. It's hard to even notice the messages from your own lab members among all the spam. Of course, you asked the department for a personal secretary multiple times but you got the response that you think too well of yourself and that the priority at the department is to increase academic output and not the convenience of the faculty. And so, they hired yet another PhD student with the same money instead.

And so you finally get through your email account on your own and proceed to lead the lab meeting. Oh, it is a journal club this time! A student presents a new, hot paper from a competitive lab. You have no idea why this paper got to *Nature* as it doesn't offer any novel solutions; it just summarizes what everyone knows for the last 20 years. Does it have anything to do with the fact that the senior author has 100,000 followers on *Twitter*? Might be! You are extremely irritated with this and you curse science on your mind, but of course, you cannot show this irritation to your lab members. Then, people in the lab ask you some questions. You have no idea how to answer some of them, yet, you need to say something as twenty pairs of eyes are staring at you. You are supposed to know everything in this area of expertise, right? So, you quickly come up with some answers and do your best to sound self-confident hoping that no one will analyze your words in detail. Or, you neglect the question saying that it's irrelevant for the research in the group—even if it's not.

Then, it's time to meet your direct boss, namely the head of the department, at the progress meeting. He kindly greets your and asks why your lab has only produced 12 publications this year while last year, the total score was 18. You wish you could say, "Because no one respects my advice in this lab, and students we got this year are not as smart as the ones we had had before." But you can't say that. So, you kindly blame yourself in front of your boss, and you promise that it will get better soon.

Then, you go through the whole round of unwanted and unnecessary meetings before you can finally take a break to get some lunch. So, you go to the canteen and bump into a group of your own PhD students sitting together at the table. When they see you, they stop chatting in split second. And then you know for sure: they just gossiped about you, just the same as any other day.

And then, in the afternoon, you finally find some time for RESEARCH. Of course, since you no longer have any time to touch any data on your own, you need to rely on your lab members to do the job. And, of course, no one comes to you with the things that work—they only knock at your door when something *does not* work. Questions, problems, troubleshooting. An intern just knocked on your door to discuss the same figure for the fifth time. It seems that this person has ignored all your previous comments, and the figure is the same ugly and non-informative as it was at the very first meeting. They smile at you with puppy dog eyes, and you are asking yourself, "Why am I doing this to myself?" Then, another student breaks in with hot news that they finally got beautiful results that we've both hoped. They scream at you, "Look! It is going to be a *Nature* paper!" You look at the figure and think, "Wonderful, maybe we can finally show that *Twitter* guy who is the boss here!" The same student walks in one hour later, saying that they just spotted a bug in the code and that there are no results.

When all the meetings end, you can finally rest. Did I say *rest*? I meant: hop on *Twitter* and respond to all these PIs who tagged you in their *Twitter* threads in the meantime. What can you do if so many people ask for your opinion on their recent hot findings in the field? Just praise everyone, and pretend that you managed to read all these papers. Oh, there are also some more emails waiting at your email account now. Some fellow PI from the same consortium is just kindly asking if you are comfortable with him taking the last position on the authorship list in your new paper. And, he adds in the Post Scriptum that his kids just got sick, so it would be nice if you take the financial report for the grant agency on your shoulders this time. You sigh and agree since you know this person for 30 years now, and you don't want to lose a valuable connection.

Time to crawl home. You sometimes wish you could live in the woods and breed goats instead of leading a research lab, but you cannot just leave everything behind: a position of a PI is not a type of job in which you could say, "I quit!" and never show up in the office again. Your lab members are bound to you, and your family is bound to you too. If you were a CEO of a bank, you might at least change the location by finding a similar position in another bank somewhere else. But if you are a PI who wants to relocate, your lab members will need to follow you. That would be a complete mess.

So, this is what a day of many PIs looks like. Of course, I know quite a few PIs who are very happy with their professional lives. But I also know quite a few who are not happy at all. And, I know about their real thoughts only because I found myself at the right time and place—I bumped into them in a bar. In fact, the rate of depression among full professors might be as high as the rate of depression among early career researchers. These numbers are unknown as the topic is still taboo in the academic community. However, some professors leaving their faculty positions are becoming vocal about their personal stories (Ernst, 2020).

The above "one-day-of-a-professor's-life" story might sound like a harmless anecdote told with a wink, but it's an illustration that you should be careful what you wish for. We often set goals for many years ahead and then extort ourselves to achieve these goals without questioning and reevaluating them regularly. This is a frequent sin of diligent and patient individuals—and academics often meet this description. Is every battle worth winning though? One good exercise is to imagine yourself as a full professor with all the inventory. Just imagine one week of your life as a typical professor trapped between grant proposals, grant reports, manuscripts, administrative meetings, and student projects. Would you enjoy your life this way? If the answer is "No," this will help you to make the ultimate decision to change the career path with no regrets.

How much time will this process take?

... to find a new harbor? To find a place where I fit and where I want to stay? When will this odyssey end? Will this be weeks, months, years? Is this even going to happen in the first place? It is a common worry of anyone who is planning a career switch.

The time course of your transition towards the next career is hard to predict. It is because the distance between you and your dream job is not subject to the same metric as geographical distance: you cannot just pin your destination on the map and march towards it. While you are marching, you change with every step, and together with your own change, your target also moves.

I would compare this weird metric to the world from *The Neverending Story* (Ende, 1979). In this fantasy novel, characters don't use any maps while traveling—they only use *intentions*. In this world, the speed at which you can relocate from point A to point B depends on your strength of will, namely on *how badly* you want to get there. So, if you wish to get point B, you take off from point A, and you need to imagine point B as sharply as you can and obsessively think how much you want to get there. And then, if you want it really bad, in some magic way you will get there much quicker than you expected. Of course, in real life, it is not as simple: strong motivation is not everything (although some public figures such as Rhonda Byrne, the author of *The Secret*, 2006, might tell you otherwise). But it is a good starting point to activate your brain and prompt it to come up with creative solutions for how to get to your goals.

Another reason why it is hard to predict how much time it will take you to adapt is that most industry careers are *less structured* than the academic career. There are no clear milestones, such as Assistant Professor, Associate Professor, or so. In industry, you need to work out your strategy for getting to the position you want: you can choose the most challenging projects to impress your employer, search for diagonal promotions, get extra qualifications that will give you an edge, and sometimes even take detours and accept a lower salary for a while to be able to work with the right people and learn a lot from them. For this reason, it's hard to give a hard estimate on how much time it will take you to get to the target position, even if you specify this target very precisely.

176

Science beyond academia?

The relation between science and academia is like the relation between religion and the Catholic church—you might be a believer and still resign from the system. Whether you become a scientist is not a binary choice anymore; you can actually choose both. A researcher is someone who does research and not someone with a university contract.

Many people employed in academia for a lifetime are not creative in fact—they just keep on producing new manuscripts recycling the same pipeline over and over again. And then, at some point, they get students and become talking heads while the students keep on producing. Would I call it research? No. On the contrary, many professionals in industry *do* research even when employed at non-R&D positions. For instance, let's assume that you work in an HR department in a corporation. You get feedback that 5% of the employees within the company report burnout, and you need to find the cause behind this situation. So, you interview these employees in confidence trying to figure out the real reasons, and think about how to improve the policies within the company to prevent this situation in the future—isn't this research? Or, you build a prototype for a new model of a passenger car and test many versions of the chassis to lower the probability that the driver will lose control over the machine at the nearest turn—isn't this research? Or, you work at the sales department of the company, and work on new strategies to talk to the client—test multiple scenarios and improve every time—isn't this research? A systematic approach to solving problems *is* research, and your systematic approach will help you at work everywhere you go.

Besides, as indicated in chapters 3-5, these days, you can officially do research in multiple different settings beyond academic institutions, from startups, through corporations, to government-funded institutions. Rathenau Instituut in the Hague, the Netherlands published a report summarizing career trajectories of PhD graduates in the Netherlands (Koier & de Jonge, 2018). The study summarized self-reports of 16,000 PhD graduates who had received their degrees in the previous 22 years revealed that the unemployment rate among all PhD degree holders is negligible (1.2-3.3%, depending on the field of study). Moreover, ~70% are employed in public and private non-academic sectors (60-83%, depending on the field of study). Furthermore, among those PhDs, the vast majority still performs research of some kind in their current job (64-86%, depending on the field of study) and they spend the majority of man-hours doing the actual research (48%-64%, depending on the field of study). All these numbers demonstrate that moving to industry doesn't mean disconnecting from research. Quite the opposite; you have more options than ever before.

But, these are not the only options. The academic market is also opening to freelance researchers these days: e.g., to Data Scientists, and other professionals who treat research as a hobby, next to their job. In the times of large, high quality open-access datasets, intensive information exchange and collaboration through *Twitter* and other media, this is possible. Today, an infrastructure to allow freelance researchers without an academic affiliation to develop research pipelines and produce new results, is already under construction. For example, Reproducible Self-Publishing (RepSeP[74]) is a research article compilation infrastructure, which allows articles to be published as fully reproducible code able to regenerate a human-readable and publishing-ready article, slide deck, or conference poster, directly from the top-level analysis code and raw data. This infrastructure is crucial both to reproducibility and decentralization in the research process.

Besides, life is also about *hustle*; most things come to your life when you don't *need* them anymore. I was surprised that I started publishing much more after my contract expired, and after I resigned from being a researcher (or at least, a researcher employed in academia in its current form), and started treating publishing papers as an innocent hobby. Since I no longer relied on publications as fundaments of my career, and at the same time, I was free to choose whom I was going to work with, I became much pickier with choosing projects and people to collaborate. And I was only going for projects which were truly interesting for me at that point, with people who were inspiring in some ways, responsive, self-motivated to work on the project, and willing to teach me something too. No wonder that my citation record—which was dead throughout all my PhD—started to go up. Of course, there are downsides to this as publishing research papers outside of academia is associated with working for free, and this doesn't suit everyone. Still, I feel that this will be my preferred way to stay in touch with science.

The take-home message

1. The top of the academic food chain might be less of a good job than you think.

2. It's hard to predict how much time it will take you to adapt to industry; most industry careers don't have clear milestones, and there are more opportunities to get promoted or modify your plans at every career stage.

3. You can be a full-fledged researcher outside academia.

---

[74] www.github.com/TheChymera/RepSeP

LAST WORDS

Shall I regret?

I lead a non-profit foundation, based in Nijmegen, the Netherlands that helps early-career researchers with career development. I often get this itchy question, "Natalia, should I regret my PhD?" The answer to this question is not all that simple.

I wish I could say, "Of course it was worth it!"—but as a matter of fact, no one knows the *what if*. What would have happened if instead of choosing the graduate school, you spent these 4-5 years of your life differently? Would you have been happier now? Wealthier? Better connected? With more opportunities for further growth? Perhaps, if you had spent the same amount of time on gaining streetwise knowledge rather than on your PhD, you would have had a way better future than now.

But as a matter of fact, none of us can tell whether it was the right choice to do a PhD—not right now. It will become much clearer 10-20 years from now. As Steve Jobs famously said in his Stanford commencement speech[75], at some point, you will start *connecting the dots*, namely, combining everything that you've experienced—including your PhD—into a unique career path.

It might also happen that your PhD will influence your career directly: you'll get a cool job because of your academic achievement and your diligence to finish the PhD project. And, your career will flourish from there. But it is also likely that when you look back at your professional career, you'll see the *indirect,* rather than the direct, influence that your PhD had on your career. Many PhDs in industry declare that the self-management skills and patience developed in graduate school helped them greatly in their industry jobs—to a much higher extent than acquiring the expertise related to their research topic. So, it is a likely scenario that your PhD might turn out useful, or even groundbreaking for your career, but for reasons other than what you originally expected. It's good to be mindful and to have the ability to extrapolate your knowledge and life experience beyond the everyday duties.

---

[75] www.ted.com/talks/steve_jobs_how_to_live_before_you_die

Perhaps one day, you will think to yourself, e.g.:

"Initially I felt that it was all for nothing, but eventually, my challenging PhD made me a stronger person who has patience and perseverance. And now, many years later, I am very successful for this exact reason."

"In my PhD, I had to face many situations in which I had to speak from a position of lower power. This is why now, I am a tough negotiator in my business."

"I wouldn't get to where I am now without the connections gained during my PhD."

"My PhD title gave me the credibility I needed to work with my clients; it is a quality stamp that positively influences my sales."

"My PhD taught me a lot about people, and about their internal motivations. Now, I can inspire others better than ever, and be a better boss/leader."

I can tell for myself that in the long run, my PhD *will* influence my career to a large extent—in all the unexpected ways. This process has already started; if not for the fact that (1) I went through a PhD; (2) it was a rocky one, this book would have never come to life. When I was starting a PhD a few years ago, I was planning to be a researcher for life. If this PhD had not happened, I might have never found out how it feels to be an author, because I probably wouldn't have such an important topic to write about. And this is just the beginning of my post-PhD journey.

It's also a good exercise to watch some interviews with elderly people who talk about their regrets in life. I can also recommend to check out the TEDx talk by Matthew Dicks[76]. One of the things you can learn from these movies is that, at the deathbed, people tend to regret the things they *didn't do* more than the things they did. So, if you are tempted to try yourself out there, in the dark, beyond the career path best known to you, perhaps you should just do it now.

Also, mind that these days, the decision to leave academia is *reversible*. If after a year or two, you will get a strong desire to come back, it is still possible in most cases. Due to the slow publication process, research publications often come out with a large delay, so you'll still have some scientific output within a year or two from the end date of your contract. Sometimes, it's good to step away for a while to check if you and academia are a good match. It's a bit similar to complicated relationships: sometimes taking a little break to get some fresh air and check whether you'll actually miss the other party is a good idea and can eventually make you happier—even if you decide to come back.

---

[76] www.youtube.com/watch?v=vnatyrn6DFE

Free parent, enslaved parent

I have recently read the famous book by Robert Kiyosaki *Rich dad, poor dad* (Kiyosaki & Lechter, 2000). At last! In this book, the author brings back memories from childhood and analyses the lessons about money received from two individuals —his own, highly educated but poor dad, and the uneducated but rich dad of his friend. While reading this book, it came to my mind that I could also learn a lot from my own parents' story.

My mother has spent the last 30 years of her life in corporate conditions, working for big companies in the automotive and aviation industries. She was born in a little village in South-Eastern Poland—a place where cars, schools, or electricity were unheard of. At the age of seven, she first saw the flash of lightbulb lightning up. She decided to become an electrical engineer on the spot. Eventually, she got to one of the top positions in a large corporation. She was managing big teams and traveling a lot for work, including a four-year contract in New Jersey, US. She also developed a little consultancy company on the side and had other constructive hobbies, such as building a house in her free time. She was always a well-organized, disciplined individual who was functioning well in large organizations. She adapted well to the corporate culture, followed the rules, and worked well with lots of different types of people. There were times when there were multiple subsequent personnel reductions in her workplace, but she was never laid off—sometimes, she was the only survivor in her whole department. She just mastered corporate life, thus, she became the top professional in the eyes of her bosses. She worked was promoted to the position of the Quality Manager and used to bring the quality procedures home. I still have a memory of our daily procedures every morning. My sister and I had a list of activities to follow glued to the wall. After opening my eyes, I had 22 minutes to brush my teeth, get dressed, have breakfast, and shut the door behind me. If I wanted to get a new toy, I had to submit a written application to my parents describing how this toy would contribute to my personal development. So, what does my mother—this well-adapted, well-composed corporate person—tell me when it comes to looking for jobs? Well, she tells me to go for my dreams, start my own company, and do everything I can so that I'm free, and I have no boss.

My father, on the other hand, is a professional chess player. He decided to go for undergrad studies in engineering just to get a degree, and he was taking some jobs on the side just for the income. But the only real thing that was ever important to him was chess. So, he went to study at the Academy of Physical Education and got the title of a professional trainer in chess. He then went on to work as both a chess player and a chess trainer. As a chess player, he was always his own boss and traveled a lot. He was a runner up in the Polish individual championships in chess, and a trainer of the Polish national team. I remember that he was barely ever present when I was a school kid. Now that he is retired and close to 70 years old, he teaches chess to kids, and he is happy that while getting retirement money... he has more time for chess. He is still hard to catch! Chess is a sport like any other; you win and get the prize, or you lose and walk away with nothing. Sometimes one imprecise move on the chessboard can lead to the ultimate loss in a two-week-long tournament. If you ask me, I would call anyone who chooses this profession, a mad person. My dad also tried to break up with chess a few times and find himself a "normal job," but was so addicted to chess that he was always back at the chessboard after a short period. I also remember him as an imaginative person who always thought out of the box: painting in his free time, writing books and articles (guess what: all about chess). Plus, he was always up for storytelling. When I was a kid, he used to be a fairy tale generator, big time: he used to come up with a new, genuine fairy tale from the top of his head every evening so that I and my sister could fall asleep. So, what does my dad—this gambler and artist—is telling me when it comes to life advice? Well, when I talk to him about jobs, he always underscores how essential safety is. He tells me that I should always take care of my education first, and then get "a good, safe, decent job on a payroll." And, he doesn't want to even hear about businesses or any other unnecessary gambling activities.

What does this teach me? Well, the grass is always greener on the other side. People often imagine that other working environments or professions are better than theirs: more enjoyable, more fulfilling, more rewarding. People tend to demonize the downsides of their job and overestimate the benefits of other jobs around. So, it is important to be objective and able to appreciate the job you've got. For instance, as a researcher, do you enjoy the fact that you *are allowed* to participate in research conferences? In many industries, attending external meetups organized beyond the company and sharing information about your projects is *forbidden*. Even if you attend an internal conference within the company, trade secrets and Non-Disclosure Agreements might prohibit you from sharing the details of what you are doing with employees from other departments. So, enjoy the research conferences for as long as you can! It is only an example; there are many other aspects of research life to enjoy— even little things such as flexible hours or no dress code. We take it for granted, but in many other professions, white-collars have way less personal freedom than us. The grass is not greener on the other side; the grass is greener where we water it.

Also, changing jobs—especially when it's a lucky escape—evokes a rapid boost in the level of job satisfaction, which then gradually decreases (Chadi & Hetschko, 2014). In the long run, we tend to get used to the perks of the current job and take them for granted. Then, we often start looking around and asking ourselves whether there is something better out there, waiting for us—especially when we see all these smiling faces of our acquaintances on *LinkedIn* who just got new jobs. This void is quite natural; it's hard to find the right balance between ambition and drive—which always prompts you to keep on improving—and gratitude for what you already have. The temptation is a part of human nature. Even if you have the perfect job, once in a while, the doubts will come—especially if you meet someone whose job has some perks that your job doesn't.

These atavistic fears and beliefs

Coming from academia, we often suffer from this obsession of going forward or getting higher in the professional hierarchy. Academia is designed in this way: you either go up, or you are out at some point—there is no middle ground.

This academic approach to careers makes us think that if we don't get promoted for some time, it's a sign of *regress*. We are so used to building up to something in our careers that everything we do in our professional lives—from taking a course to giving a talk—must happen for a reason and become yet another bullet point on our CV. Also, since we strongly identify ourselves with our jobs, in case we don't update our CV (or, resume) for some time, we feel like our self-development has stopped.

Of course, industry follows this way of thinking to a certain extent. Even if you work in a corporation, it might be frowned upon you if you stay in the same position for twenty years and if you don't develop your professional skills any further. Pressure for growth and progress is an evolutionary mechanism, and it will always be there in the society—especially in the times when automatization of many jobs slowly decreases the demand for human employees in many areas of the job market, and the supply of jobs starts falling, respectively. But sometimes, it is better to let go, stop thinking about your next promotion opportunity, and to focus on *enjoying the process* of becoming a professional instead.

In most countries of the world, high social status is no longer *necessary* to live a good life. You can do well as a "regular employee"—and it doesn't mean that you are not ambitious! We often have atavistic fears that being just a "regular employee" is not good enough. In ancient times, when people were still living in tribes, individuals at the top of the hierarchy had better entitlement to food, shelter, and mating than the rest of the tribe. Back then, social status had a crucial influence on all other aspects of life and could even considerably prolong life. Running away from being at the bottom of the ladder often literally meant running away from death. Now, this is no longer the case; there is no more need to be a leader to be safe and sound.

You don't need to fear failure also because the world is *abundant*. In academia, resources are highly limited: not everyone can land a faculty position, and it's often the case that you need to *compete* against your own friends for the same award or the same job. Academia can feel very claustrophobic, given the lack of space and opportunity for growth for everyone—academics are often like a bunch of tigers closed together in a cage. It's just much less space than they deserve.

Beyond academia, however, you have much more space for development and you can experience much more synergy with others. Typically, you don't need to *compete* with people around you but rather quite the opposite: you are rewarded for being a team player and a supporter to others. The more you offer to others, the more indispensable you become, and the more you get back. Furthermore, even if you experience a ceiling effect in your current job, you are free to change your employer without any repercussions—and in most professions, you can easily find multiple employers within commuting distance. Thus, you will never feel the same captivity again.

Most researchers have a never-ending curiosity and drive for self-growth. For this reason, as a researcher, it is hard to earn this feeling of *settling down*. Let me explain. Some people out there can get *comfortable* with their current jobs so much that they never reconsider changing positions. As researchers, we are often on the more restless end; as soon as we are comfortable in some place, we start thinking, "OK, so what can I improve on now? Where to go next?" And, if nothing changes in our scope of duties, or in our position title for a long time, we get very uncomfortable, or even anxious, on our minds. It is hard for us to let go and just be happy.

Next to this restlessness, we also often suffer from some cognitive errors and detrimental beliefs when it comes to jobs. For instance, many people give up a wish to find their dream job and settle for something just *good enough* for them. They assume that they just miss the *luck* necessary to get the dream job. Well, some people out there *are* lucky and happen to meet their destiny at their very first job. However, most people need to try at least a few jobs before they find their place on Earth, so if this happens to you, you need to know that it's normal.

How to help PhDs?

As discussed throughout this book, PhDs don't have an easy job transitioning to industry. They often land in this uncomfortable position where they are considered too highly educated and too expensive for low-level industry positions, not enough experienced for the high-level positions. At the same time, they are often too well-educated and "privileged" to get help with finding the next job from the government agencies. It is a very hard situation to find yourself in, especially given that next to finding the source of income, you need to reconceptualize your whole career and find a new role to play in society.

It's not a secret that most PhDs are not getting enough prepared for industry jobs during their PhD programs. There is a huge need to develop better *training programs* for PhDs (Clair et al., 2017) that would help them to better adapt to the free job market early on in their careers rather than learning about the job market in panic when their contract is close to the end. On most occasions, PhDs aren't helped career-wise anymore when their contract expires and when they need this help the most. This problem should be addressed by creating dedicated training programs for unemployed PhDs.

I'd like to draw your attention to two points here. Firstly, as mentioned in *Introduction*, it is the classic *tragedy of the commons* problem that should be solved through regulation on the institutional level. It is easy to blame PIs for their lack of involvement—but they need to make daily choices that make their lab competitive on the academic market. In fact, it's an *economical* rather than ethical problem as most PIs are genuinely interested in helping their employees career-wise; they just afford it. Perhaps, giving either more (e.g., financial) incentives for sending PhDs to the professional training early on, or introducing sanctions for not doing that, would change the calculus of risks and rewards in the PIs' books.

Secondly, there is still little awareness among employers and recruiters about what a PhD is, and what competencies it entails. Twenty years ago, PhDs were still rare in the open job market. It's a matter of the last two decades when a broad stream of young and highly educated people started leaving academia. Awareness of this upward trend could be raised by creating a publicly available booklet to inform those who have never worked in academia what PhD is about. Such a booklet might help small and middle-sized companies who are still unfamiliar with the academic culture. Also, it would be an interesting experiment to research if PhDs provide better "revenue per salary" to companies by any chance—after all, this is the ultimate argument to hire any employee.

Lastly, as mentioned in *Introduction*, for most PhD graduates, there is not enough room to stay in academia. And this problem is, to my mind, caused by capitalism: PIs will always choose to hire yet another PhD student who is a cheap machine to produce manuscripts, rather than hiring as a lab assistant, a Postdoc, a secretary, and such.

So, what is a solution to this problem? I believe that the only solution to capitalism is even more aggressive capitalism—this is also why I wrote this book. If more early career researchers realize that there are good jobs waiting for them outside academia—and that they don't need to compromise on their professional life and accept poor working conditions—academic employers will finally need to make more effort to keep good people around. And, the working conditions in academia will probably improve with time as well.

Other resources for PhDs transitioning to industry

Fortunately, in recent years, many independent resources have appeared on the scene—from books and blogs, through podcasts and webinars, courses, to the whole online communities and content platforms. There are lots of great, both free and commercial, online resources listing tips on how to network, how to present yourself during job interviews, and how to land your dream job. It is good to brace yourself and to go through some of these materials before job interviews! I listed all the resources I'm familiar with in *Appendix 1*.

So, how does it feel after transitioning beyond the academic career track?

As mentioned in *Introduction* academic literature dedicated to post-PhD academic tracks is a black hole: so far, there were only a few—either quantitative or qualitative—studies dedicated to professional development after leaving academia. Thus, not much is known about the *typical* career paths after moving to industry and how to best utilize your academic experience in industry.

To approach this question, I asked several friends who shifted from academia to industry to share their impressions with me and to give their advice to those who still hold academic positions but are hesitating on what to do next. Twenty-three former academics have completed the survey. Since I only asked friends and friends of friends, the results cannot be treated as a scientific study. Yet still, I believe that the conclusions are interesting.

For example, I asked about the level of satisfaction from the job right before switching career tracks and right after making the switch. In the group I interviewed, there was not a single person who reported that their quality of life had dropped after leaving academia! Only one person among 23 participants declared that they have regrets about leaving academia. I summarized some of the outcome statistics in Fig. 8. I also placed the full testimonials from the participants of this survey in *Appendix 2*.

Some of the survey participants decided to stay anonymous while some other participants have put their names on their testimonials.

Additionally, I also interviewed five individuals who *came to academia* from industry—I placed the full testimonials in *Appendix 3*. As you can see from these testimonials, it can also be a good career move, and none of the interviewed academics regret the decision they made.

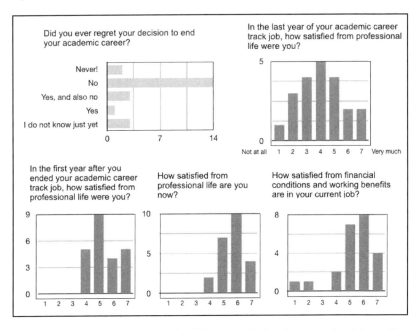

Figure 8 The results of the survey featuring 23 former academics who now work in industry. Most respondents never regretted transitioning to industry, and they declare their quality of professional life to be *higher* compared to the times when they were finishing their last academic contract.

The last piece of advice

The last piece of advice might sound a bit surprising and contradictory to everything said before, but hopefully, it makes sense at second glance.

So, the last thing is: freedom is a *lonely road*. As Sigmund Freud famously said, "Most people don't want freedom, because freedom involves responsibility, and most people are frightened of responsibility." You will never be able to find anyone who can guide you by hand and tell you with 100% confidence which career choices you should make. If you are too dependent upon advice from other people, you'll most likely regret many of your decisions. Most probably, all the answers to your questions

186

are already there in the back of your head, you just have no access to them at the moment.

Therefore, my last piece of advice is this: don't listen to anyone. It's good to ask for advice or opinion, but eventually, you should still make your own decisions. Living intuitively and taking calculated risks usually work better than going only for statistics and strongly following advice from senior people. If I can point to the one thing I regret from my twenties, it would be exactly that: listening to advice much more often than necessary. In the end, all the decisions I made against my own intuition, turned out to be wrong.

The decision to write this book was also an intuitive move for me. I don't have any family members who are authors of any book other than a book about chess, and neither do I have many friends who are authors. Thus, there was no one I could ask for advice. I was hesitating about this decision for a long time—writing a book might mean exposure to a wider audience, which was not the case in my life before. While to some people, attention and recognition are additional perks, to me, they are the *costs* I need to bear to convey the message. At the same time, a book dedicated to careers written by an anonymous person wouldn't be credible. One of the key take-home messages coming from this book is that it's *worth* it to be bold and to try new things in your life. It would be hypocrisy not to try... Eventually, I decided to put this book together under my name, hoping that this move won't change much in my daily life.

Furthermore, the topic seemed monstrous and overwhelming. I was questioning myself: is it better to write down what I know now, or to wait for five years until I know much more about this topic? Is it better to give heuristic advice, or not to give any advice at all? Yet, I eventually decided to take up the challenge and describe the problem together with the scope of possible solutions and tips to the best of my abilities. What helped me make this final decision, was many PhDs were asking me the same questions. At some point, I thought to myself, "Maybe better to write a book, otherwise, I always need to repeat the same pieces of advice over and over again." I also decided to publish this book online to make it as available to early-career researchers as possible—regardless of which corner of the world they live in.

I also decided to put this book together quickly, as a writing sprint in the scope of a few weeks. I knew that the more time I would think about the fact that I am writing about a big societal problem, the more stress it would bring—so, I was doing my best to finish the manuscript and post it online before the adrenaline kicks in and freezes me. And now, when I see the endpoint, I'm really happy with my decision to take this avenue.

So, I wish you all the very best with your career. I hope you make good, independent decisions in your professional life, and. I would be happy to hear that you are doing well. If you have some career story which you would be willing to share with me, please drop me a message (see: *Feedback information*).

If you enjoy my writing…

… I write a personal blog as well[77]. It concerns a wide variety of topics, but recently, I turned towards analyzing and commenting on the global changes in the job market. I hope that you can find some interesting content there!

If you feel like you need more guidance and hands on training…

… in career development after your PhD, we also offer intensive career orientation courses for researchers transitioning to industry in *Welcome Solutions*[78]. As research shows, such courses effectively help PhDs in launching their new careers (Layton et al., 2020).

In our course, we follow the philosophy introduced in this book: you and your job are two pieces of a puzzle, and the most challenging stage of the transition is to find the right match. Therefore, we combine comprehensive knowledge about the job market for PhDs with self-discovery exercise. We offer intensive two-day on-site workshops and 4-week workshops online. These workshops are highly interactive, contain many group activities as well as individual self-discovery exercises and aptitude tests. The ambitious goal behind our workshops is to help you discover what type of job and which environment fits you best and to give you practical information on how to get there. Don't spend your time on a lonely odyssey through the job market!

We also talk to PhDs and other professionals in industry who tell us about their industry careers, and we post this content online. Please subscribe to our open *YouTube* channel[79] to watch the materials and learn from those who made it!

If you would like to actively contribute to careers of other researchers…

… you might consider joining the Advisory Board of *Stichting Solaris Onderzoek en Ontwikkeling*. Solaris operates according to a novel scheme. Firstly, people contacting the organization and searching for help with their careers are offered consultancy with a confidential, international panel of advisors. In a way, it's a form of group mentoring, in which the panelists can debate the problem and propose various solutions at a time. We make sure that all the panelists sign a confidentiality clause and that everyone's opinion is respected equally. We also collect a lot of information about possibilities for PhDs (especially in the Netherlands) and post it on our websites. We are open to any suggestions for how to develop further!

---

[77] www.nataliabielczyk.com

[78] www.welcome-solutions.com

[79] www.youtube.com/c/welcomesolutions

Lastly, if you feel that this book has inspired you…

… I would be grateful for some warm words about the book on *Amazon*[80] and/or *Goodreads*[81]. By supporting this book, you support independent, self-published authors. Also, sharing positivity and recommending good content is the best way to spread the news and reach more potential readers who need this content. And, good karma always comes back!

---

[80] www.amazon.com/dp/B08DD7GMH4

[81] www.goodreads.com/book/show/49707754-what-is-out-there-for-me-the-landscape-of-post-phd-career-tracks?

REFERENCES

Basalla, S. & Debelius, M. (2014). *"So What Are You Going to Do with That?": Finding Careers Outside Academia.* University of Chicago Press. ISBN: 978-0-226-20040-8

Berdahl, M & Malloy, J. (2018). *Work Your Career: Get What You Want from Your Social Sciences or Humanities PhD.* University of Toronto Press, Higher Education Division. ISBN: 978-1-487-59426-8

Bielczyk, N. Z., Ando*, A., Badhwar*, A., Caldinelli*, C., Gao*, M., Haugg*, A., Hernandez*, L. M., Ito*, K., Kessler*, D., Lurie*, D., Makary*, M. M., Nikolaidis*, A., Veldsman*, M., Allen, C., Bankston, A., Bottenhorn, K. L., Braukmann, R., Calhoun, V., Cheplygina, V., Costa Boffino, C., Ercan, E., Finc, K., Foo, H., Khatibi, A., La, C., Mehler, D. M. A., Narayanan, S., Poldrack, R. A., Raamana, P. R., Salo, T., Goddard-Sebillotte, C., Uddin, L. Q., Valeriani, D., Valk, S. L., Walton, C. C., Ward, P. G. D., Yanes, J. A., Zhou, X., OHBM Student and Postdoc Special Interest Group. (2020). Effective self-management for early career researchers in the natural and life sciences. *Neuron, 106*(2): 212–17. doi:10.1016/j.neuron.2020.03.015

Bielczyk, N. Z. & Bonet-Carne, E. (2020). Safety or freedom? On the post-PhD career tracks. *eLife blog.* Retrieved from www.ecrlife.org/academic-career-landscape/

Briggs-Myers, I. & Myers, P. B. (1995). *Gifts Differing: Understanding Personality Type.* Mountain View, CA: Davies-Black Publishing. ISBN: 978-0-89106-074-1

Brown Urban, J. & Linver, M. R. (2018). *Building a Career Outside Academia: A Guide for Doctoral Students in the Behavioral and Social Sciences.* American Psychological Association. ISBN: 978-1-433-82952-9

Bruskin, J. (1973). What are Americans Afraid Of? The Bruskin Report: A Market Research Newsletter. *New York Times.*

Bruzzese, A. (2018). How to Tailor a Resume for a Specific Job. Retrieved from www.livecareer.com/resources/resumes/how-to/write/resume-tailoring

Bumpus, N. (2015). Moving toward inclusion. *Science.* doi: 10.1126/science.caredit.a15002 73

Byrne, R. (2006). *The Secret.* Atria Books. ISBN: 978-1-58270-170-7

Caccipuoti, C. & Keohane-Burbridge , E. (2020). *Independent Scholars Meet the World: Expanding Academia beyond the Academy (Rethinking Careers, Rethinking Academia).* University Press of Kansas. ISBN: 978-0-700-62991-6

Caterine, C. (2020). *Leaving Academia: A Practical Guide.* Princeton University Press. ISBN: 978-0-691-20019-4

Chadi, A. & Hetschko, C. (2014). The Magic of the New: How Job Changes Affect Job Satisfaction. *Journal of Economics & Management Strategy, 27*(1). doi: 10.1111/jems.12217

Cheng, B., Kan, M., Levanon, G., Ray, R. L. (2014). Job Satisfaction: 2014 Edition. Retrieved from www.conference-board.org/publications/publicationdetail.cfm? publicationid=2785

Cheplygina, V., Hermans, F., Albers, C., Bielczyk, N., Smeets, I. (2020). Ten simple rules for getting started on Twitter as a scientist. *PLoS Computational Biology, 16*(2): e1007513. doi: 10.1371/journal.pcbi.1007513

Clair, R., Hutto, T., MacBeth, C., Newstetter, W., McCarty, N. A. & Melkers, J. (2017). The "new normal": Adapting doctoral trainee career preparation for broad career paths in science. *PLoS One, 12*(5), e0177035. doi: 10.1371/journal.pone.0177035

Clark, A. E. (2015). What makes a good job? Job quality and job satisfaction. *IZA World of Labor, 215,* doi: 10.15185/izawol.215

Columbus, L. (2018, 29th January). Data Scientist Is the Best Job In America According Glassdoor's 2018 Rankings. Retrieved from www.forbes.com/sites/louiscolumbus/2018/01/29/data-scientist-is-the-best-job-in-america-according-glassdoors-2018-rankings/#1d6840985535

Cornthwaite, C. (2020). *Doctoring: Building a Life With a PhD.* Independently published. ISBN: 979-8-673-05738-4

Dirnhuber, J. (2017, 31st May). Children turn backs on traditional careers in favour of internet fame, study finds. Retrieved from www.thesun.co.uk/news/3617062/children-turn-backs-on-traditional-careers-in-favour-of-internet-fame-study-finds

Dohmen, B. (2018, June 23rd). Is Intuition A Form Of Intelligence? Retrieved from www.forbes.com/sites/investor/2018/06/23/is-intuition-a-form-of-intelligence/#7c495e0015fd

Dwyer, K. K. & Davidson, M. M. (2012). Is Public Speaking Really More Feared Than Death? *Communication Research Reports, 29*(2), 99-107. doi: 10.1080/08824096.2012.667772

Ende, M. (1979). *Die unendliche Geschichte (The Neverending Story)*. Thienemann Verlag. ISBN: 978-3-522-12800-1

Ernst, Z. (2020, 14th May). Leaving academia for the private sector: Seven years later. Retrieved from www.medium.com/@zacernst/leaving-academia-for-the-private-sector-seven-years-later-fbb7849182f6

Facer-Childs, E. R., Campos, B. M., Middleton, B., Skene, D. J., & Bagshaw, A. P. (2019). Circadian phenotype impacts the brain's resting-state functional connectivity, attentional performance, and sleepiness. *Sleep, 42*(5), zsz033. doi: 10.1093/sleep/zsz033

Franks, S. (2019, 27th June). One in Four U.S. Companies Reports Losing Business Due to Language. Retrieved from https://blog.languageline.com/one-in-four-u.s.-employers-reports-losing-business-due-to-language

Fruscione, J. & Baker, K. J. (2018). *Succeeding Outside the Academy: Career Paths beyond the Humanities, Social Sciences, and STEM*. University Press of Kansas. ISBN: 978-0-700-62688-5

Gallagher, A. H. & Gallagher, M. P. (2020). *The Portable PhD: Taking Your Psychology Career Beyond Academia*. American Psychological Association. ISBN: 978-1-433-83125-6

Gigerenzer, G. (2008). *Gut Feelings: The Intelligence of the Unconscious*. Viking. ISBN: 978-0-670-03863-3

Giltner, D. (2010). *Turning Science Into Things People Need: Voices of Scientists Working in Industry*. Self-published. ISBN: 978-1-935-68904-1

Godin, S. (2010). *Linchpin: Are You Indispensable?* Penguin Group Inc. ISBN: 978-1-101-19631-1

Godin, S. (2020). *Tribes: We Need You to Lead Us*. Little, Brown Book Group. ISBN: 978-0-749-93975-5

Goldberg, L. R. (1993). The structure of phenotypic personality traits. *The American Psychologist, 48*(1): 26–34. doi: 10.1037/0003-066X.48.1.26

Grant, A. M. (2012). An integrated model of goal-focused coaching: An evidence-based framework for teaching and practice. *International Coaching Psychology Review, 7*(2), 146–65.

Gritsenko, D. (2015). *Changing Hats: A book for academics looking beyond academia.* Amazon.com Services LLC. ASIN: B01MR7FCHQ

Hanseke, G. (2018). Good jobs, good pay, better health? The effects of job quality on health among older European workers. *The European Journal of Health Economics, 19*(1), 59-73. doi: 10.1007/s10198-017-0867-9

Hardin, G (1968). The Tragedy of the Commons. *Science, 162*(3859), 1243–8. doi: 10.1126/science.162.3859.1243

Higgins, M (2014, 14th March). Using the Star technique to shine at job interviews: a how-to guide. Retrieved from www.theguardian.com/careers/careers-blog/star-technique-competency-based-interview

Hunt, V., Layton, D. & Prince, S. (2015). Why Diversity Matters. Retrieved from www.mckinsey.com/business-functions/organization/our-insights/why-diversity-matters

Kiyosaki, R. & Lechter, S. L. (2000). *Rich Dad, Poor Dad.* Warner Books Ed. ISBN: 978-0-446-67745-0

Kelsky, K. (2015). *The Professor Is In: The Essential Guide To Turning Your PhD Into a Job.* Three Rivers Press, ISBN: 978-0-553-41942-0

Koier, E. & J. de Jonge (2018). The impact of a doctorate. The careers and job prospects of doctorate holders in the Netherlands. *The Hague: Rathenau Instituut.*

Kubler-Ross, E. (1969). *On Death and Dying.* Routledge. ISBN: 978-0-415-04015-9

Kuss, D.J. & Griffiths, M.D. (2017). Social networking sites and addiction: Ten lessons learned. *International Journal of Environmental Research and Public Health,* 14, 311. doi: 10.3390/ijerph14030311

Layton, R. L., Solberg, V. S. H., Jahangir, A. E., Hall, J. D., Ponder, C. A., Micoli, K.J., Vanderford, N. L. (2020). Career planning courses increase career readiness of graduate and postdoctoral trainees. *F1000 Research,* doi: 10.12688/f1000research.26025.1

Lilienfeld, S. O., Lynn, S. J., Lohr, J. M. (2014). *Science and Pseudoscience in Clinical Psychology.* Guilford Publications. ISBN: 978-1-462-51751-0

Linder, K. E.,, Kelly, K., Tobin, T. J., Kim. J. (2020). *Going Alt-Ac: A Guide to Alternative Academic Careers.* Stylus Publishing. ISBN: 978-1-620-36830-5

Magnimind (2019, 17th April). Why data scientists are future jobs in the world? Retrieved from www.becominghuman.ai/why-data-scientists-are-future-jobs-in-the-world-9eeec9c8f617

Marker, S. (2015, 22th February). How many jobs will the average person have in his or her lifetime? Retrieved from www.linkedin.com/pulse/how-many-jobs-average-person-have-his-her-lifetime-scott-marker

Marston, W. M. (1928). *Emotions of Normal People*. K. Paul, Trench, Trubner & Co. Ltd.

Mather-L'Huillier, N. (2015). Non-academic Careers for PhD Holders. Retrieved from www.findaphd.com/advice/doing/phd-non-academic-careers.aspx

Miller, K., Chmiel, J., Whitehead, L. & Jet (2014). *Moving On: Essays on the Aftermath of Leaving Academia*. Amazon.com Services LLC. ASIN: B00HOH011A

Moffitt, T. E., Arseneault, L., Belsky, D., Dickson, N., Hancox, R. J., Harrington, H., ... Caspi, A. (2011). A gradient of childhood self-control predicts health, wealth, and public safety. *Proceedings of the National Academy of Sciences, 108*(7), 2693–8. doi: 10.1073/pnas.1010076108

Mulvey, J. (2015). *How to Find a Career With Your Humanities Degree in 126 Days: A Guide for Lost Humanities Majors*. Selloutyoursoul.com. ASIN: B0165T5Y6Y

Nelson, M. R. (2014). *Navigating the Path to Industry: A Hiring Manager's Advice for Academics Looking for a Job in Industry*. Annorlunda Books, Inc. ISBN: 978-0-990-74452-8

Newport, C. (2016). *Deep Work: Rules for Focused Success in a Distracted World*. Grand Central Publishing. ISBN: 978-1-455-58669-1

Ordóñez, L. D., Schweitzer, M. E., Galinsky, A. D., Bazerman, M. (2009). Goals Gone Wild: The Systematic Side Effects of Over-Prescribing Goal Setting. *Academy of Management Perspectives, 23*. doi: 10.2139/ssrn.1332071

Ostrom, E. (1990). *Governing the Commons: The Evolution of Institutions for Collective Action*. Cambridge: Cambridge University Press. ISBN: 978-0-521-40599-8

Peabody, R. (2014). *The Unruly PhD: Doubts, Detours, Departures, and Other Success Stories*. Palgrave MacMillan. ISBN: 978-1-137-37310-6

Pegoraro, M., Picot, E., Hansen, C. N., Kyriacou, C. P., Rosato, E., & Tauber, E. (2015). Gene expression associated with early and late chronotypes in *Drosophila melanogaster. Frontiers in Neurology, 6*:100. doi: 10.3389/fneur.2015.00100

Persson, T. (2020). *The PhD Career Coaching Guide: Job Search Strategies, Interview Techniques, and Life Lessons for Achieving Success*. Passage2pro AB. ISBN: 978-9-151-94264-3

Pickle, N. (2019). Post-PhD job searches are tough. Here's how I escaped Dr. Seuss's 'Waiting Place'. *Science*. doi: 10.1126/science.caredit.aaz8833

Pryal, K. (2019). *The Freelance Academic: Transform Your Creative Life and Career.* Blue Crow Books. ISBN: 978-1-947-83435-4

Puritty, C., Strickland, L. R., Alia, E., Blonder, B., Klein, E. Kohl, M. T. et al. (2017). Without inclusion, diversity initiatives may not be enough. *Science, 357*(6356),1101–2. doi: 10.1126/science.aai9054

Raia, A. P. (1965). Goal Setting and Self-Control: An Empirical Study. *Journal of Management Studies* **2**(1):34–53. doi: 10.1111/j.1467-6486.1965.tb00564.x

Rath, T. (2007). *Strengths finder 2.0*. Simon And Schuster UK. ISBN: 978-1-595-62015-6

Raven, J. C. (1936). Mental tests used in genetic studies: The performance of related individuals on tests mainly educative and mainly reproductive. *MSc Thesis*, University of London.

Ries, E. (2011). Lean startup. *How Today's Entrepreneurs Use Continuous Innovation to Create Radically Successful Businesses*. Penguin Books Ltd. ISBN: 978-0-670-92160-7

Robbins, M. (2017). *The 5 Second Rule: Transform your Life, Work, and Confidence with Everyday Courage*. Savio Republic. ISBN: 978-1-682-61238-5

Robbins, T. (1991). *Awaken the Giant Within: How to Take Immediate Control of Your Mental, Emotional, Physical and Financial Destiny!* Free Press. ISBN: 978-0-671-79154-0

Roenneberg, T., Kuehnle, T., Juda, M., Kantermann, T., Allebrandt, K., Gordijn, M., & Merrow, M. (2007). Epidemiology of the human circadian clock. *Sleep Medicine Reviews, 11*(6), 429–38. doi: 10.1016/j.smrv.2007.07.005

Rogers, K. L. (2020). *Putting the Humanities PhD to Work: Thriving in and beyond the Classroom*. Duke University Press. ISBN: 978-1-478-00954-2

Ruts, H.-J. (2019). Belastingplan verkleint fiscaal verschil werknemers en zelfstandigen, vooral bij hogere inkomens. Retrieved from www.zipconomy.nl/2019/11/belastingplan-verkleint-fiscaal-verschil-werknemers-en-zelfstandigen-vooral-bij-hogere-inkomens

Sarner, M. (2018). How burnout became a sinister and insidious epidemic. Retrieved from www.theguardian.com/society/2018/feb/21/how-burnout-became-a-sinister-and-insidious-epidemic

Savage, M. (2019, July 26th). Burnout is rising in the land of work-life balance. Retrieved from www.bbc.com/worklife/article/20190719-why-is-burnout-rising-in-the-land-of-work-life-balance

Schillebeeckx, M., Maricque, B., & Lewis, C. (2013). The missing piece to changing the university culture. *Nature Biotechnology, 31,* 938–41. doi: 10.1038/nbt.2706

Schrijvers, J. (2002). *Hoe word ik een rat? De kunst van het konkelen en samenzweren.* SCRIPTUM. ISBN: 978-9-055-94255-8

Schwarzenegger, A. (2013). Total Recall: My Unbelievably True Life Story. *Simon & Schuster.* ISBN: 978-1-451-66244-3

Shanafelt, T.D., West, C. P., Sloan, J. A.,Novotny, P. J., Poland, G. A., Menaker, R., Rummans, T. A., Dyrbye, L. N. (2009). Career Fit and Burnout Among Academic Faculty. *Archives of Internal Medicine, 169*(10), 990–5. doi: 10.1001/archinternmed.2009.70

Sherlock, M. & Wagstaff, D. L. (2018). Exploring the Relationship Between Frequency of Instagram Use, Exposure to Idealized Images, and Psychological Well-being in Women. *Psychology of Popular Media Culture, 8(*4), 482–90. doi: 10.1037/ppm0000182

Silver, D., Schrittwieser, J., Simonyan, K., Antonoglou, I., Huang, A., Guez, A., Hubert, T., Baker, L., Lai, M., Bolton, A., Chen, Y., Lillicrap, T., Fan, H., Sifre, L., van den Driessche, G., Graepel, T., Hassabis, D. (2017). Mastering the game of Go without human knowledge. *Nature, 550*(7676), 354–59. doi: 10.1038/nature24270

Sinche, M. V. (2016). *Next Gen PhD: A Guide to Career Paths in Science.* Harvard University Press. ISBN: 978-0-674-50465-3

Sinche, M., Layton, R. L., Brandt, P. D., O'Connell, A. B., Hall, J. D., Freeman, A. M., Harrell, J. R., Cook, J. G., Brennwald, P. J. (2017). An evidence-based evaluation of transferable skills and job satisfaction for science PhDs. *PLoS ONE, 12*(9), e0185023. doi: 10.1371/journal.pone.0185023

Slack, M. (2019). 5 Problems with The Ladders' 6 Second Resume Study. Retrieved from www.resumegenius.com/blog/resume-help/5-problems-with-the-ladders-6-second-resume-study

Sowray, B, & Murray, D. (2019, March 21st). The Handbags You Won't Regret Investing In. Retrieved from www.elle.com/uk/fashion/what-to-wear/a30859/best-investment-bags

Tardelli, M. (2020). *The Salmon Leap for PhDs. Swimming upstream: A transition from academia to industry.* Independently published. 979-8-681-26796-6

Tomasello, D. L. (2019). Addressing Isolation in the Scientific Community. *Molecular Medicine, 25(*11), 931-32. doi: 10.1016/j.molmed.2019.08.007

Tracy, B. (1993). *Maximum Achievements: Strategies and Skills That Will Unlock Your Hidden Powers to Succeed.* Simon Schuster. ISBN: 978-0-684-80331-3

Vohs, K. D. (2018). Barnum Effect in psychology. *Encyclopedia Britannica.* Retrieved from www.britannica.com/science/Barnum-Effect

de Vries, M., Holland, R. W., Witteman, C. L. M. (2008). Fitting decisions: Mood and intuitive versus deliberative decision strategies. *Cognition & Emotion, 22*(5), 931–43. doi:10.1080/02699930701552580

Wapnick, E. (2017). *How to Be Everything: A Guide for Those Who (Still) Don't Know What They Want to Be When They Grow Up.* HarperOne. ISBN: 978-1-538-41760-7

Warren, E. & Warren-Tyagi, A. (2005). *All Your Worth: The Ultimate Lifetime Money Plan.* Simon & Schuster Inc. ISBN: 978-0-743-26988-8

Wiseman, R. (2004). *The Luck Factor: The Scientific Study of the Lucky Mind.* Arrow. ISBN: 978-0-099-44324-4

Wigert, B. & Agrawal, S. (2018, July 12th). Employee Burnout, Part 1: The 5 Main Causes. Retrieved from www.gallup.com/workplace/237059/employee-burnout-part-main-causes.aspx

Wills, E. (2018). Iceland has made it illegal to pay women less than men. The Business Insider. Retrieved from www.businessinsider.com/iceland-has-made-it-illegal-to-pay-women-less-than-men-2018-1?international=true&r=US&IR=T

Witters, (2011). In U.S., Government Jobs Pay in Well-Being. Retrieved from news.gallup.com/poll/148340/Government-Jobs-Pay-Well-being.aspx

Woolston, C. (2018). Science PhDs lead to enjoyable jobs. *Nature, 555,* 277. doi: 0.1038/d41586-018-02696-6

Woolston, C. (2019). PhDs: the tortuous truth. *Nature, 575,* 403–6. doi: 10.1038/d41586-019-03459-7

Wrześniewski, A., McCauley, C., Rozin, P., & Schwartz, B. (1997). Jobs, careers, and callings: People's relations to their work. *Journal of Research in Personality, 31*(1), 21–33. doi: 10.1006/jrpe.1997.2162

FEEDBACK INFORMATION

Feedback on the book

If you would like to provide feedback on this book, you are most welcome to drop an email to *Welcome Solutions*, at welcome.solutions.nijmegen@gmail.com

If your feedback is used in the future editions of the book or for any other (commercial or non-commercial) purposes, you'll get notified by email and acknowledged. In that case, please also include the following statement in your email (otherwise, we won't be able to use the information that you provided):

"I agree that my data is processed and stored according to the W*elcome Solutions* GDPR policy. I agree to be further contacted by a representative of *Welcome Solutions*."

Sharing your story

If you would like to tell us your own post-PhD story—either ups, downs, or both—please also drop us an email at welcome.solutions.nijmegen@gmail.com. We will read your email! We might also get back to you and ask you for permission to use exempts from your story to publish them at our website www.welcome-solutions.com or in the future editions of the book. In that case, please also include the following statement in your email (otherwise, we won't be able to use the information that you provided):

"I agree that my data is processed and stored according to the *Welcome Solutions* GDPR policy. I agree to be further contacted by a representative of *Welcome Solutions*."

APPENDICES

Appendix 1: All the online resources for PhDs transitioning into industry

A) Books:

1. *Turning Science Into Things People Need: Voices of Scientists Working in Industry* (Giltner, 2010): Anthology introducing career stories of ten respected researchers who have successfully built new careers in industry.

2. *Navigating the Path to Industry: A Hiring Manager's Advice for Academics Looking for a Job in Industry* (Nelson, 2014): Advice on how to optimize your job application process as a researcher: how to network, conduct informational interviews, turn your academic CV into an industry resume, write a cover letter, and go through the job interviews with confidence.

3. *The Unruly PhD: Doubts, Detours, Departures, and Other Success Stories* (Peabody, 2014): Anthology introducing career stories of researchers who have successfully built new careers in industry.

4. *Moving On: Essays on the Aftermath of Leaving Academia* (Miller et al., 2014): Antology introducing careers stories of fourteen former graduate students, adjuncts, and tenure-track professors who have successfully built new careers in industry.

5. *"So What Are You Going to Do with That?": Finding Careers Outside Academia* (Basalla & Debelius, 2014): Career advice for PhDs including discussion on transferable skills, strategies to pass job interviews, and examples of researchers who have successfully made the transition.

6. *Changing Hats: A book for academics looking beyond academia* (ebook, Gritsenko, 2015): Demystifying stereotypes about transitioning to industry including practical tips and success stories.

7. *The Professor Is In: The Essential Guide To Turning Your PhD Into a Job* (Kelsky, 2015): Advice on how to optimally develop your research career and how to transition beyond academia when the time comes.

8. *How to Find a Career With Your Humanities Degree in 126 Days: A Guide for Lost Humanities Majors* (Mulvey, 2015): The book contains a 126-day career-orientation

program, focused on finding a direction in the job market, building the skill set, and landing the job.

9. *Next Gen PhD: A Guide to Career Paths in Science* (Sinche, 2016): Overview of the career landscape facing science PhDs, combined with guidelines on how to identify personal strengths and interests, network, and successfully get through the job application process.

10. *Succeeding Outside the Academy: Career Paths beyond the Humanities, Social Sciences, and STEM* (Fruscione & Baker, 2018): A collection of essays dedicated to emotional, intellectual, and financial aspects of making a transition from academia to industry.

11. *Work Your Career: Get What You Want from Your Social Sciences or Humanities PhD* (Berdahl & Malloy, 2018). The book is dedicated to PhD students in social sciences and humanities in Canada, and presents a systematic approach to build successful career outcomes, both in academia and industry.

12. *Building a Career Outside Academia: A Guide for Doctoral Students in the Behavioral and Social Sciences* (Brown Urban & Linver, 2018): Collection of essays dedicated to how to make the right career decision, what the scope of possibilities is, and how to prepare for job interviews as a researcher in behavioral and/or social sciences.

13. *The Freelance Academic: Transform Your Creative Life and Career* (Pryal, 2019): The author tells her professional story and gives practical advice for how to develop the career you want, and how to effectively use your creativity and your strengths at work.

14. *The PhD Career Coaching Guide: Job Search Strategies, Interview Techniques and Life Lessons for Achieving Success* (Persson, 2020): Advice on how to find a good job, attract employers, and successfully get through the job application process.

15. *Going Alt-Ac: A Guide to Alternative Academic Careers* (Linder et al., 2020): General career advice for researchers who consider transition to industry, based on case stories by the authors and other researchers who successfully transferred to industry.

16. *The Portable PhD: Taking Your Psychology Career Beyond Academia* (Gallagher & Gallagher, 2000). A guidebook for PhD graduates in psychology who think about working beyond academia: in public policy, education, healthcare, and business.

17. *Putting the Humanities PhD to Work: Thriving in and beyond the Classroom* (Rogers, 2020): An overview of the options in the job market for PhDs in humanities: how graduate training can lead to meaningful and significant careers beyond the academy for graduates, and how to find out which path you should take.

18. *Doctoring: Building a Life With a PhD* (Cornthwaite, 2020): Personal story of transition to industry by the author, aiming to empower researchers who think about taking the big leap towards industry and doubt in their value.

19. *The Salmon Leap for PhDs: Swimming upstream: A transition from academia to industry* (Tardelli, 2020): The summary of the best strategies for swimming in different waters towards landing an industry position. PhDs are in high demand outside academia, yet they need to learn how to speak the language of industry

recruiters. This book summarizes practical tips on how to transition from academia to industry.

20. *Leaving Academia: A Practical Guide* (Caterine, 2020): Advice for researchers thinking about the transition, focused on overcoming psychological difficulties, translating academic experience to the language of business, and adapting to the first job in industry.

21. *Independent Scholars Meet the World: Expanding Academia beyond the Academy (Rethinking Careers, Rethinking Academia)* (Caccipuoti & Keohane-Burbridge, 2020): An antology of personal stories and a compilation of advice from academics who successfully developed careers both in academia and in industry.

B) Blogs:

1. *Nature Careers* column[82]: Career column listing short blog posts providing broad advice for developing careers both in academia and beyond.

2. *BiomedBadass* blog[83] by Victoria Sherwood, PhD: Advice on how to successfully develop an industry career as a researcher in STEM.

3. *Post-PhD Career* blog series[84] at *TalkPlant* by Rupesh Paudyal, PhD: General career tips for researchers leaving academia and profiles of researchers who successfully transitioned to industry.

4. Blog section[85] at *PostPhdCareer.com* by Olga Pougovkina, PhD: General career tips for researchers leaving academia.

5. *What Are All the PhDs? Sharing the Career Path of All The PhDs*[86]: Self-submitted silhouettes of PhDs who successfully transitioned to industry.

6. *PhD Career Guide*[87]: Information about the most popular post-PhD career tracks and a set of advice on how to enter these career tracks.

7. *Beyond the Professoriate* blog[88] by L. Marein Wood: General career tips for researchers leaving academia.

8. *PhD to Life* blog[89] by Jennifer Polk, PhD: General career tips for researchers leaving academia.

9. *Roostervane* blog[90] by Chris Cornthwaite, PhD: General career tips for researchers leaving academia and leadership.

---

[82] www.go.nature.com/3aQl0Cq

[83] www.biomedbadass.com

[84] www.talkplant.com/introducing-post-phd-career-blog-series-at-talkplant

[85] www.postphdcareer.com/blog

[86] www.whatareallthephds.tumblr.com

[87] www.phdcareerguide.com

[88] www.beyondprof.com/blog

[89] www.fromphdtolife.com/blog

[90] www.roostervane.com/blog

10.*Genes to Genomes*[91] by the Genetics Society of America: A blog about career perspectives for researchers working in genetics, both in academia and beyond.

11.*Jobs on Toast* blog[92] by Chris Humphrey, PhD: A blog reviewing careers for PhDs in business, charities, industry and government, exploring topics such as the scope of careers for PhDs, pitching to employers, and how to find the right moment to move to industry.

12.*Sell Out Your Soul*[93] blog: A blog dedicated to PhDs and MS graduates in humanities. A guidebook how to quickly find and land a good position in industry with education in humanities majors.

C) Podcasts/YouTube channels:

1.*Welcome Solutions* YouTube channel[94]: Career talks featuring interviews with researchers who successfully transitioned to industry, other professionals with interesting career paths, and career experts.

2.*Papa PhD Podcast*[95] by David Mendes, PhD: Interviews with researchers who successfully transitioned to industry and career experts.

3.*PhD Careers Podcast*[96] by Caroline Ritchie, PhD: Interviews with researchers who successfully transitioned to industry.

4.*"What are you going to do with that?" Podcast*[97] by Danni Reches, PhD: Interviews with researchers who successfully transitioned to industry.

5.*PhD Career Stories Podcast*[98]: Silhouettes of researchers who successfully transitioned to industry: interviews and recordings of personal stories.

6.*PhDs at Work Podcast*[99] by Michelle Erickson, PhD: Interviews with researchers who successfully transitioned to industry.

7.*Passage2Pro Podcast*[100] by Tina Person, PhD: Tips for landing a good job in industry as an academic.

8.*BiomedBadass* YouTube channel[101] by Victoria Sherwood, PhD: Tips for landing a good job in industry as a STEM researcher.

---

[91] www.genestogenomes.org/tag/decoding-life

[92] www.jobsontoast.com

[93] www.selloutyoursoul.com

[94] www.youtube.com/c/welcomesolutions

[95] www.papaphd.com

[96] www.scientificphd-nowwhat.com/phd-careers-podcast

[97] www.whatareyougoing2do.wixsite.com/website

[98] www.phdcareerstories.com

[99] www.bit.ly/34mTewZ

[100] www.passage2pro.com/podcast

[101] www.youtube.com/channel/UCWzKoXua0A_uBLIqOZ4j14w

9. *Hopkins Biotech Podcast*[102] hosted by Roshan Chikarmane, PhD and Jenna Glatzer, PhD: Exploring non-academic career options for life scientists by interviewing researchers working in pharmaceuticals, biotechnology, consulting, venture capital, and other areas.

10. *Once a Scientist Podcast*[103] by Nick Edwards, PhD: a resource for young scientists to learn about different careers. The series consists of informal conversations where scientists can relax and speak about why they love their jobs and how they got to the point where they are now.

11. *Self-Compassionate Professor Podcast*[104] by Danielle De La Mare, PhD: Podcast helping academics and former academics in finding wellness, meaning, purpose, and freedom in their careers and lives. The podcast features those who have navigated their careers with creativity and self-compassion.

12. *Turning Science* YouTube channel[105] by David M. Giltner, PhD: Advice for PhDs in science and engineering who are searching to design and build rewarding careers in industry.

13. *The Scientistt Podcast*[106] by Jamie Slevin, PhD: A podcast to explore the realities of research life in the most honest and informative way.

D) Content platforms/Online communities:

1. *Cheeky Scientist*[107] platform by Isaiah Hankel, PhD: Member-only content platform + online community supporting researchers transferring to academia.

2. *Beyond the Professoriate*[108] platform by L. Maren Wood, PhD: Content platform listing courses + coaching offer.

3. *From PhD to Life*[109] platform by Jennifer Polk, PhD: Content platform listing courses + coaching offer.

4. *Roostervane*[110] platform by Chris Cornthwaite, PhD: Member-only content platform + online community supporting researchers transferring to academia.

5. *PhDs at Work*[111] by Michelle Erickson, PhD: Open online community for professionals with a PhD.

---

[102] www.hopkinsbiotechpodcast.com

[103] www.onceascientist.net

[104] www.podcasts.apple.com/us/podcast/self-compassionate-professor/id1500328836

[105] www.youtube.com/channel/UCrkeHUyE_HNulhdC7nhp6Vg

[106] www.scientistt.net/pages/podcast

[107] www.cheekyscientist.com

[108] www.beyondprof.com

[109] www.fromphdtolife.com

[110] www.roostervane.com

[111] www.phdsatwork.com

6. *Smart Tribe*[112] platform: Online community providing mentors for researchers in the process of transitioning to industry.
7. *Versatile PhD*[113] platform: Member-only content platform + online community supporting researchers transferring to academia.
8. *Graduate Career Consortium*[114]: Member-only content platform + online community supporting careers of PhD graduates from research universities and medical schools within the U.S. and Canada.
9. *The Dropout Club*[115]: Member-only content platform + online community for graduates from medical schools.
10. *Free The PhD*[116] platform by Vay Cao, PhD: Content platform listing courses + coaching offer.
11. *PhD Career Networking Group*[117] by Parag Mahanti, PhD: Open *LinkedIn* group offering mutual career support for professionals with a PhD.
12. *PhDs - Industry Hub*[118]: Open *LinkedIn* group offering mutual career support for professionals with a PhD.
13. *The Professor Is In*[119] platform by Karen L. Kelsky, PhD: Member-only content platform supporting researchers transferring to academia.
14. *Passage2Pro*[120] platform by Tina Persson, PhD: Content platform listing courses + coaching offer.
15. *Turning Science*[121] platform by David M. Giltner, PhD: Courses and coaching for PhDs in science and engineering who are searching to design and build rewarding careers in industry.
16. *Imagine PhD*[122] platform: Free career exploration and planning tools for the Humanities and Social Sciences.
17. *NaturalScience.Careers*[123] platform: A platform offering career development resources for PhDs in natural sciences.

[112] www.smarttribe.io

[113] www.versatilephd.com

[114] www.gradcareerconsortium.org

[115] www.docjobs.com

[116] www.freethephd.com

[117] www.linkedin.com/groups/8476427

[118] www.linkedin.com/groups/12451614

[119] www.theprofessorisin.com

[120] www.passage2pro.com

[121] www.turningscience.com/essential-guide

[122] www.imaginephd.com

[123] www.naturalscience.careers

18. *Researching.io*[124]: An online community matching PhDs working in academia with PhDs working in industry.
19. *Scientistt.net*[125] platform: Open online community listing new career opportunities and career elopement resources for researchers both in academia and industry.
20. *Industry Link*[126]: Open platform for PhD graduates based in Ontario, Canada, offering company tours, part-time internships, and consulting services.

E) Independent online courses for PhDs:

1. *4-week Intensive Online Career Development Course for Researchers in Transition to Industry*[127] by Welcome Solutions (Coach: Natalia Bielczyk, PhD): Intensive course focused on combining the knowledge about yourself with the knowledge about the job market, and learning effective strategies for networking and landing contracts.
2. *16-week Career Booster Program* by Success Beyond The Lab[128] (Coach: Dr. Amani Said, PhD): Online program focused on creating your professional Identity, identifying your ideal career path, and learning the tools to land any job.

---

[124] www.researching.io

[125] www.scientistt.net

[126] www.macindustrylink.com

[127] www.welcome-solutions.com/index.php/career-training-services

[128] www.successbeyondthelab.com

Appendix 2: Testimonials from former PhDs who took a decision to transition beyond the academic career track

Some of the responders finished their PhDs recently (or are still finishing their thesis!), while others have been working in industry for many years now. All the contributors express their own opinions, and not their current or previous employers'.

1. Anonymous Contributor

In what area did you do your PhD?
Cognitive Neuroscience

In which country did you complete your PhD?
United Kingdom

In what type of working environment are you working right now?
Working in a corporation/middle size company (>= 50 employees)

In which market sector are you working right now?
Software Development

Could you share your position title, and briefly describe (2-3 sentences) what your current scope of responsibilities is?
Data Scientist

How did you find your current job?
LinkedIn

Can you name the three biggest pros versus the three biggest cons of your current job?
Pros:
➢Much better working conditions (office space, available resources, etc.),
➢High salary,
➢Permanent contract.
Cons:
Not much so far :)

Can you briefly describe what a typical day at the office looks like in your current job?
I am working in a small team of Data Scientists in a middle-sized software company. It's an open office, and I interact with many people—which is a nice change compared to my last academic job where I felt very isolated. Every day, my team starts with a stand-up where we discuss our progress and goals for the day. I work on small data analysis projects as well as longer, more complex ones. I go to meetings. I eat lunch with colleagues, I socialize.

What was the biggest surprise to you once you started this job?
Everyone is very friendly and much less formal than I expected.

What experience obtained in academia helped you the most in your current job? Did the personal contacts developed in academia, help you in any way? From your current perspective, was PhD worth going through (compared to the alternative scenario in which you would have spent the same amount of time working in your current market sector)?
I didn't need to use personal contacts. PhD title looks good on the CV and was helpful in landing a data science job where everyone expects you to be smart. I am using a lot of skills from my PhD, mostly statistics (hypothesis testing, modeling) and programming.

What were the major reasons behind your decision to leave the academic career track? Was it a rapid decision, or perhaps, was this a long process of self-discovery? Or maybe, you are still hesitating and might come back to academia in the future?
I enjoyed my PhD and while going through my PhD program I thought I would stay in academia. I found a Postdoc contract very quickly but it turned out this time I did not feel so good about my lab, my supervisor and my project. I started thinking about the alternatives. Most of all I wanted a permanent position that would also allow me to do something interesting and use my skills. After doing some research on data science jobs I decided this was a good option for me. After that, I made up my mind very quickly and didn't hesitate to leave.

Do you feel that you have reached your destination job already in terms of professional development, or are you still planning to change professions in the future?
I want to develop within my current profession.

If you could turn back time and change something in your own PhD track to better prepare for your current job, what would it be?
I would switch from Matlab to Python.

What would you like to advise those who hesitate whether they should leave academia?
Don't be scared or worried, there are plenty of options and you have the skills.

2. Marlieke van Kesteren, PhD
In what area did you do your PhD?
Cognitive Neuroscience

In which country did you complete your PhD?
The Netherlands

In what type of working environment are you working right now?
I work in a small company with around 20 employees.

In which market sector are you working right now?
Grant Advising

Could you share your position title, and briefly describe (2-3 sentences) what your current scope of responsibilities is?

Grant Consultant. I advise academics and companies on their grant submissions.

How did you find your current job?
LinkedIn

Can you name the three biggest pros versus the three biggest cons of your current job?
Pros:
➢Short and to-the-point projects,
➢Learning about a lot of different science,
➢Lots of strategical thinking.
Cons:
➢It can get a bit stressful close to the deadline,
➢Sometimes you do boring stuff like copy-paste or write obvious statements,
➢Managing a large group of different people.

Can you briefly describe what a typical day at the office looks like in your current job?
I get to the office around 8:30 am, chat a bit with the colleagues that are present, check emails, and start work on a certain project. This can be contacting clients, writing, editing, or merging comments, discussing with colleagues about strategy or the budget, etc. We also have meetings within our company, about new projects and clients or changes to funding schemes. We often meet with the client, either at their university or company or through Skype. With our company, we always have lunch jointly and often take a stroll through the neighborhood afterward, or we play a game of table tennis. Most of the time, we work on multiple projects at the time, as they last about 2 months on average. When a project has just finished, I work on writing blogs, learning about funding schemes, and keeping in touch with former clients. I leave for home around 5 pm, sometimes work a bit in the evening but not often. Every day is different, and I like short projects and the fact that we can help people get funding for their research!

What was the biggest surprise to you once you started this job?
The fact that I would be able to get a permanent contract very quickly.

What experience obtained in academia helped you the most in your current job? Did the personal contacts developed in academia, help you in any way? From your current perspective, was PhD worth going through (compared to the alternative scenario in which you would have spent the same amount of time working in your current market sector)?
Applying for, and obtaining grants. Having a PhD is a very big plus in this job.

What were the major reasons behind your decision to leave the academic career track? Was it a rapid decision, or perhaps, was this a long process of self-discovery? Or maybe, you are still hesitating and might come back to academia in the future?
It was a long process, which already started during my first Postdoc project. The reasons were mostly the academic climate, short contracts, and stress.

Do you feel that you have reached your destination job already in terms of professional development, or are you still planning to change professions in the future?
I think anything is possible, but I think I'll stick to my current job for a while.

If you could turn back time and change something in your own PhD track to better prepare for your current job, what would it be?
I did do quite some extra things, but I would've liked it to be more accepted that people follow an alternative career path. This is changing now though, fortunately!

What would you like to advise those who hesitate whether they should leave academia?
Network! Talk to people, and have informational meetings. It is fun and tells you way more than reading or searching on the internet.

Any additional notes and comments you would like to share with the readers of the book:
You are not alone. It is OK to not follow an academic career track after being a (successful) PhD student!

3. Anonymous Contributor
In what area did you do your PhD?
Mathematics

In which country did you complete your PhD?
I went through the whole PhD program but I did not defend my thesis.

In what type of working environment are you working right now?
Working in a corporation/middle size company (>= 50 employees)

In which market sector are you working right now?
Advertising

Could you share your position title, and briefly describe (2-3 sentences) what your current scope of responsibilities is?
Software Engineer. I work on designing, building and maintaining large-scale systems.

How did you find your current job?
I was contacted by a recruiter.

Can you name the three biggest pros versus the three biggest cons of your current job?
Pros:
➤Flexibility in terms of the geographic location of my workplace,
➤Flexibility in terms of team/problem domain I work on,
➤Big impact.
Cons:
➤Big company and big impact sometimes slows you/projects down, while you can have a big absolute impact,
➤It's hard to change the course of a big company.

Can you briefly describe what a typical day at the office looks like in your current job?
Some overheads (email, etc.), meetings, some "actual" work (designs/coding, etc.).

What was the biggest surprise to you once you started this job?
It takes disproportionally big effort (in relation to actually building a feature) to scope, work across teams and get agreement on medium and larger projects.

What experience obtained in academia helped you the most in your current job? Did the personal contacts developed in academia, help you in any way? From your current perspective, was PhD worth going through (compared to the alternative scenario in which you would have spent the same amount of time working in your current market sector)?
Working independently during my PhD helped me the most in my current job. I didn't use any academic contacts for work. I feel that PhD was worth going through—on its own it was pleasant and interesting.

What were the major reasons behind your decision to leave the academic career track? Was it a rapid decision, or perhaps, was this a long process of self-discovery? Or maybe, you are still hesitating and might come back to academia in the future?
Opportunity.

Do you feel that you have reached your destination job already in terms of professional development, or are you still planning to change professions in the future?
No, and no.

If you could turn back time and change something in your own PhD track to better prepare for your current job, what would it be?
I would have done it in a field related to my line of work.

What would you like to advise those who hesitate whether they should leave academia?
Switching to industry doesn't necessarily mean being told what to do. There are a lot of jobs, also in corporations, in which one can be a leader and do creative work. Scientists aren't more or less ethical than people working in industry, and due to the way academic system is set up, in a lot of countries it is probably easier to become a victim of workplace abuse/discrimination in academia than in industry (when you switch jobs in industry you don't need letter of recommendation from your previous job and in academia period of non-productiveness may taint your whole career).

4. Chris Hartgerink
In what area did you do your PhD?
Methods and statistics

In which country did you complete your PhD?
The Netherlands

In what type of working environment are you working right now?

Entrepreneurship (co-owning a company with more than one person involved)

In which market sector are you working right now?
Scholarly communication/IT-services

Could you share your position title, and briefly describe (2-3 sentences) what your current scope of responsibilities is?
Founder, I think? My responsibilities range from everything to everything :) (I just started!) This includes setting up the company, finding an office, furnishing the office, making a business plan, strategic planning, hiring people, networking to find those people, doing reading to stay up-to-date with the field.

How did you find your current job?
I was able to do this after I received a considerable amount of funding from the Shuttleworth Foundation. The process of formulating the vision, and applying for funding took approximately one year. It was a high-risk situation that paid off.

Can you name the three biggest pros versus the three biggest cons of your current job?
Pros:
➤I get to instill the values into the work I'm doing, without negotiating or politics,
➤I get to see much more than just the specific research work I'm doing, which helps me learn about the world in different ways and that feeds back into how I construct questions of interest for research,
➤I am finding out I am much better at non-research things than I thought.
Cons:
➤I need to find my way of managing people that aligns with my values, but also still allows me to realize the vision in an efficient way,
➤There is a lot of things to do, so I must be organized and say no to many things. If I wasn't structured and at the point that I could say no without insecurity, I think that would be much more difficult, but it still requires energy,
➤Realizing that communication is much harder and repetitive than simply explaining your idea to someone once :)

Can you briefly describe what a typical day at the office looks like in your current job?
At this point, I'm not in a typical scenario, but on average it consists of taking several calls per day, having several meetings, doing writing for the business (which forces me to let go of the relative perfectionist mindset of academic writing), and hoping for some time left to do dreaming, visioning, and strategizing.

What was the biggest surprise to you once you started this job?
Non-research aspects are so much fun! Building not just on a research line for a change, but something that is starting to exist in the real world, and has a direct impact, brings much more joy and energy than I had imagined.

What experience obtained in academia helped you the most in your current job? Did the personal contacts developed in academia, help you in any way? From your current perspective, was PhD worth going through (compared to the alternative scenario in which you would have spent the same amount of time working in your current market sector)?

I think that my track record in academia was already quite particular, where I struggled with internal politics, resistance to my activism, and my unlikable research topic. This emotionally strengthened me over the years and helped me built a network of supportive people to go through these times. I know my boundaries well enough through those experiences that I can recognize when I am nearing them. Additionally, my PhD has taught me a level of rigorous, flexible analytic thinking that is extremely useful in any situation that I find myself in. It was definitely worth going through the PhD in that sense, but recommending it is another thing (I no longer talk to my dad, which also brought me much but I wouldn't recommend the situation to other people).

What were the major reasons behind your decision to leave the academic career track? Was it a rapid decision, or perhaps, was this a long process of self-discovery? Or maybe, you are still hesitating and might come back to academia in the future?

This was a long process, but I am confident in my decision to leave. I am prepared to go back at some point if my conditions are met, but I expect those will never be and I find it hard to formulate those explicitly. My major reasons revolve around the misuse of power to exploit people when in reality there's a conflict that needs to be worked through in an adult and emotionally responsible manner. This vulnerability and openness were unavailable to me in difficult situations, which the management may or may not have realized depending on the situation. Combined with several other personal factors, this resulted in severe depression with suicidal ideation at one point. These power abuses occurred several other times afterward, but by then I'd already made my decision to leave. These specific situations are again appalling in how these were dealt with and ultimately resulted in my getting overworked before finishing my PhD (after my contract ended). As a result, I only handed in my PhD quite recently, one year after getting overworked. Even after truly attempting to improve the situation from my end and being emotionally honest and vulnerable, did I receive little to no understanding.

Do you feel that you have reached your destination job already in terms of professional development, or are you still planning to change professions in the future?
Yes

If you could turn back time and change something in your own PhD track to better prepare for your current job, what would it be?
I would try to see it more as an education program, where I get the space to explore and learn the skills I want to learn. Supervisors, of course, have a plan for your research, but letting them exploit you 100% detracts from your own potential.

What would you like to advise those who hesitate whether they should leave academia?
If you're hesitating, leave, and see whether you want to go back. Don't stay out of fear. Academia isn't the only place to do science. Academia isn't all that it's glorified to be. You

can still have the freedoms outside of it, without a whole bunch of the toxicity. It might not be in the first job, but you have leverage. You're worth more than you think, and companies will recognize that in various ways if you force them to. There's a lot of haggling in wage, benefits, etc—use it.

Any additional notes and comments you would like to share with the readers of the book:
"When you were applying for jobs at the end of your academic career track, did your academic title" was irrelevant, because I didn't have my title during this phase, and even if I wouldn't use it 🙅

My perspectives might be particular to the Netherlands, where PhD candidates are seen as employees and have certain rights. Additionally, my final year in academia (the academic year 2017-2018) was already a transition phase because I received external funding and was an independent researcher for four out of five days in the week.

5. Anonymous Contributor

In what area did you do your PhD?
Cognitive Neuroscience

In which country did you complete your PhD?
The Netherlands

In what type of working environment are you working right now?
Working in an institution funded by the government—working in academia, but on a position without a career track

In which market sector are you working right now?
Governmental/Service Institute

Could you share your position title, and briefly describe (2-3 sentences) what your current scope of responsibilities is?
Program leader; I am part of the policy and communication department; I am involved in multiple (international) projects where I manage projects, organize meetings and training (around research data, data management, and Open Science).

How did you find your current job?
I got in contact with the organization on a national day for PhD students. I really liked what they do, and I contacted them about the possibilities to work for them. During my PhD I was able to do an internship with them which led to my current position.

Can you name the three biggest pros versus the three biggest cons of your current job?
Pros:
➤Flexible working hours,
➤Great colleagues,
➤Great secondary employment conditions (vacation hours, pension, travel reimbursements).
Cons:

➤Travel time (my job is in another city),

➤Unequal distribution of work during the year (peaks and high workload in March/October but little work during the summer),

➤A lot of traveling (for EU projects) which can be stressful.

Can you briefly describe what a typical day at the office looks like in your current job?
We start the day with a meeting of our department to discuss everyone's work and what we are currently focusing on, then I have a couple of virtual meetings with my EU project partners discussing the project's progress. The rest of the day, I prepare a presentation for a workshop we are giving tomorrow, help my colleague with the last edits for a project deliverable we are working on together, and I then finalize my travel schedule for a consortium meeting that I am going to at the end of the week.

What was the biggest surprise to you once you started this job?
How similar the skills are that you need in and outside academia. It most often comes down to solving a complex problem and organizing your work properly to transform a large task into smaller manageable sub-steps.

What experience obtained in academia helped you the most in your current job? Did the personal contacts developed in academia, help you in any way? From your current perspective, was PhD worth going through (compared to the alternative scenario in which you would have spent the same amount of time working in your current market sector)?
A PhD was required for my current position, and my work is still related to academia—so for me, it was very useful. My network was a big plus in finding people that have chosen other career paths so that helped me a lot. The biggest skill I learned during my PhD is dealing with insecurity, solving complex problems and handling multiple projects at the same time.

What were the major reasons behind your decision to leave the academic career track? Was it a rapid decision, or perhaps, was this a long process of self-discovery? Or maybe, you are still hesitating and might come back to academia in the future?
I know during my last year of PhD that I didn't want to continue in academia because I didn't want to move abroad (and the likelihood for me to find a position in the Netherlands was small), and I didn't want the insecurities and high workload that come with an academic job. I also want to have a family, and find it very hard to combine and academic unstable job with satisfying family life. I did like my PhD and I know lots of people who are still in research so I do miss the world of research and sometimes doubt whether I should try and find an academic position again.

Do you feel that you have reached your destination job already in terms of professional development, or are you still planning to change professions in the future?
I am at a junior, temporary position currently so I am pretty sure that I'll develop further. I don't have a destination in mind, however, as I have lots of interest I could explore. I enjoy the way rather than working towards a specific goal or position.

If you could turn back time and change something in your own PhD track to better prepare for your current job, what would it be?
I am pretty happy with how things went so I wouldn't change anything.

What would you like to advise those who hesitate whether they should leave academia?
Go out and talk to people that work at places that interest you! Ask yourself what kind of work you like and how important other things like stability, salary and work-life balance are for you. Then chose a job that ticks the most boxes.

Any additional notes and comments you would like to share with the readers of the book:
Don't underestimate your value as an academic scholar. There are so many cool things out there that you can do!

6. Anonymous Contributor
In what area did you do your PhD?
Musicology

In which country did you complete your PhD?
The Netherlands

In what type of working environment are you working right now?
Working in an institution funded by the government, I'll work at an IT company from 1 December 2019.

In which market sector are you working right now?
Data management

Could you share your position title, and briefly describe (2-3 sentences) what your current scope of responsibilities is?
Project Manager. I'm managing a H2020 project about infrastructure for data, organize calls and meetings, prepare financial and administrative documents and monitor the progress of the project.

How did you find your current job?
Networking

Can you name the three biggest pros versus the three biggest cons of your current job?
Pros:
➤Still surrounded by academics,
➤Flexible working hours,
➤Work in an international environment.
Cons:
➤No fixed contract,
➤Rather boring job,
➤Not enough (or full) responsibility.

Can you briefly describe what a typical day at the office looks like in your current job?
Attending and chairing meetings and calls, working on documents, setting up agendas, sending emails, talking to the financial department.

What was the biggest surprise to you once you started this job?
It was a surprise to me that most of my colleagues' work pace was so slow.

What experience obtained in academia helped you the most in your current job? Did the personal contacts developed in academia, help you in any way? From your current perspective, was PhD worth going through (compared to the alternative scenario in which you would have spent the same amount of time working in your current market sector)?
Efficiency and the ability to write comprehensive texts helped me the most. I couldn't make use of my personal contacts made during my PhD. From the job perspective, it was definitely not worth doing a PhD.

What were the major reasons behind your decision to leave the academic career track? Was it a rapid decision, or perhaps, was this a long process of self-discovery? Or maybe, you are still hesitating and might come back to academia in the future?
No real career perspectives in my field, the academic life was too lonely for me. It was a long(er) but quite a natural process of figuring out that I wasn't made for academia.

Do you feel that you have reached your destination job already in terms of professional development, or are you still planning to change professions in the future?
The current job was a great starting point but by no means my dream job. In two months from now, I'll start a new job in industry. I hope to do this new job for a couple of years.

If you could turn back time and change something in your own PhD track to better prepare for your current job, what would it be?
Deal with data and software to record and clean data better.

What would you like to advise those who hesitate whether they should leave academia?
It's a very personal decision whether to leave academia. It's important to be honest with oneself and to dare to think about happiness and what one needs to be happy and feel appreciated.

Any additional notes and comments you would like to share with the readers of the book:
The working environment (where? how? with whom?) is as important as the content.

7. Adriana Bankston, PhD
These answers represent the interviewee's personal views and not the views of their employer, University of California.

In what area did you do your PhD?
Biochemistry, Cell and Developmental Biology

In which country did you complete your PhD?
USA

In what type of working environment are you working right now?
Doing federal government relations for a university

In which market sector are you working right now?
Academic, but on the policy side

Could you share your position title, and briefly describe (2-3 sentences) what your current scope of responsibilities is?
Principal legislative analyst for the University of California (UC). I serve as an advocate for UC with Congress, the Administration and federal agencies: follow research issues that affect UC campuses at various levels, and position the campuses for future funding opportunities.

How did you find your current job?
Networking as well as prior experience in the area

Can you name the three biggest pros versus the three biggest cons of your current job?
Pros:
➤Working on a lot of different issues,
➤Learning from people from different backgrounds,
➤Going to interesting meetings.
Cons:
➤Figuring out how to manage all the projects,
➤Time difference between the East and the West coast of the US,
➤A lot of responsibility (which is also good).

Can you briefly describe what a typical day at the office looks like in your current job?
A lot of meetings and emails, reading and summarizing different issues, working with various team members on projects. Mostly in the office, but also going to meetings at various venues to learn about the latest developments (for example within federal agencies).

What was the biggest surprise to you once you started this job?
I was surprised how naturally it came to me and how well I was doing from the beginning. I thought it would be much more of a learning curve (which it was) but also it felt like a really good fit right from the start.

What experience obtained in academia helped you the most in your current job? Did the personal contacts developed in academia, help you in any way? From your current perspective, was PhD worth going through (compared to the alternative scenario in which you would have spent the same amount of time working in your current market sector)?
Definitely project management and being able to give presentations, working in teams and networking with people. Mostly the contacts developed outside of academia helped me.

What were the major reasons behind your decision to leave the academic career track? Was it a rapid decision, or perhaps, was this a long process of self-discovery? Or maybe, you are still hesitating and might come back to academia in the future?
I didn't feel like the academic life satisfied my desire to make an impact, and it also took a long time to get the results. I realized that I am the kind of person who likes more instant gratification and likes working on multiple projects and variety, whereas academic life sometimes is more monotonous and it takes a long time to get a result. It was a gradual decision starting about 6 months into my Postdoc, and a definite decision after my second Postdoc. I definitely wouldn't go back, but I do use a lot of the skills I learned in my PhD.

Do you feel that you have reached your destination job already in terms of professional development, or are you still planning to change professions in the future?
I think I'm in the right field, but people change jobs in policy after several years (don't typically stay in a position for 20 years) so I might end up in a different type of policy position in the future, or in a different setting.

If you could turn back time and change something in your own PhD track to better prepare for your current job, what would it be?
Starting to prepare for it sooner and doing more informational interviews earlier on than I did.

What would you like to advise those who hesitate whether they should leave academia?
Academia is a lifestyle, so if that suits you, then you should do it. You have to love it to do it, so if you don't, you should leave. Life is too short to do something that you don't enjoy. I realized that policy gives me much more the type of lifestyle I want, as well as the kinds of things I want to be thinking about on daily basis. The best piece of advice I can give is one of the Steve Jobs quotes which I like "If today were the last day of my life, would I want to do what I am about to do today?" And whenever the answer has been "no" for too many days in a row, I know I need to change something." This is very useful to think about in terms of how you feel about your job when you first get up in the morning, that says a lot.

Any additional notes and comments you would like to share with the readers of the book:
Don't be afraid to experiment with your career options, it can be exciting and lead you to new directions you never thought of.

8. Piotr Migdał, PhD
In what area did you do your PhD?
Quantum Physics

In which country did you complete your PhD?
Spain

In what type of working environment are you working right now?
Freelancing (owning a one-person company)

In which market sector are you working right now?
Machine Learning

Could you share your position title, and briefly describe (2-3 sentences) what your current scope of responsibilities is?
Deep Learning Consultant. Hand-crafted hands-on machine learning and deep learning workshops for companies and universities. Dedicated deep learning projects.

How did you find your current job?
I self-employed myself.

Can you name the three biggest pros versus the three biggest cons of your current job?
Pros:
➤More flexibility (locations, projects I take),
➤Fast-paced,
➤No bureaucracy.
Cons:
➤Less predictability,
➤No office,
➤No collaborators-by-default.

Can you briefly describe what a typical day at the office looks like in your current job?
It can be very different, depending on a project. Usually, working from random places to prepare a project, workshop, etc.

What was the biggest surprise to you once you started this job?
It is easy to maintain a relationship with academia (e.g. at the moment, I am participating in a 3-month project at Centrum for Quantum Technologies, National University of Singapore).

What experience obtained in academia helped you the most in your current job? Did the personal contacts developed in academia, help you in any way? From your current perspective, was PhD worth going through (compared to the alternative scenario in which you would have spent the same amount of time working in your current market sector)?
Contacts—yes (some of them from the pre-PhD phase); some contracts were based on that. The title sometimes helps. The heavy mental toll of PhD is hard to compare with other factors. Had I known I would end up not in academia, I wouldn't have pursued PhD.

What were the major reasons behind your decision to leave the academic career track? Was it a rapid decision, or perhaps, was this a long process of self-discovery? Or maybe, you are still hesitating and might come back to academia in the future?
Slow-paced, internal politics, and paperwork, low freedom (sic! e.g. to move to a different place), grant system and tenure path.

Do you feel that you have reached your destination job already in terms of professional development, or are you still planning to change professions in the future?

No. I am still investigating options, to do even more impactful projects.

If you could turn back time and change something in your own PhD track to better prepare for your current job, what would it be?
I would start preparing for internships at companies sooner.

What would you like to advise those who hesitate whether they should leave academia?
Take a few internships in companies. Or, ideally: a year of working outside of academia. No matter what is your decision, you'll learn some skills. If you have never worked outside of academia, you don't know what are the other options. And don't get fooled that all work that matters, is intellectually fulfilling, etc is only in academia.

Any additional notes and comments you would like to share with the readers of the book:
https://p.migdal.pl/2015/12/14/sci-to-data-sci.html for motivation and https://p.migdal.pl/2016/03/15/data-science-intro-for-math-phys-background.html for a how-to guide

9. Anonymous Contributor
In what area did you do your PhD?
Cognitive Neuroscience

In which country did you complete your PhD?
the Netherlands

In what type of working environment are you working right now?
I'm currently contacting various corporations/middle sized companies for jobs

In which market sector are you working right now?
IT (currently looking for a job)

Could you share your position title, and briefly describe (2-3 sentences) what your current scope of responsibilities is?
The range of jobs I'm interested in is quite broad: Data Scientist, Data/Business Analyst, Software Engineer; but all within IT.

How did you find your current job?
I'm utilizing my network to arrange job interviews, it's all about whom you know.

Can you name the three biggest pros versus the three biggest cons of your current job?
Pros:
➢The sector provides more stability in terms of contract extension,
➢It pays better,
➢The work doesn't require as much intrinsic motivation as a research job.
Cons:
➢It's still a very male business (but maybe so is research),
➢It's all about money (but so is research),
➢I cannot think of a third con... :)

Can you briefly describe what a typical day at the office looks like in your current job?
I cannot answer this question yet, because I'm currently still working on my PhD.

What was the biggest surprise to you once you started this job?
I cannot answer this question yet, because I'm currently still working on my PhD.

What experience obtained in academia helped you the most in your current job? Did the personal contacts developed in academia, help you in any way? From your current perspective, was PhD worth going through (compared to the alternative scenario in which you would have spent the same amount of time working in your current market sector)?
I sometimes regret having done a PhD, because so far, I don't get the feeling people outside academia (specifically recruiters) appreciate it as (relevant) working experience. They don't understand what PhD is, and appear to see me as someone who just took a very long time to graduate from university. I have to convince people that I've obtained very broad and intensive work experience, and that I have very relevant transferable skills.

What were the major reasons behind your decision to leave the academic career track? Was it a rapid decision, or perhaps, was this a long process of self-discovery? Or maybe, you are still hesitating and might come back to academia in the future?
I felt kind of rejected by academic life, because my life choices (having a family, settling down) don't fit with the demands our field puts on researchers (moving from country to country, working on short contracts). I realized that I cannot fight it, and just had to let go of the idea that I could stay at my university to do research and teach. Letting go did feel very relaxed in a way, because I know there are a lot of opportunities for me outside academia. It still makes me sad, though, because I'll miss it here.

Do you feel that you have reached your destination job already in terms of professional development, or are you still planning to change professions in the future?
I think the company I'm currently negotiating with will be a nice place to work, and I think the job itself will be very nice and possibly challenging. However, I can imagine that I'll be going on after about 5 years.

If you could turn back time and change something in your own PhD track to better prepare for your current job, what would it be?
I could have approached it in a much more structured and "agile" way, although that's quite difficult when you are working on a project all by yourself.

What would you like to advise those who hesitate whether they should leave academia?
First make sure you believe in yourself! Make a list of all your transferable skills, have a look at a lot of different job advertisements, and try to see how your transferable skills could fit their requirements. Don't be afraid to "exaggerate" your skills to fit the requirements, because academics tend to downplay their abilities (to the extreme).

Any additional notes and comments you would like to share with the readers of the book:
Right now, making the switch feels like I'm turning my back on academics forever.

This was one of my biggest hurdles, and even though it might not be true, I've made peace with it. It's scary to leave the comfortable setting of the university and to "start working for real," but in the end it will all work out.

10. Mark Melnykowycz, PhD

In what area did you do your PhD?
Mechanical Engineering and Materials Science

In which country did you complete your PhD?
Switzerland

In what type of working environment are you working right now?
Working in a startup (< 50 employees), Entrepreneurship (co-owning a company with more than one person involved)

In which market sector are you working right now?
Biomedical/Medtech

Could you share your position title, and briefly describe (2-3 sentences) what your current scope of responsibilities is?
Artist-Engineer. As I'm involved in multiple organizations, this job title seems to be an umbrella to cover them. I work mainly in engineering for data science, but also work on setting up business models and UX design of products. It depends on the specific company I'm working in, and at which stage of development they are.

How did you find your current job?
Networking

Can you name the three biggest pros versus the three biggest cons of your current job?
Pros:
➤Flexibility,
➤Growth/impact potential,
➤Fulfillment.
Cons:
➤Uncertainty financially,
➤Low resource availability,
➤Energy needed to build things.

Can you briefly describe what a typical day at the office looks like in your current job?
I work mainly from home at the moment: I wake up, have calls, code, work on project management, go to meetings as needed.

What was the biggest surprise to you once you started this job?
You only need certain level of knowledge to work in different fields, beyond that it's your desire to adapt and learn that seems to make the difference.

What experience obtained in academia helped you the most in your current job? Did the personal contacts developed in academia, help you in any way? From your current perspective, was PhD worth going through (compared to the alternative scenario in which you would have spent the same amount of time working in your current market sector)?

The general desire to learn and build and the development of this motivation was probably the most important. This is not bounded by a specific technology or market sector and can be broadly applied in whichever direction I choose to go. Research and Art are pretty similar in the way a person works. The ability to build analogies between what you know and the knowledge you need to build to accomplish new challenges is the most important. This allows you to explore different industries and build "unique" solutions by taking ideas from one sector and applying them to another, essentially remixing them.

What were the major reasons behind your decision to leave the academic career track? Was it a rapid decision, or perhaps, was this a long process of self-discovery? Or maybe, you are still hesitating and might come back to academia in the future?

I never had an academic career track; I saw a PhD as a way to stay in Switzerland and explore smart materials. However, I was always more interested in combining engineering with business as opposed to pure research. After learning about product design, I could adapt to many fields.

Do you feel that you have reached your destination job already in terms of professional development, or are you still planning to change professions in the future?

No, I see it as continuous learning and development. This is the interesting part—as well as being able to take on new challenges.

If you could turn back time and change something in your own PhD track to better prepare for your current job, what would it be?

I would have focused on biomedical engineering.

What would you like to advise those who hesitate whether they should leave academia?

It depends on what you want to do, and if you know what you want or not. If it fulfills you and you see yourself grow in academia, then stay there. If not, then move on.

11. Anonymous Contributor

In what area did you do your PhD?
Cognitive Neuroscience

In which country did you complete your PhD?
the Netherlands

In what type of working environment are you working right now?
Working in a corporation/middle size company (>= 50 employees)

In which market sector are you working right now?
IT

Could you share your position title, and briefly describe (2-3 sentences) what your current scope of responsibilities is?
Data Science Consultant. My current employer is an IT consultancy company, so other companies can hire your services. I got hired by the Nederlands Woning Waarde Instituut (NWWI) who asked me to develop validation tools for property valuation reports. I'm developing apps and models that get integrated in their data infrastructure to make decisions or create insights about property valuations and appraisers.

How did you find your current job?
Online

Can you name the three biggest pros versus the three biggest cons of your current job?
Pros:
➤Relatively good starter salary,
➤People perceive me as the expert in data analytics (I feel respected and valued),
➤Lots of learning opportunities and experience in my field.
Cons:
➤Work seems a bit superficial sometimes,
➤Less flexibility in working hours (40 hours, 9-to-5 job) which makes it hard to do other stuff like going to the doctor,
➤It is expected of you to work at least 45 hours a week, because after you leave the client at 5pm there are meetings and other responsibilities that you have to follow up on.

Can you briefly describe what a typical day at the office looks like in your current job?
I get to the client at 9 am. I start to work, make a plan for the day, catch up on emails and talk to people that I need to collaborate with on that day (asking the internal employers at the NWWI whether they have time to do things with me). At 9:45 we have a "stand up" in which the whole IT department of the NWWI comes together and discusses their plans for the day. There are days when I work alone, because I am the only Data Scientist there. So, whenever I develop a model in R, I work alone. However, when the model needs to go into testing in production, I need to work together with colleagues at the department so that they can help me to integrate the model into their infrastructure, e.g. I ask the Database Manager to write a database script with me that meets all requirements of their environment. At 12:15 pm most people at the department go on a walk to get some lunch together. After lunch I meet with someone from the compliance department to discuss the changes that I made to an interface a couple of days ago. I've built a shiny app that measures appraiser performance such that the compliance department can check on appraisers. After the meeting I write a document that summarizes their feedback and how I'm planning to implement new changes. Later, I continue to work on the data model until 5 pm. Then, I have to catch the train to Nieuwegein to attend a meeting or training at the headquarters of my current employer. This happens once or twice a week, but it's been less often the case in the summer months. Since I'm a consultant that got hired by the client, I work at their office almost all the time. So, these meetings at my employer's office are a good chance to catch up with my colleagues from my employer. At 8pm I go home.

What was the biggest surprise to you once you started this job?
There were no real big surprises. It was all pretty much as I expected. The only thing that surprised me was how hard it is to finish your PhD once you start working outside of academia full time.

What experience obtained in academia helped you the most in your current job? Did the personal contacts developed in academia, help you in any way? From your current perspective, was PhD worth going through (compared to the alternative scenario in which you would have spent the same amount of time working in your current market sector)?
Every day I do things for the first time, and I need to look up how to do them. It helps that I did a PhD because I learned how to do stuff that I haven't done before during that time; not sure what your question is about, but I'd rather say no. The contacts obtained during my PhD didn't help me find my current job, and they also did not help me to develop most of the skills that I'm using today. This is actually a question that I have been asking myself a lot lately! I guess that it's not worth the trouble for everybody immediately after their PhD, but I do think that your chances of being considered for a "higher position" later in your career are higher if you have a PhD. I personally benefited from the PhD right away. I was offered a position at the end of a junior pay scale because my PhD in neuroscience does count as working experience in the field of data science. Starters usually have to enter careers at my employer with a 2-year traineeship, which I was allowed to skip because of my experience in data analysis and programming. There are also studies pointing out that especially women benefit from higher salaries after they completed a PhD. So, I would do PhD again, probably.

What were the major reasons behind your decision to leave the academic career track? Was it a rapid decision, or perhaps, was this a long process of self-discovery? Or maybe, you are still hesitating and might come back to academia in the future?
Two years into the PhD I started thinking about my career after the PhD. It was a really serious decision. My promoters even offered me a part-time Postdoc position, but I also applied for jobs right after my contract ended, which is a sign that I really needed to do something else, I think. I'm however not 100% sure that I'll never want to go back to academia—but I'll leave that to chance for now.

Do you feel that you have reached your destination job already in terms of professional development, or are you still planning to change professions in the future?
I would like to gain a lot of experience and then start my own company. But if I get a really nice job in my current profession in the future, I might just want to stick to that.

If you could turn back time and change something in your own PhD track to better prepare for your current job, what would it be?
I would do a lot of datacamp tutorials; I would enter competitions (e.g., *Kaggle*) or build a data science portfolio with public data.

What would you like to advise those who hesitate whether they should leave academia?
If you never have taken any action to leave academia, you're probably not up for it.

But if you find yourself taking courses and do other things that are secretly preparing you for transitioning to industry, perhaps you've already made up your mind then?

12. Anonymous Contributor
In what area did you do your PhD?
Cognitive Neuroscience

In which country did you complete your PhD?
the Netherlands

What is the type of job you are performing right now?
Working in a corporation/middle size company (>= 50 employees)

In which market sector are you working right now?
IT/Data services

Could you share your position title, and briefly describe (2-3 sentences) what your current scope of responsibilities is?
Data Science Consultant. I am building dashboards (interactive interfaces) to assist managers in gaining an overview of their data. Normally this job is called Data Analyst; my colleagues work mostly with machine learning to gain insights from data for our clients.

How did you find your current job?
I was introduced by an ex-academic colleague. :)

Can you name the three biggest pros versus the three biggest cons of your current job?
Pros:
➢ Accountability (your daily work means something to someone),
➢ Job security (after a year the job becomes permanent, plus you'll always have work to do in this sector),
➢ Everything that comes with job security (e.g., I can get a mortgage, my child won't need to change schools).
Cons:
➢ Work floor atmosphere (less comradery than I experienced in my research institute; people don't identify with the company as much as I'd thought),
➢ Accountability sometimes means stress (you cannot get away with "It didn't work out" anymore in your biweekly update),
➢ Pay (contrary to gossip, my salary has stayed level after switching from scientific staff, partly because such a side-step means you start as a "junior" again).

Can you briefly describe what a typical day at the office looks like in your current job?
Commute in company car, grab a free coffee at the office/client's office, program in R all day, with some help from an experienced colleague, present progress to the client about once a week.

What was the biggest surprise to you once you started this job?
Even though my department has about 50% PhDs, the atmosphere is much less nerdy and in-group than I had expected.

What experience obtained in academia helped you the most in your current job? Did the personal contacts developed in academia, help you in any way? From your current perspective, was PhD worth going through (compared to the alternative scenario in which you would have spent the same amount of time working in your current market sector)?
Programming knowledge in general helped me the most. More R, Python, Git and database stuff (SQL) would have been good, but not a must. It was through an introduction that I landed my job. None of the interviews without internal contacts panned out. My PhD was not worth going through; if I had entered this job market then, climbing the salary scale, and not worked for free after my PhD contract ended, I would be about €60,000 wealthier and much less stressed.

What would you like to advise those who hesitate whether they should leave academia?
It was a long process, and not easy to say goodbye.

Do you feel that you have reached your destination job already in terms of professional development, or are you still planning to change professions in the future?
I aim to continue to grow within this niche.

Any additional notes and comments you would like to share with the readers of the book:
Learn Git, Python, and spend a few hours a week working in what recruiters think of as a "professional environment" (e.g., for a start-up).

13. Anonymous Contributor
In what area did you do your PhD?
Cognitive/Clinical Neuroscience

In which country did you complete your PhD?
Norway

In what type of working environment are you working right now?
Working in an institution funded from government

In which market sector are you working right now?
Government

Could you share your position title, and briefly describe (2-3 sentences) what your current scope of responsibilities is?
(Senior) Advisor/Analyst

How did you find your current job?
Norwegian job forum

Can you name the three biggest pros versus the three biggest cons of your current job?
Pros:
➤Job security (permanent position),
➤High salary,
➤"Flexible" working hours.
Cons:
➤Too many meetings,
➤Lots of tasks/projects to work with at the same time,
➤The subject matter is not something I am (very) interested in (but that is partly my fault, and knew somewhat before starting).

Can you briefly describe what a typical day at the office looks like in your current job?
One meeting per project (for at least an hour) with co-workers in the same workplace, or video-meetings with colleagues across the country (or sometimes, other countries). Otherwise, sitting in front of the computer working with data analysis (although more "experienced"/senior colleagues have to spend more time with meetings that data analyses).

What was the biggest surprise to you once you started this job?
The number of meetings and people I have to deal with on a daily basis. The amount of traveling to different work locations that is expected from me.

What experience obtained in academia helped you the most in your current job? Did the personal contacts developed in academia, help you in any way? From your current perspective, was PhD worth going through (compared to the alternative scenario in which you would have spent the same amount of time working in your current market sector)?
The PhD was absolutely worth going through. I wouldn't have been able to get my current job, or similar data analyst roles without my PhD. One thing to keep in mind is that in Norway, one receives a fairly decent salary for doing a PhD (roughly €45,000), as opposed to most other countries.

What were the major reasons behind your decision to leave the academic career track? Was it a rapid decision, or perhaps, was this a long process of self-discovery? Or maybe, you are still hesitating and might come back to academia in the future?
It involved a lot of introspection, and to be honest, some inner turmoil. The main reason for leaving academia was the prospects of career stability. The path to tenure in academia is incredibly difficult, and that realization made me think hard about what the next step should be. However, I may yet come back to academia in the (near) future, although only for a few years (Postdoc). It is not something I advise, but I truly would like to continue working with brain imaging for a few more years if possible. But again, bear in mind that the salary for a Postdoc in Norway is substantially higher than in other countries (up to €60,000).

Do you feel that you have reached your destination job already in terms of professional development, or are you still planning to change professions in the future?
Not necessarily change professions, but change employer/workplace.

If you could turn back time and change something in your own PhD track to better prepare for your current job, what would it be?
Attempt to spend more time learning programming languages such as Python and SQL.

What would you like to advise those who hesitate whether they should leave academia?
Try to really think about where and what you want to do in the next 5 to 10 years. If job security/stability is important, then leaving academia is definitely the right option.

Any additional notes and comments you would like to share with the readers of the book:
I might be one of the few people who are not completely satisfied with my current job situation, despite all its benefits (and truly, my colleagues seem to love their job). What I would advise is to keep in mind that you may not land your "dream job" right away, but at the very least, take it as an experience that will lead you there at some point. If the PhD life isn't too overwhelming, it's a good idea to plan ahead, so that you can (a) figure out what sorts of jobs outside of academia might interest you, and (b) develop the necessary skills.

14. Marzia Scelsi

In what area did you do your PhD?
Neuroscience and Genetics

In which country did you complete your PhD?
United Kingdom

In what type of working environment are you working right now?
Working in a corporation/middle size company (>= 50 employees)

In which market sector are you working right now?
Pharmaceutical

Could you share your position title, and briefly describe (2-3 sentences) what your current scope of responsibilities is?
Statistical scientist: responsible for exploratory analysis as well as design and analysis of clinical trial data.

How did you find your current job?
In the past, I did an internship in the same company, and learned about the recruiting process during my time there—so decided to apply.

Can you name the three biggest pros versus the three biggest cons of your current job?
I don't know, I haven't started yet and I only have limited experience from my time as an intern which I don't think really counts.

Can you briefly describe what a typical day at the office looks like in your current job?
9-to-5, but also quite flexible at times, including around an hour-long lunch break with colleagues. On Mondays and Fridays, the office is quite empty because many employees take advantage of the opportunity to work from home.

What was the biggest surprise to you once you started this job?
The number of female employees. Not particularly in my function (still a STEM role so quite male-dominated), but more generally in the company.

What experience obtained in academia helped you the most in your current job? Did the personal contacts developed in academia, help you in any way? From your current perspective, was PhD worth going through (compared to the alternative scenario in which you would have spent the same amount of time working in your current market sector)?
Yes, the PhD was totally worth going through in terms of hard skills acquired to get this job. With only my MS title (in Physics) I would have never been able to land such a job. Very few personal contacts developed in academia helped me along the way, the rest was all thanks to research and study that I had undertaken as a personal interest.

What were the major reasons behind your decision to leave the academic career track? Was it a rapid decision, or perhaps, was this a long process of self-discovery? Or maybe, you are still hesitating and might come back to academia in the future?
A decision that took two years in the making. The culture of rejection and job instability in academia were the main reasons.

Do you feel that you have reached your destination job already in terms of professional development, or are you still planning to change professions in the future?
I am not actively planning to change professions yet, but I am always open to career changes in the future if I end up not being satisfied with my job.

If you could turn back time and change something in your own PhD track to better prepare for your current job, what would it be?
I wouldn't change anything.

What would you like to advise those who hesitate whether they should leave academia?
Put some effort and take the leap. Sometimes we don't do it just out of laziness, because staying in academia is the comfortable option.

15. Anonymous Contributor
In what area did you do your PhD?
Physics (Theoretical, Particle Physics and Cosmology)

In which country did you complete your PhD?
Poland

In what type of working environment are you working right now?
Working in a corporation/middle size company (>= 50 employees)

In which market sector are you working right now?
Fintech

Could you share your position title, and briefly describe (2-3 sentences) what your current scope of responsibilities is?
Senior Data Scientist: customer behavior analytics, e.g. predictive modeling of customer churn/customer segmentation

How did you find your current job?
Through a professional recruitment agency

Can you name the three biggest pros versus the three biggest cons of your current job?
Pros:
➤Interesting job,
➤Lots of freedom,
➤Steep learning curve.
Cons:
➤My work belongs to the company, not to myself,
➤I cannot easily jump on the out-of-job project due to contract restrictions of a full-time role.

Can you briefly describe what a typical day at the office looks like in your current job?
I code all day, talk to people I work with from time to time, occasionally go to some bigger meetings. As I am new in this company, I am not yet involved in too many projects and it's very relaxed.

What was the biggest surprise to you once you started this job?
No major surprises.

What experience obtained in academia helped you the most in your current job? Did the personal contacts developed in academia, help you in any way? From your current perspective, was PhD worth going through (compared to the alternative scenario in which you would have spent the same amount of time working in your current market sector)?
I have no fear of learning new things—regardless if it is mathematics or any other type of complex problem (algorithmic, software, etc.). I know if I have learned quantum field theory, I can master Python/algorithms/probability/statistics/whatever I want.

What were the major reasons behind your decision to leave the academic career track? Was it a rapid decision, or perhaps, was this a long process of self-discovery? Or maybe, you are still hesitating and might come back to academia in the future?
It was quite rapid actually. I was on a year-long Postdoc contract in London with my husband and my daughter (then around 2.5 years old). I got offered a contract in Melbourne—great institute and team, it would have been amazing career-wise. However, the logistics of moving again with all my family just after 12 months, my husband finding a job and VISA with a work permit, seemed very, very complicated. Or, a contract in a (also great) institute in Denmark, in a very small town with little job prospects for my other half. Or a possibility to apply for a scholarship (with slim chances to get one) that would allow me to stay in London for another few years. I started to really hate my research work and find it completely

pointless. I made a quick choice, spent 3 months preparing for job interviews, and got a job as a Data Scientist.

Do you feel that you have reached your destination job already in terms of professional development, or are you still planning to change professions in the future?
I am not sure.

If you could turn back time and change something in your own PhD track to better prepare for your current job, what would it be?
I would get a software engineer summer job/internship a startup/tech company to learn coding and proper engineering practices before I even started my PhD.

16. Anonymous Contributor

In what area did you do your PhD?
Developmental Biology

In which country did you complete your PhD?
United Kingdom

In what type of working environment are you working right now?
Freelancing (owning a one-person company)

In which market sector are you working right now?
Academic reform

Could you share your position title, and briefly describe (2-3 sentences) what your current scope of responsibilities is?
Freelancer working on changing the academic system for the better.

How did you find your current job?
I set up my company after the completion of my last job.

Can you name the three biggest pros versus the three biggest cons of your current job?
Pros:
➤Intellectual freedom,
➤Flexibility,
➤It doesn't compromise my morality.
Cons:
➤Isolating,
➤Requires hustling for work,
➤Requires self-administration of e.g. taxes, corporate liabilities.

Can you briefly describe what a typical day at the office looks like in your current job?
Answering email queries e.g. to journalists, working on the website, working on current research projects, e.g., working on proposals/research papers/talks.

What was the biggest surprise to you once you started this job?
That it isn't necessary to be in an academic institution to be a scholar.

What experience obtained in academia helped you the most in your current job? Did the personal contacts developed in academia, help you in any way? From your current perspective, was PhD worth going through (compared to the alternative scenario in which you would have spent the same amount of time working in your current market sector)?
Research skills were definitely useful. PhD was worth doing; Postdocs—less so.

What were the major reasons behind your decision to leave the academic career track? Was it a rapid decision, or perhaps, was this a long process of self-discovery? Or maybe, you are still hesitating and might come back to academia in the future?
It is still somewhat a transition; I may return to academia. However, I was keen to work on improving academia, which I realized was not easy in an academic position, and an opportunity came along to do so.

Do you feel that you have reached your destination job already in terms of professional development, or are you still planning to change professions in the future?
Still planning to move in the future.

If you could turn back time and change something in your own PhD track to better prepare for your current job, what would it be?
More involvement with non-profits/fundraising

What would you like to advise those who hesitate whether they should leave academia?
I understand it can be tough as there is always some sort of a role that you can be employed in (for little compensation) in academia; but you are worth more than you think you are outside of academia, and you need to think about what aspects of your work are interesting and applicable to other (perhaps more interesting) career paths.

17. Miriam de Boer, PhD
In what area did you do your PhD?
Cognitive Neuroscience

In which country did you complete your PhD?
The Netherlands

In what type of working environment are you working right now?
Working in academia, but on a position without an academic career track

In which market sector are you working right now?
Science Education

Could you share your position title, and briefly describe (2-3 sentences) what your current scope of responsibilities is?

Project leader: leading projects on translating scientific breakthroughs to primary schools meaning coordinating teams of teachers and scientists coaching teachers for inquiry-based learning; expert on inquiry-based learning; editor of a book on science education.

How did you find your current job?
I worked with them during my PhD time and stayed in touch.

Can you name the three biggest pros versus the three biggest cons of your current job?
Pros:
➤ Shorter projects,
➤ Different topics but still in-depth understanding of different scientific fields necessary,
➤ Societal relevance.
Cons:
➤ Still temporary contract,
➤ Less clear on how you can grow career-wise,
➤ Loads of practical admin work.

Can you briefly describe what a typical day at the office looks like in your current job?
A kind of a 9-to-5 approach: entering the office, answering emails; having meetings with colleagues; writing texts for books; preparing meetings content-wise and in practice.

What was the biggest surprise to you once you started this job?
I was surprised that I felt quite confident in this job as an academic whereas I knew next to nothing about project management, which during my PhD it felt the other way around; that I did pretty well as a PhD student.

What experience obtained in academia helped you the most in your current job? Did the personal contacts developed in academia, help you in any way? From your current perspective, was PhD worth going through (compared to the alternative scenario in which you would have spent the same amount of time working in your current market sector)?
What helped me the most, was the in-depth knowledge of how science works. Yes, contacts from academia were the reason I found the job and I think it helps to understand how the university works; also, the title helps when working with other academics and teachers, they know you know what doing research is, helps in growing career-wise in academia. Yes, PhD was very relevant.

What were the major reasons behind your decision to leave the academic career track? Was it a rapid decision, or perhaps, was this a long process of self-discovery? Or maybe, you are still hesitating and might come back to academia in the future?
It was an extremely long process; rather difficult because it is hard to find out what else is out there. I knew I really liked science but also wanted more interaction with people, more direct impact on society. I might come back to academia in the future, but then in a different field.

Do you feel that you have reached your destination job already in terms of professional development, or are you still planning to change professions in the future?

Noooooooooo, not at all, might change professions but guess I'll keep on doing "something with people" and "something with science," luckily there are plenty of opportunities.

If you could turn back time and change something in your own PhD track to better prepare for your current job, what would it be?
Doing fewer things than I intuitively knew I wasn't pretty good at. Then, I would have obtained the title anyway but without challenging myself so much, thus faster.

What would you like to advise those who hesitate whether they should leave academia?
Maybe the attitude: leaving academia is not a failure, and there are plenty of opportunities to do sciency stuff outside universities.

18. Anonymous Contributor
In what area did you do your PhD?
Computational Neuroscience/Machine Learning

In which country did you complete your PhD?
Canada

In what type of working environment are you working right now?
Entrepreneurship (co-owning a company with more than one person involved)

In which market sector are you working right now?
Computational Biology

Could you share your position title, and briefly describe (2-3 sentences) what your current scope of responsibilities is?
CEO

How did you find your current job?
CDL incubator

Can you name the three biggest pros versus the three biggest cons of your current job?
Pros:
➢Flexibility,
➢Motivation,
➢Independence.
Cons:
➢Risk,
➢Pay,
➢Long hours.

Can you briefly describe what a typical day at the office looks like in your current job?
No one day is the same. Investors, projects, clients call, internal calls, conferences, project and tech development, hiring, etc.

What was the biggest surprise to you once you started this job?
Much harder than it seems.

What experience obtained in academia helped you the most in your current job? Did the personal contacts developed in academia, help you in any way? From your current perspective, was PhD worth going through (compared to the alternative scenario in which you would have spent the same amount of time working in your current market sector)?
The PhD help build my technical skills, and having a PhD brings trust and credibility so that all helps. It was worth it.

What were the major reasons behind your decision to leave the academic career track? Was it a rapid decision, or perhaps, was this a long process of self-discovery? Or maybe, you are still hesitating and might come back to academia in the future?
It wasn't very applied, low impact, low pay.

Do you feel that you have reached your destination job already in terms of professional development, or are you still planning to change professions in the future?
I'm happy now, but who knows.

If you could turn back time and change something in your own PhD track to better prepare for your current job, what would it be?
Get more industry experience.

What would you like to advise those who hesitate whether they should leave academia?
Talk to people!

Any additional notes and comments you would like to share with the readers of the book:
It's a personal journey.

19. Anonymous Contributor
In what area did you do your PhD?
Life Sciences

In which country did you complete your PhD?
Romania

In what type of working environment are you working right now?
Working in a startup (< 50 employees)

In which market sector are you working right now?
Utilities/Asset management

Could you share your position title, and briefly describe (2-3 sentences) what your current scope of responsibilities is?

I am now a Data Scientist, helping companies to make data-driven decisions in the asset management field. This implies research, gathering domain knowledge, communication skills, apart from hard skills like programming, stats, math, algorithms, etc.

How did you find your current job?
While being part of a Microsoft program that ran for 4 months in Amsterdam.

Can you name the three biggest pros versus the three biggest cons of your current job?
Pros:
➤I can use the hard skills I was already developing while doing the PhD,
➤I got a chance to show my creativity,
➤I got a chance to be acknowledged for my results.
Cons:
➤A totally new field, different from the one I was previously trained in,
➤Lack of structure in the day to day work routine,
➤Not so much teamwork.

Can you briefly describe what a typical day at the office looks like in your current job?
I usually start by having a very bitter plain dark coffee :) After that, I read 1-2 papers from the data-oriented asset management field, get to check my agenda for the day. I usually have 1/2 meetings per day. During the meetings, we discuss what the business partner would like to see/know about their data, and maybe by the end of the day, we have a more tangible result to show to the business partner. If not, well, tomorrow is another day :)

What was the biggest surprise to you once you started this job?
The lack of understanding from other people what it means to work hard for a PhD.

What experience obtained in academia helped you the most in your current job? Did the personal contacts developed in academia, help you in any way? From your current perspective, was PhD worth going through (compared to the alternative scenario in which you would have spent the same amount of time working in your current market sector)?
Maybe being responsible for the outcome is one of the biggest lessons learned in academia and being a "lonely wolf." No, personal contacts did not help me. No, the PhD was not worth going through.

What were the major reasons behind your decision to leave the academic career track? Was it a rapid decision, or perhaps, was this a long process of self-discovery? Or maybe, you are still hesitating and might come back to academia in the future?
I did not feel like I belonged to academia anymore, the rules of the system wouldn't fit at all my career prospects. No, it was not a rapid decision. No, I am not hesitating, and I won't go back to Academia as a full-time investment—maybe as a mentor to PhD students from the outside world.

Do you feel that you have reached your destination job already in terms of professional development, or are you still planning to change professions in the future?

I still plan to change professions in the future to increase access to career opportunities.

If you could turn back time and change something in your own PhD track to better prepare for your current job, what would it be?
More focus on speaking up, more focus on communicating messages for a wide public, more focus on tech skills.

What would you like to advise those who hesitate whether they should leave academia?
Time is the most important resource for a human. Treat your time as an investment for profit :)

20. Raimon Pruim, PhD
In what area did you do your PhD?
Neuroimaging

In which country did you complete your PhD?
The Netherlands

In what type of working environment are you working right now?
Working in a (non-profit) institution partly funded partly by the government, and partly by industry

In which market sector are you working right now?
Information Technology

Could you share your position title, and briefly describe (2-3 sentences) what your current scope of responsibilities is?
Research scientist on computer vision and deep learning. Doing research and finding new solutions for computer vision problems using deep learning (~TRL 4-6). Focusing on the domain of defense and security.

How did you find your current job?
Google search

Can you name the three biggest pros versus the three biggest cons of your current job?
Pros:
➤Research that is close to implementation,
➤Diversity of projects,
➤Working together with highly skilled colleagues.
Cons:
➤Project diversity has the cost of lack of specialization,
➤Less focus on publication and CV building,
➤More short-term goals requiring quick results rather than quality.

Can you briefly describe what a typical day at the office looks like in your current job?
Mostly you work on multiple projects and focus on one or two projects every day. You meet with colleagues of the project team discussing progress. Rest of the day you spend on finding new solutions, implementing (open source) tools, data processing and building deep learning models that fit the project goals.

What was the biggest surprise to you once you started this job?
The level of expertise of colleagues

What experience obtained in academia helped you the most in your current job? Did the personal contacts developed in academia, help you in any way? From your current perspective, was PhD worth going through (compared to the alternative scenario in which you would have spent the same amount of time working in your current market sector)?
Critical mindset in setting up the research and being able to quickly interpret, value and filter new developments in the research field and relate them to current work.

What were the major reasons behind your decision to leave the academic career track? Was it a rapid decision, or perhaps, was this a long process of self-discovery? Or maybe, you are still hesitating and might come back to academia in the future?
Focus on implementation as an end product rather than a publication. And more structure/ certainty of a permanent job in contrast to the uncertainty of relying on funds and writing research proposals.

Do you feel that you have reached your destination job already in terms of professional development, or are you still planning to change professions in the future?
No, I'll never feel as if I have reached a "destination job"—ambitions are always renewed.

If you could turn back time and change something in your own PhD track to better prepare for your current job, what would it be?
Focus more on efficient coding and open sourcing the developed work during the PhD (i.e., do your work such that it transferable to other—this is relevant for future team work).

What would you like to advise those who hesitate whether they should leave academia?
Follow your gut feeling. At least don't think that the world outside academia is 100% commercially driven—there are plenty of opportunities out there to do societal relevant research outside academia (even with the option to publish).

21. Anonymous Contributor
In what area did you do your PhD?
Neuroscience

In which country did you complete your PhD?
The Netherlands

In what type of working environment are you working right now?
Working in a startup (< 50 employees)

In which market sector are you working right now?
Biotech

Could you share your position title, and briefly describe (2-3 sentences) what your current scope of responsibilities is?
Scientist: I make mathematical models of single-cell metabolism.

How did you find your current job?
By sending applications on *LinkedIn*, specifically to jobs which I don't need a cover letter for.

Can you name the three biggest pros versus the three biggest cons of your current job?
Pros:
➤A start-up gives you exposure to multiple aspects of running a company, leading to an accelerated learning curve.
Cons:
➤Possible insecurity that comes with working in an early-stage startup.

Can you briefly describe what a typical day at the office looks like in your current job?
It does look quite like a regular PhD day. I still read a lot of articles for my work and run the analysis.

What was the biggest surprise to you once you started this job?
The whole start-up funding scenario does astonish me.

What experience obtained in academia helped you the most in your current job? Did the personal contacts developed in academia, help you in any way? From your current perspective, was PhD worth going through (compared to the alternative scenario in which you would have spent the same amount of time working in your current market sector)?
I gained a lot of confidence in expressing and trusting my opinions. I find it difficult to foresee a situation where, retrospectively, I would choose <u>not</u> to do a PhD.

What were the major reasons behind your decision to leave the academic career track? Was it a rapid decision, or perhaps, was this a long process of self-discovery? Or maybe, you are still hesitating and might come back to academia in the future?
I want to explore options, academic and otherwise. The start-up I work for gives me that option.

Do you feel that you have reached your destination job already in terms of professional development, or are you still planning to change professions in the future?
I still need to finish my PhD. I doubt that I am a person who actually *chooses* a profession.

If you could turn back time and change something in your own PhD track to better prepare for your current job, what would it be?
I was more than adequately prepared for this job.

What would you like to advise those who hesitate whether they should leave academia?
I would advise setting out time for explicit introspection, and a book *A job to love* by Alain de Boton.

22. Anonymous Contributor
In what area did you do your PhD?
Biological Sciences

In which country did you complete your PhD?
USA

In what type of working environment are you working right now?
Tutoring & working at a restaurant while I wait for my Belgian residence visa to be approved. I'll be working as a research scientist at a pharmaceutical company in Belgium.

In which market sector are you working right now?
Currently: education & services. In a few months from now: the pharmaceutical industry.

Could you share your position title, and briefly describe (2-3 sentences) what your current scope of responsibilities is?
Currently:
Biology tutor with high school students: weekly one-on-one sessions in which I help with homework, preparation for tests, and clarifying confusing concepts.
Food runner: I bring food from the kitchen to customers at a busy local restaurant, keep order tickets organized, and help out the rest of the crew where I can.
In a few months: Research Scientist. I'll be working in the R&D department of a mid-size Belgian pharmaceutical company to help develop new treatments for neurodegenerative disorders.

How did you find your current job?
Current positions: Craigslist; Research Scientist position: *LinkedIn*.

Can you name the three biggest pros versus the three biggest cons of your current job?
Current job pros:
➤Great work-life balance,
➤Working with people,
➤New skills to learn.
Cons:
➤Low pay,
➤Less meaningful than I find my scientific career,
➤Not flexible in the case of the restaurant job.

Can you briefly describe what a typical day at the office looks like in your current job?
I tutor and work at the restaurant in the afternoons and the evenings. Usually, I prepare for tutoring the day before or in the morning: reviewing concepts that the students are studying, finding relevant handouts that I can give them. For tutoring, I drive to students' homes and

spend an hour with them working on whatever they're having trouble with or on current assignments. The restaurant job has, perhaps surprisingly, some similarities to working in a lab. I need to multitask a great deal: bringing out plates, managing the ticket board, polishing washed dish-ware, keeping track of supplies that might be running low. I'm also on my feet for 5 hours at a time, going up and down stairs constantly. Interacting with customers is, of course, another part of the job. I feel like I'm part of a team at the restaurant, which I enjoy.

What was the biggest surprise to you once you started this job?
For the restaurant work: how much it reminded me of very busy lab days. For tutoring: Being seen as an authority figure felt quite strange at first.

What experience obtained in academia helped you the most in your current job? Did the personal contacts developed in academia, help you in any way? From your current perspective, was PhD worth going through (compared to the alternative scenario in which you would have spent the same amount of time working in your current market sector)?
For current positions:
Tutoring: biology knowledge, teaching experience, time-management
Food running: multitasking, working under stressful conditions, being used to picking up new knowledge
For research scientist position (my best guess, since it hasn't begun yet): all of my technical skills, independent thinking, communicating research findings to others, my knowledge about neurodegeneration, organization & time-management.
For me, my PhD was absolutely worth doing. In the pharmaceutical world, there seems to be a divide between "PhD-level" scientists and those that have not completed a PhD. I want to pursue a career in drug discovery research, and, to advance in this sector, I think a PhD is very useful. If I wanted to work as a tutor/in the restaurant business full-time, then no, the PhD wouldn't have been worth doing (though it would certainly have still been an interesting life experience).

What were the major reasons behind your decision to leave the academic career track? Was it a rapid decision, or perhaps, was this a long process of self-discovery? Or maybe, you are still hesitating and might come back to academia in the future?
It was a long process: I considered many possible careers before making my decision. My reasons for leaving were as follows:
1. Academia felt too solitary; I craved the feeling of being part of a team.
2. Academia feels very competitive to me right now; if you get unlucky and your project doesn't go smoothly/give you the big findings you were hoping for, you won't publish in a high-impact factor journal, which will making funding harder to get, which will make it harder for you to carry out your research, which will affect your publications, and so on in a vicious cycle. There seems to be little room for error these days, and experiments may not go as hoped. That's part of the excitement of science, not knowing what discoveries lie ahead. But I found that uncertainty stressful in academia; it's very unpleasant to feel like your career is riding on the outcome of your western blot.
3. Probably as a result of reason #2, the work-life balance in academia is more skewed towards work than I would like.

4. I was drawn to translational science in graduate school, and I decided I wanted to be closer to making disease-modifying therapies a reality; hence the move to pharma.

Do you feel that you have reached your destination job already in terms of professional development, or are you still planning to change professions in the future?
As mentioned above, tutoring and restaurant work are temporary. Concerning R&D work in pharma, I'll have to see how I feel about it once I'm there. I don't currently plan to change careers from working as a research scientist, but I wouldn't be surprised if future life experiences guide me in some other direction eventually.

If you could turn back time and change something in your own PhD track to better prepare for your current job, what would it be?
For the research scientist position: I wish that I had learned to code (I'm not sure it'll be super important, but it would probably help in assessing bioinformatics papers!).

What would you like to advise those who hesitate whether they should leave academia?
Assuming you're deciding whether to pursue a professorship, ask yourself: how important is it for me to be able to design my research program without the influence of a profit motive? If it's important enough to outweigh the long hours, stress, uncertainty, responsibility for the publications & careers of your lab members, criticism from reviewers, then put in the work and go for it. Otherwise, figure out what your favorite and least favorite aspects of your academic job are and try to find another industry that maximizes the favorite aspects and minimizes the least favorite ones.

Any additional notes and comments you would like to share with the readers of the book:
Though I didn't discuss it much here, taking a year off to travel and volunteer was a fantastic experience. I highly recommend it if you're in a position to do it. If you can do it having already lined up a job for when you get back (unlike me), all the better!

23. Ruud Berkers, PhD
In what area did you do your PhD?
Cognitive Neurosciences / Medical Sciences

In which country did you complete your PhD?
The Netherlands

In what type of working environment are you working right now?
Working in a specialized mental healthcare clinic

In which market sector are you working right now?
Mental Healthcare

Could you share your position title, and briefly describe (2-3 sentences) what your current scope of responsibilities is?

I am a trainee now as a clinical psychologist/therapist, hoping to continue specializing as a clinical psychologist. Currently, I am not paid a salary, as it is more of an internship, but I hope to continue in a paid position in the next half year.

How did you find your current job?
Through a professor (networking).

Can you name the three biggest pros versus the three biggest cons of your current job?
Pros:
➤Lots of contact with people (patients and colleagues),
➤Lots of visible results from your hard work,
➤Learning a lot about myself and people in general.
Cons:
➤Low flexibility at work,
➤Sometimes the results can be disappointing,
➤Low pay (currently).

Can you briefly describe what a typical day at the office looks like in your current job?
I get into the office at 8:15, then we have the first meeting to update each other on how each of the patients admitted to the clinic is doing (what sort of evening, night and morning they had), then we have group therapy, we discuss exposures they are going to do for the day, help them with their exposures, go for lunch, have group cognitive therapy, discuss how their exposures went for the day, and perform intake/anamnesis interviews with potential new patients referred to the clinic. And in-between all the sessions we write our reports about all the group sessions and write reports about psychological anamnesis/intake sessions we did with patients that were referred to the clinic.

What was the biggest surprise to you once you started this job?
How competent, critical and energetic my colleagues would be, and how well the theory is translated into clinical practice.

What experience obtained in academia helped you the most in your current job? Did the personal contacts developed in academia, help you in any way? From your current perspective, was PhD worth going through (compared to the alternative scenario in which you would have spent the same amount of time working in your current market sector)?
I learned a lot about myself in academia, and I learned to overcome a lot of frustration. In the end, the most confrontational thing is that in the end I had to take full responsibility for making the research work, making my PhD project work. I had to think ahead and plan, which did not always go well, but making mistakes in that way has taught me a lot. And of course, the personal contacts were and are still very useful as academic experience is still important for specialized mental healthcare institutions.

What were the major reasons behind your decision to leave the academic career track? Was it a rapid decision, or perhaps, was this a long process of self-discovery? Or maybe, you are still hesitating and might come back to academia in the future?

The reasons were: no clear career prospects in science, low motivation to work a lot for little recognizable results, lack of direct contact with people, lack of contact with daily practice ("the ivory tower"). It was always on the back of my mind that I'd rather work in a clinical setting and outside academia. At some point, I had to decide that if I wanted to retrain as a clinical psychologist I should not wait too long. Maybe in the future, I'll do science again, but only in combination with clinical work.

Do you feel that you have reached your destination job already in terms of professional development, or are you still planning to change professions in the future?
I want to follow a (lengthy) track of specializing in becoming a licensed clinical psychologist. Currently, I am an intern (for 6 months) which of course is unsustainable in the long run. I'd like to switch soon.

If you could turn back time and change something in your own PhD track to better prepare for your current job, what would it be?
I would have focused my research more on clinical populations and clinical practice, rather than conducting more fundamental science.

What would you like to advise those who hesitate whether they should leave academia?
I think many people are hesitant to leave science as they think they can never go back into science. I think this is an unproductive way of thinking. First, if you are not sure whether science is the right line of work for you or if there is a career for you in science, you must try other things to find out. It is possible to go back into science if you are committed to it. But there are alternative paths that can be just as or even more fulfilling than a career in academia. Second of all, I think you can only be happy in science or have a successful career if you are fully committed to it, and if you love the work. If you notice you are wavering, you are probably doing yourself a favor by trying something else.

247

Appendix 3: Testimonials from current academics who took a decision to come to academia from industry

1. Anonymous Contributor
For how many years did you work in industry?
2 years

In what area of science are you now working, and on what position?
neuroscience/PhD candidate

In which country did you work in industry?
Poland

In which country do you live now?
United Kingdom

What type of job did you perform before moving to academia?
Working in a corporation/middle size company (>= 50 employees)

In what market sector were you working?
FMCG (fast-moving consumer goods)

Could you share your last industry position title, and briefly describe (2-3 sentences) what your scope of responsibilities was?
Junior Brand Manager; I managed a line of cosmetics, overlooking all aspects of product management, from design to advertising.

Can you briefly describe how a typical day at the office looked like in your industry job?
Meetings, writing emails, communicating with stakeholders, problem-solving, meetings, writing texts, trying to persuade colleagues to prioritize my product over other products, meetings.

How did you find your current academic job?
I applied for a scholarship.

Can you name the three biggest pros versus the three biggest cons of your current academic job, compared to your prior industry experience?
Pros:
➤I feel more ownership of my work,
➤I feel I'm doing something important,
➤Work is more creative.
No cons so far!

What was the biggest surprise to you once you started your academic job?
There were no surprises.

What experience obtained in industry helped you the most in your current academic job? Did the personal contacts developed in industry, help you in any way? From your current perspective, was your previous industry job worth going through?

Soft skills like project management, working to meet deadlines, resilience to stress. Yes, it was worth it: I learned a lot of transferable skills, and it also allowed me to appreciate academia more.

What were the major reasons behind your decision to embark on the academic career track? Was it a rapid decision, or perhaps, was this a long process of self-discovery? Or maybe, you are still hesitating and might come back to industry in the future?

I was unhappy in industry and deep down I knew I want to go back to academia.

Did you ever regret your decision to come to academia?

No.

Do you feel that you have reached your destination job already in terms of professional development, or are you still planning to change professions in the future?

I plan to stay in academia but there is still a lot to achieve.

What would you like to advise those who hesitate whether they should come to academia from industry?

They should give it a try and they always can come back. Professional decisions are rarely forever nowadays.

2. Mirjam Bloemendaal, PhD

For how many years did you work in industry?

1.5 years. In a way, I *came back* to academia, as I completed my PhD before starting my job in industry.

In what area of science are you now working, and on what position?

Postdoc in gut-brain research

In which country did you work in industry?

The Netherlands

In which country do you live now?

The Netherlands

What type of job did you perform before moving to academia?

Working in a corporation/middle size company (>= 50 employees)

In what market sector were you working?

Medical food

Could you share your last industry position title, and briefly describe (2-3 sentences) what your scope of responsibilities was?

My job title was a Clinical Studies Researcher. This means I was involved in research related activities around the clinical trials testing medical food products that this company produced. This was a wide range of tasks; from discussing the design of a new clinical trial, through literature search on suitable questionnaires to include in a trial, comparing results and effect sizes of medical food trials to pharmaceutical trials, to looking for responder profiles in the data of these clinical trials. These were hands-on research-related tasks, not including data collection which was done locally at a.o. hospitals and not including statistical analyses, which was done by statisticians and programmers dedicated to this task.

Can you briefly describe how a typical day at the office looked like in your industry job?
This would, for example, start with a team meeting within the clinical studies team, updating each other on the progress of the tasks to be divided within the team. Part of the day I may work independently on data cleaning, making a data analysis plan or literature search. I would often have meetings outside my own team with Data Managers, Medical Doctors, statisticians, as within the company many individuals with each a specific role were involved in projects. Also, meetings outside the company with academic partners could happen. Often, there were also company-wide announcements or celebrations.

How did you find your current academic job?
Through Academic Transfer.

Can you name the three biggest pros versus the three biggest cons of your current academic job, compared to your prior industry experience?
Pros:
➤Ownership,
➤Training possibilities,
➤Freedom.
Cons:
➤My current academic job is associated with a longer commuting time,
➤Coffee is of lesser quality,
➤Slightly lower pay.

What was the biggest surprise to you once you started your academic job?
None.

What experience obtained in industry helped you the most in your current academic job? Did the personal contacts developed in industry, help you in any way? From your current perspective, was your previous industry job worth going through?
It has broadened my view of research, from fundamental academic research towards clinical trials with its extensive regulations, legislation, and budgets. I also learned a lot about how a big company is organized, the internal dynamics and how a company operates within a competitive field. My experience in industry helped me to obtain my current position. I maintain good contacts with my former colleagues though practically my contacts did not result in any benefit (to answer this question). It was a very good learning experience, though I was eager to learn more than industry could offer me.

What were the major reasons behind your decision to embark on the academic career track? Was it a rapid decision, or perhaps, was this a long process of self-discovery? Or maybe, you are still hesitating and might come back to industry in the future?
My motivation to learn and be more independent in managing projects resulted in a move (back to) academia. For a management role within research projects, I would consider going back to industry, one day.

Did you ever regret your decision to come to academia?
No.

Do you feel that you have reached your destination job already in terms of professional development, or are you still planning to change professions in the future?
I currently feel very much in place.

What would you like to advise those who hesitate whether they should come to academia from industry?
Before starting: ask detailed questions about what your role entails, what are your responsibilities, what are practically your tasks. Ask about working conditions, e.g. how big a team you'll work in, company culture, the way of working, is it team-based or project-based. Know in what kind of working environment you thrive, big or small team, working independently or together. However, the only way to find out if something is for you is by trying. Be honest and explicit about your wishes, if no one knows what you aspire, no one will think of you when the opportunity arises.

Any additional notes and comments you would like to share with the readers of the book:
When choosing a job, follow your interests and intrinsic motivation. Don't let fears, insecurities or practical considerations keep you from this.

3. Anonymous Contributor
For how many years did you work in industry?
1 year

In what area of science are you now working, and on what position?
Computational Neuroscience / Senior Lecturer

In which country did you work in industry?
Australia

In which country do you live now?
Australia

What type of job did you perform before moving to academia?
Working in a corporation / middle size company (>= 50 employees)

In what market sector were you working?
Semiconductor industry

Could you share your last industry position title, and briefly describe (2-3 sentences) what your scope of responsibilities was?
Research Scientist. R&D for low power and low area wireless LAN chips for mobile devices

Can you briefly describe how a typical day at the office looked like in your industry job?
Developing signal processing algorithms, writing and testing code

How did you find your current academic job?
I contacted several professors who shared my research interest about modeling of brain networks

Can you name the three biggest pros versus the three biggest cons of your current academic job, compared to your prior industry experience?
Pros:
➤Independence to work on whatever I like,
➤I decide on my working schedule,
➤Meeting interesting researchers and students.
Cons:
➤There is only one: that I earn less than what I could in industry.

What was the biggest surprise to you once you started your academic job?
None. I knew it very well as was engaged in research for many years as Master's and PhD student

What experience obtained in industry helped you the most in your current academic job? Did the personal contacts developed in industry, help you in any way? From your current perspective, was your previous industry job worth going through?
In industry there is no stopping, there are deadlines after deadlines which are firm. You are working as a large team so if you fail the whole team fails and millions of dollars can get wasted if the component of the chip you are working on has a failed tape-out. Of course, this is specific to what I was working at and will different in other sectors of industry.
I don't think that personal contact in industry helped me in my academic job.
Yes, it was worth going through as now I know that I am not the type that fits in industry. So, I'm not going back—but I do have plans for my tech startup!

What were the major reasons behind your decision to embark on the academic career track? Was it a rapid decision, or perhaps, was this a long process of self-discovery? Or maybe, you are still hesitating and might come back to industry in the future?
The major reason is that I didn't like the fast pace of a large multinational corporation where the work never stops as they employ people in each and every time zone. You finish your day's work and someone picks up from where you left in another time zone.

I only worked in industry for about 8 months to realize it wasn't for me. There is no hesitation at all and I am very happy with what I do now!

Did you ever regret your decision to come to academia?
Not yet!

Do you feel that you have reached your destination job already in terms of professional development, or are you still planning to change professions in the future?
No change for immediate future but you never know.

What would you like to advise those who hesitate whether they should come to academia from industry?
It is really difficult to give general advice. It depends on what your current role is. What are the long-terms prospects in your current industrial role? At what career stage are you in? In academia, your options are a Research Assistant, Postdoc or faculty member. If it is faculty, is it a tenured position? Surviving in academia can be as tough if not more than in industry so career in academia has to be very carefully planned.

4. Stephan Heunis
For how many years did you work in industry?
4 years

In what area of science are you now working, and on what position?
PhD candidate in Neuroimage Processing methods (Electrical Engineering)

In which country did you work in industry?
The Republic of South Africa

In which country do you live now?
The Netherlands

What type of job did you perform before moving to academia?
Working in a corporation / middle size company (>= 50 employees)
Working in a startup (< 50 employees)

In what market sector were you working?
Job 1: automation and control systems for machines, plant and factory
Job 2: enterprise mobile software systems

Could you share your last industry position title, and briefly describe (2-3 sentences) what your scope of responsibilities was?
I was a member and eventually the head of the Solution Delivery Team at a software engineering startup that provided Software as a Service (SaaS) enterprise mobility solutions for companies across multiple industries worldwide. My role was to lead a team of 9 Solution Delivery Engineers in the process of building around 40 enterprise mobile applications to customers. This role included managing team culture and growth sustainably,

hiring new engineers and programmers, running day to day team and project management activities (including designing and building mobile business process applications myself), interfacing with partners and customers regularly, and interfacing with leaders and teams of other internal business units (sales, lead generation, product and platform, support) in order to help scale our business.

Can you briefly describe how a typical day at the office looked like in your industry job?
At the software startup, life was quite crazy. Shortly after I joined the company (of around 7 people at that stage) we received our first round of funding from a venture capital firm in Silicon Valley. After this we went into overdrive and worked very hard for a very long time. I didn't sleep much. As is typical for a startup, you have to juggle multiple responsibilities and apply different skills daily, all at a very fast pace, which I found quite exhilarating at the time. I typically had several meetings a day, sometimes related to project management, other times to project support, or 1-on-1s with team members. In between I helped out with software designs, debugging code, writing project documentation, customer support, sales support and strategic planning. Oh, and I wrote way too many emails. The free lunch and sun-roasted ground coffee was great, though :P

How did you find your current academic job?
I cannot remember which website it was exactly, but I came across an online application for this position. I applied for more positions than I care to admit, all in the broad field of neuroimage/signal processing, and this is the one I was lucky enough to end up with :)

Can you name the three biggest pros versus the three biggest cons of your current academic job, compared to your prior industry experience?
This is a difficult question for me because doing a PhD, in my experience, is a bit like having a temperamental demeanor. At times, things are great and I'm positive about the whole scientific enterprise and about my prospects in it. At other times I end up in dark places questioning my very existence and pondering the futility of it all. Depending on one's position on this spectrum, pros and cons could vary widely.

That being said, I think the best thing about my current academic job is the freedom: in terms of flexibility of both working hours and intellectual endeavors. Where else would I have had the flexibility of time to be able to spend meaningful time raising a baby and a toddler while having full-time job responsibilities? Where else would I be granted such opportunities to direct my own course and maintain several collaborations in parallel, outside of the scope of the problem that I am employed to solve? Certainly not to the same extent in my previous industry positions. Of course, the freedom is not infinite, it's highly dependent on one's circumstances, and it could also have a detrimental effect in some cases. But I am lucky enough to be in a position where the freedom afforded to me sits well with my (possibly self-destructive) need to be In Control Over Things. This is different from the situation I had with my industry job. There, I initially felt like things were great ("we're a meritocracy, y'all!") but I eventually ended up banging my head too many times against the wall of steel that is the key-performance-indicator-driven executive team.

The other worthwhile positive aspect is that I get to generate knowledge (queue: clouds opening up, glorious rays of sun shining through, and angels harmonizing beautifully). I find this concept fascinating! I get to meticulously investigate phenomena, build and design ways to test them, try to understand them at their roots, and try to describe them in a concise yet insightful way, thus pushing the boundaries of what we consider known about the natural world. And I get to do this in the fascinating field of neuroscience while working at the forefront of technological development and human understanding. It is a privilege and a delight, and I should remind myself of this way more often than I currently do.

The biggest disadvantage of my current academic job, in my (admittedly limited) experience, is the fact that it moves very slowly, to my taste. To be clear, I think scientific research has to be thorough, meticulous and iterative to get us closer and closer to the truth over time, which necessitates serious time investment, of course. Much more time, for example, than solving the type of limited-scope engineering problems that are more ubiquitous in industry. But even so, I think in academia we waste an unnecessary amount of time by doing things inefficiently —by not focusing enough on working together or learning from each other.

Secondly, academia is *on average* exceptionally bad (again, in my opinion) at structuring a group of people around solving challenging problems efficiently. Academia doesn't (yet) value teamwork, collaboration, personal skill building, project management, and leadership as much as industry does, and this shows.

Lastly, I despise the apparent need for competitiveness. As we are climbing the crooked ranks of academia, we continuously have to prove that we are better than our "competition". We need to have more articles published in higher impact factor journals, higher citation counts, be the first to create a new method, achieve the highest classification accuracy with our improved algorithm, be novel, be better. Be the best. And I think this is antithetical and counterproductive to the goals of improving our common understanding of the world for the benefit of our planet and all species living on it, humanity being a small but not insignificant part. For that, I feel, we need collaboration.

What was the biggest surprise to you once you started your academic job?
How little checks there are on our accountability as academics. Accountability towards the public, towards our funders, and towards our colleagues, employees, and trainees. We are incentivized (by the self-perpetuating system that is ourselves) to promise novelty and groundbreaking results, to publish-or-perish, to get out on top whatever the cost. This is an unhealthy environment that allows exclusivity, bullies, harassers, and sloppy science to thrive. It seems like we should be doing everything we can to change this system. However, surprisingly, it seems that most academics are either unaware of or ignoring this.

What experience obtained in industry helped you the most in your current academic job? Did the personal contacts developed in industry, help you in any way? From your current perspective, was your previous industry job worth going through?
I am currently working in the field of functional MRI processing methods development, whereas my training and previous jobs were in engineering and project management.

Topically, my industry job did not prepare me for my current scientific interest. However, the project work and management experience alone has made my time in industry extremely useful, in my opinion. Much of what we have to do in a PhD is related to project management: defining goals, creating an execution plan, making decisions given too many unknown factors, dealing with disappointment, recovering and restructuring after a setback. Academic programs typically don't provide the training that I think is necessary to do this efficiently, so I feel very lucky to have had this experience and training prior to starting my PhD.

What were the major reasons behind your decision to embark on the academic career track? Was it a rapid decision, or perhaps, was this a long process of self-discovery? Or maybe, you are still hesitating and might come back to industry in the future?
I feel like I've wanted to do this "kind of thing" for a very long time, certainly since I was in high-school. But practical challenges, cultural pressures, youthful ignorance, personal motivations and just life in general took me along the route that I have followed until now. While working my industry jobs, however, I definitely experienced a level of intellectual dissatisfaction. I always had an extra hobby, inventing things, building things. I also read a lot, especially popular neuroscience and philosophy books. Over time these hobbies started shaping my thoughts and became more and more difficult to ignore. At the risk of succumbing to hindsight bias, I would say this process probably played a big role in my decision to change careers. As did the fact that my previous working environment was becoming too toxic for my taste.

Did you ever regret your decision to come to academia?
Yes. Regularly. Although not (yet?) to the extent that I'd necessarily decide to go back to the alternatives. I still like my current job much more than I did my previous one, although I wouldn't mind a higher salary and a system that acknowledges and incentivizes things other than the number of publications, impact factor, novelty, statistical significance, and white-dude-ishness.

Do you feel that you have reached your destination job already in terms of professional development, or are you still planning to change professions in the future?
What does it feel like to have reached your destination job? I imagine that my current experience is not that. I certainly feel like I have much more to learn and that I would like to grow and develop new skills, collaborations, and meaningful friendships along the way. If this means changing professions in the future, that is what I'll likely do. However, as far as working within the broad field of science and doing meaningful work to improve research transparency, reproducibility, inclusivity and collaboration, I'm pretty sure this is where I want to be for the foreseeable future.

What would you like to advise those who hesitate whether they should come to academia from industry?
My advice would depend on the specific needs and aspirations of the person, and also the relation between their current job and their possible future academic job. If, for all the failures of academia, the new job is still an improvement over the old one, go for it. That is

unless you have encountered obvious red flags regarding the new working environment. Personally, I find the freedom of time and intellectual stimulation of my current academic job extremely attractive, and I would highlight these positive aspects in my advice to like-minded people. However, if job security, low-pressure working conditions, predictability and time for self-care are very important to the person, I would advise that they think carefully before moving to academia, where these aspects are few and far between.

5. Anonymous Contributor

For how many years did you work in industry?
10 years

In what area of science are you now working, and on what position?
Neuroscience / Assistant Professor

In which country did you work in industry?
The Netherlands

In which country do you live now?
The Netherlands

What type of job did you perform before moving to academia?
Working in a corporation / middle size company (>= 50 employees)

In what market sector were you working?
Pharmaceutical industry

Could you share your last industry position title, and briefly describe (2-3 sentences) what your scope of responsibilities was?
Senior Scientist. Responsible for biological lead optimization activities and preclinical proof of concept studies. Actively led public-private partnership networks.

Can you briefly describe how a typical day at the office looked like in your industry job?
Supervision of technicians and staff. Discussion of experiments to be performed. Prioritization of targets in collaboration with other colleagues. Active discussion within working groups dedicated to a target on the lead compound selection and optimization from both chemical and biological perspectives. Management of internal and external staff working on research projects.

How did you find your current academic job?
Through persistence. Coming back to academia is challenging due to publication record often not being a priority in some companies. I sought to look for positions that combined my management expertise with academic flair.

Can you name the three biggest pros versus the three biggest cons of your current academic job, compared to your prior industry experience?

Pros:
- ➤ Freedom of research direction,
- ➤ Possibility to develop research with immediate rather than long-term impact,
- ➤ Research recognition.

Cons:
- ➤ Academia is less well-paid,
- ➤ The nature of the competitive grant funding system encourages individual rather than team research (team research in industry is a big plus),
- ➤ Rewards in academia are individual rather than team-based.

What was the biggest surprise to you once you started your academic job?
The lack of management expertise by some academics put in positions of management responsibility. The skills needed to be a good manager are very different from that of being a good academic.

What experience obtained in industry helped you the most in your current academic job? Did the personal contacts developed in industry, help you in any way? From your current perspective, was your previous industry job worth going through?
Management expertise both in content and personnel management. The industrial position also enabled the development of a large network which has been very helpful in developing academic collaborations and grant possibilities.

What were the major reasons behind your decision to embark on the academic career track? Was it a rapid decision, or perhaps, was this a long process of self-discovery? Or maybe, you are still hesitating and might come back to industry in the future?
It was a gradual evolution. I often felt I had the talents to perform well both as an academic and as an industry-based researcher/manager. Positions that enable both are attractive to me in either setting.

Did you ever regret your decision to come to academia?
No

Do you feel that you have reached your destination job already in terms of professional development, or are you still planning to change professions in the future?
Professional development is always an evolution. A colleague once told me his strategy to change position every 5 years to stay fresh in terms of knowledge and to be able to contribute to the function. It is important a position stays dynamic and you can still grow.

What would you like to advise those who hesitate whether they should come to academia from industry?
If you are thinking about it, try ... you can always consider if you like to continue in industry later as you'll already have an industrial career track record. It is difficult however to go from industry back to academia. You have a set of skills that are different from those with academic-only career trajectories and lack their publication record. Many coming from industry try but fail to enter academic tenured positions. (Re-entering at Postdoc levels is

easier—above this is more challenging). If you really want this, keep trying. Don't give up. You just need a little bit of luck and the right opportunity.

Any additional notes and comments you would like to share with the readers of the book:
Develop a network and learn how to formulate your ideas/proposals in succinct clearly formulated ways that are realistic.

Appendix 4: About the author

Dr. Natalia Bielczyk is an entrepreneur, researcher, author, and philanthropist. She was born in Katowice, Poland in 1986. In 2004, she joined the College of Inter-Faculty Individual Studies in Mathematics and Natural Sciences at the University of Warsaw, Poland. Within the College, she obtained three Master's titles. First, in February 2010, she graduated from MA in Psychology, specialized in Applied Psychometrics which concerns building and standardizing tests and questionnaires. During her undergraduate studies, she developed a questionnaire of Machiavellism which was further commercially used by recruiting companies in Warsaw. In her Master's thesis in Psychology, she was investigating whether creativity is Gaussian-distributed in the population. She was also looking for correlates between different creative traits and other personal traits such as political views or a sense of humor. Creativity proved to be a bimodal trait, and no correlates with other variables were found. Later that year, in July, Natalia graduated from MS in Mathematics (specialized in Applied Mathematics). In her Master's Thesis, she was investigating systems of differential equations with delay and applying those systems to study relations between people. Finally, in September 2012, she graduated from MS in Physics (specialized in Medical Physics). Her Master's Thesis in Physics was a methodological work on new, automated EEG data analysis with the use of Directed Transfer Function, which returns causal relationships between pairs signals from EEG recordings. In the meantime, in September 2011, she also received the title of Young Master of Business Administration from the Warsaw School of Economics. During her studies, Natalia also became a blogger, and she is actively blogging until this day[129].

In 2013-2017, Natalia conducted a PhD project at the Donders Institute for Brain, Cognition and Behaviour and the Radboud University Nijmegen Medical Center under the supervision of prof. dr. Jan K. Buitelaar and prof. dr. Christian F. Beckmann. During her PhD, she was working on developing new methods for signal detection, functional and effective connectivity research in functional Imaging Resonance Imaging[130]. She successfully developed a novel test for testing the normality of distribution, as well as a range of other methods dedicated to sparsifying functional connectomes and determining causal connections within the human connectome. She also holds the Basiskwalificatie in Onderzoekstages (BKO), a professional Dutch academic teaching qualification obtained for the successful supervision of undergraduate student projects.

However, one thing Natalia also has learned during her PhD, is that researchers are a labor group suffering from high-stress levels and lack of assistance in career development, which is a subject that needs a lot of attention. Therefore, during her PhD, Natalia also got involved in the Organization for Human Brain Mapping (OHBM) Student and Postdoc Special Interest Group as a Career Development and Mentoring Manager (2017-2019). Within this function, she worked as a coordinator of the OHBM International Online Mentoring Program (~600 participants in the program so far), in which she was matching mentors with mentees.

---

[129] www.nataliabielczyk.com

[130] www.scholar.google.com/citations?user=WHhMbWUAAAAJ&hl=en

In 2018, she launched a public foundation, Stichting Solaris Onderzoek en Ontwikkeling aiming to improve on the quality of life for early career academics: developing new schemes for mentoring in academia, and helping researchers in finding jobs outside academia. The foundation creates an online repository of resources for researchers thinking of a career switch and offers free counseling to early career researchers. The organization operates according to a novel scheme: to approach complex career-related questions, online teams are summoned: recommendations are formulated by online expert panels consisting of researchers and former researchers from all around the world. Recently, the foundation received the ANBI status and as such, it is recognized as an institution for the public good in the Netherlands. In 2019-2020, Natalia was also serving as an eLife Associate, and as such, she is helping in career training for eLife Ambassadors, an international network of early career researchers in the natural sciences who are preparing for science leadership roles in the future. In May 2019, she also received a prestigious Mozilla Science Mini-Grant for the project Avengers for Better Science[131]: a retreat organized with the purpose of training future research leaders in management, mentoring and using open science tools.

Lastly, in the summer of 2019, Natalia has become an entrepreneur: she established a company Welcome Solutions based in Nijmegen, the Netherlands. The company offers workshops and coaching services for early career researchers who are looking for new career opportunities and planning a career switch to industry. Natalia is also working on a battery of aptitude tests, and a novel recruitment tool dedicated to highly educated professionals who are looking for a new career path.

In free time, she spends time with friends, reads about blockchains, dances, tase care of plants in her own garden or chills in the nearby spa.

---

[131] www.avengers-for-better-science.github.io

COPYRIGHT

What Is out There for Me? The Landscape of Post-PhD Career Tracks
Second Edition

Printed in Great Britain
by Amazon

57853188R00173